THE MULTILEVEL COMMUNITY ENGAGEMENT MODEL

THE MULTILEVEL COMMUNITY ENGAGEMENT MODEL

School, Community, Workplace Engagement and Service-Learning

BY

MUHAMMAD HASSAN RAZA
Missouri State University, USA

United Kingdom – North America – Japan – India
Malaysia – China

Emerald Publishing Limited
Emerald Publishing, Floor 5, Northspring, 21-23 Wellington Street, Leeds LS1 4DL

First edition 2024

Copyright © 2024 Muhammad Hassan Raza.
Published under exclusive licence by Emerald Publishing Limited.

Reprints and permissions service
Contact: www.copyright.com

No part of this book may be reproduced, stored in a retrieval system, transmitted in any form or by any means electronic, mechanical, photocopying, recording or otherwise without either the prior written permission of the publisher or a licence permitting restricted copying issued in the UK by The Copyright Licensing Agency and in the USA by The Copyright Clearance Center. Any opinions expressed in the chapters are those of the author. Whilst Emerald makes every effort to ensure the quality and accuracy of its content, Emerald makes no representation implied or otherwise, as to the chapters' suitability and application and disclaims any warranties, express or implied, to their use.

British Library Cataloguing in Publication Data
A catalogue record for this book is available from the British Library

ISBN: 978-1-83797-698-0 (Print)
ISBN: 978-1-83797-697-3 (Online)
ISBN: 978-1-83797-699-7 (Epub)

INVESTOR IN PEOPLE

I dedicate my book to my family which is as follows:[1]

Zeenat Raza (My wife)
Hussain Raza (My older son)
Rasti Raza (My daughter)
Ali Raza (My younger son)

---

[1] For additional information, resources, and questions about the book, please contact the author at twosoulsonereflection@gmail.com

CONTENTS

Abstract		*ix*
1.	The Background and Context of the Book	1
2.	The Multilevel Community Engagement Model: A Conceptual Framework	13
3.	The Process of MCEM Framework Development, Operationalization, and Empirical Testing	31
4.	The Role of MCEM Framework in School, Community, Workplace Engagement and Service-Learning	41
5.	The MCEM Programs	61
6.	The MCEM Stakeholders	77
7.	The MCEM Stakeholders' Resources and Vulnerabilities	87
8.	The Review of Literature	99
9.	The MCEM Program Vision, SAMREEN Goals, and Objectives	109
10.	The MCEM Program Curriculum and Delivery	129
11.	Cultural and Ethical Challenges	149
12.	The SAMREEN Evaluation	159
13.	The MCEM Program Review and Share	173
14.	The MCEM Program Reflection and Trustworthiness	181
15.	The MCEM Program Sustainability, Lessons Learned, and Future Directions	189
About the Author		*201*
Appendix		*203*
References		*221*
Index		*275*

ABSTRACT

This book provides students, instructors, researchers, practitioners, administrators, government, and nongovernment organizations with the specific guidelines to use The Multilevel Community Engagement Model as a conceptual framework and systematically develop, implement, and evaluate programs on any topics, effectively work with all groups of the population, and carried out these programs in various settings, such as school, community, and workplace in societies around the world.

1

THE BACKGROUND AND CONTEXT OF THE BOOK

The objective of this chapter is to present the purpose of this book. It provides information on the Multilevel Community Engagement Model (MCEM) and how it can be used to systematically develop, implement, and assess programs in societies around the world. It also presents a rationale and significance of using the MCEM framework in promoting service-learning (SL) and community engagement.

THE BACKGROUND OF THE BOOK

This book provides a paradigm shift for SL and community engagement in school, community, and workplace engagement by offering a crucial balance between rigor (scientific and systematic procedures) and relevance (real-life experience of program stakeholders) in the process of developing, implementing, and evaluating programs. This book provides its target audiences (e.g. students, instructors, administrators, researchers, practitioners, government personnel, nongovernment organizations, community leaders, employers, donor agencies) with a step-by-step guide to use the MCEM as a conceptual framework and systematically develop, implement, and evaluate the MCEM programs in various settings, such as classrooms, school settings, university campuses, local communities, and workplaces, to achieve various short- and long-term goals and objectives. Although the book provides step-by-step guidelines and systematic process to learners, it also facilitates and supports the choices and decisions that learners make to develop, implement, and evaluate their program. Thus, it empowers learners but simultaneously facilitates them and program stakeholders to consider and maintain a certain degree of scientific rigor to ensure the accuracy, transparency, and trustworthiness of their program.

Each chapter focuses on a specific step/phase that learners can take to carry out a successful program process. Each chapter is connected and interrelated with the other to guide a systematic process of program development, implementation, and evaluation. The author provided all specific definitions in each chapter, which are explained with examples and additional details. Each chapter has a case study, which provides learners with insightful information and substantial opportunities to relate and apply the knowledge they learn from the chapter to solve real-world problems presented in the case study and successfully accomplish a step/phase of their program. At the end of each chapter, specific assignments associated with each topic which learners can complete to foster their understanding of the contents and grow knowledge and skills in developing, implementing, and evaluating the MCEM programs. Additionally, discussion questions are also provided to facilitate in-depth discussions about the topic among learners and program stakeholders. Due to its self-explanatory quality, this book does not require learners (the audience) to have any specialized knowledge or prior experience of SL and community engagement in developing, implementing, and evaluating programs for their SL projects.

Through each chapter, learners gain an extensive understanding of the MCEM framework and learn its use to systematically develop, implement, and evaluate their MCEM programs. The MCEM framework is broader enough that can be used in many disciplines, such as family science and human development, community and social psychology, sociology, social work, education, anthropology, counseling, medicine, health services, business, hospitality, STEM, etc. The advantage of the MCEM framework is that learners can use it to develop a program on almost any topic or issue, work in any settings, and with any group of the population by carrying out an inclusive and engaged process among all program stakeholders in any country, society, and community, which provides appropriate support, infrastructure, and caring environment for the MCEM programs. Although the MCEM framework is broad enough that can be used and applied to diverse communities and societies globally, due to its effective operationalization, learners can easily use the MCEM framework to develop and implement their programs. Similarly, the MCEM framework also informs a rigorous, continuous, and multilevel assessment to assess various aspects and elements of a program throughout the program process. There are numerous examples of topics provided in this book that learners can choose from to develop their programs.

A few examples of the MCEM programs, which have been successfully developed, implemented, and evaluated by learners in the past are money and happiness, Infidelity, cultural awareness, divorce and breakups, interracial relationships, stepfamilies, promoting gender equality in classrooms, making classrooms inclusive, mass violence, child abuse and neglect, types of listening, workplace communication, personality traits and communication, promoting diversity literature in early childhood classrooms, etc.

Instructors can use this book in their classrooms who aim at providing their students with real-life and applied experiences through community engagement and SL. Students can use this book to self-direct themselves in developing, implementing, and evaluating their programs. When students use this book as a guide in their classroom, they may need fewer guidance and directions from the instructor because this book is self-explanatory and a step-by-step guide for students to complete the development, implementation, and evaluation of their programs. The MCEM programs are not only taught and developed in regular courses including online, seated, and hybrid, thesis and dissertation students can also choose them as an option than doing a research study and develop, implement, and evaluate a MCEM program. Due to the adaptability, flexibility, and effective operationalization of the MCEM framework, the MCEM program can be quite complex, long-term, and extensive, and they can also be quite simple, brief, and short-term.

This book and the MCEM program process facilitate and promote continuous, critical, and engaged conversation among learners and program stakeholders throughout the program life cycle. Learners' reflections are also essential at every step of the program to ensure the transparency and trustworthiness of the program. Hence, instructors can determine the extent and nature of direction, discussion, and engagement among students in their classrooms based on the time, scope, requirements, and purpose of student SL projects. Additionally, practitioners, government, and nongovernmental organizations, and employers can also use this book as a resource to develop, implement, and evaluate their programs with their employees, clients, and local community individuals, families, and groups. The MCEM program process promotes diversity, culture, and inclusion. It recognizes the voices of all stakeholder groups regardless of their knowledge, skills, and/or social status in society and provides them with equal opportunities to participate in the decision-making process. Hence, it also addresses the issues of equity and social justice and makes the MCEM programs more inclusive and representative of all stakeholders including the program participants. The use of the MCEM framework not only helps learners to successfully accomplish their program by achieving their program goals and/or objectives, it also helps to identify and utilize strengths and resources of all program stakeholders that they exchange, share, and use after the formal completion of program, which ensures the sustainability of the MCEM programs.

This book guides and facilitates learners in performing all kinds of SL, such as direct SL through which learners directly work with program participants and have a face-to-face contact with them. For instance, when learners directly work with their program stakeholders including the program participants (who are the target beneficiaries of a program) to develop, implement, and evaluate their program, they perform a direct service to the community. Due to the advancement of technology, learners can either choose to work in-person with program stakeholders including program participants or they also work with them online. The online SL is particularly important because many institutions are offering courses online and students complete their course assignments including their SL assignments online. Students are also likely to work on their thesis and dissertation online. Moreover, since the recent Pandemic, online learning has been quite prevalent among institutions and learners. It is important to integrate SL into online courses to provide students with experiential and applied experience in their online classes. As mentioned earlier, this book also facilitates learners to accomplish SL projects in online classes and facilitate quite similar engagement and participation of program stakeholders. Hence, learners can perform indirect SL for which they do not directly work with their program participants. For instance, rather than carrying out any in-personal or online face-to-face workshops or educational sessions to implement a program, learners can develop a resource (manual, educational videos, brochure, flyer, pamphlet, etc.) and disseminate that resource among program participants or target beneficiaries. It is worth mentioning, that for the MCEM program process, learners still collaborate and engage with program stakeholders including program participants even if they choose to develop a resource and disseminate among program participants instead of directly educating them by conducting any in-person or online workshops or educational sessions.

In some situations, it becomes difficult for learners to reach out and engage some stakeholders during the time period in which they need to complete their SL project, in those situations, learners can gather information about these stakeholders, their roles, and influences on the program from those who learners can access to, speak with, and engage them for their program. Additionally, learners can also read and research about those stakeholders who are not accessible to learn about their roles and influences on their program and participants. Usually, stakeholders are quite accessible and since the MCEM programs offer and promotes a collaborative process, when stakeholder groups from different engagement levels interact with each other, communicate, and work together for the program, they explore and find out ways to access and engage those stakeholders who are difficult to access and engage in the program. For examples, government personnel and/or representatives who are responsible for forming public policies and procedures and take important decisions which directly or indirectly affect program participants are quite busy and sometimes it becomes difficult to reach out to them and engage them in the program within the due course of time.

Further, learners can perform advocacy-based SL in which they focus on a specific issue and raise awareness about it among program participants, reach out to decision-makers, and carry out campaigns to address or eliminate that problem from the community or society, such as gender disparities, child abuse, domestic violence, health and safety, environmental sustainability, and income inequalities. For instance, learners advocate for a new policy for the welfare of children and families. For this purpose, they can write letters and reach out to their local, state, or federal level personnel who are influential and responsible for creating such policies. It is worth mentioning that for the MCEM program process, a collaborative and engaged process helps learners to achieve positive program outcomes. In this case, learners identify and engage all possible stakeholders who determine their strategy to advocate for a new policy. Although government personnel and/or representatives, who are influential and responsible for creating such policies are relevant stakeholders may or may not be engaged in the process of developing a strategy or campaign, they can become a part of it once they are reached out by the stakeholders who are identified, engaged, and utilized by the learner for this purpose. Finally, learners conduct research or support research efforts and/or write grants to study a particular problem to learn its causes for addressing and eliminating it from communities. Again, for the MCEM program process, active engagement, participation, and collaboration is essential for the success and sustainability of a program. For instance, if learners plan on writing and submitting a grant proposal for their local community families, it is crucial for learners to engage these families and other relevant stakeholder groups and gather information about their important problems and essential needs to learn about their intensively, significance, prevalence, and incidence, and focus on important and immediate issues and needs of these families on their grant proposal. Any baseline survey or assessment (formal or informal) data about target families can substantially strengthen the grant proposal. For this purpose, learners need to identify program stakeholders and engage them through the process of writing a grant. Hence, this book provides learners with many options and opportunities to perform all kinds of SL to serve local communities, gain applied and experiential learning experience, and bring positive changes in local communities, society, and globally.

This book brings people of various qualities, backgrounds, and cultures together and provide them with opportunities to learn about each other, respect each other's perspectives, and engage in a collaborative process to systematically develop, implement, and evaluate their program to achieve short-term and long-term goals and objectives. The MCEM program process promote and value peoples' qualities, resources, experiences, and expertise that they can potentially offer and share in developing, implementing, and evaluating programs in various settings. Hence, this book is a comprehensive but simple roadmap for students, instructors, researchers, practitioners, and organizations, Since the MCEM program process invites and engages all relevant stakeholders from different engagement levels, recognize their voices, utilize their knowledge and expertise, and provide them with opportunities to actively participate in the decision-making process throughout the program lifecycle, it addresses important issues of inclusion, diversity, and social justice.

This is the first book which presents the MCEM framework, its' effective operationalization, and a systematic process to develop, implement, and evaluate the MCEM programs on all topics, populations, and settings to foster SL and community engagement in societies around the world. Existing books (e.g. Darling et al., 2022; Duncan & Goddard, 2017; Linder & Hayes, 2018; Ornstein & Hunkins, 2013; Strait & Nordyke, 2015; Tinto, 1993) on SL and community engagement are quite general, which provide a review of existing literature and share general strategies and resources about SL and community engagement. This book shows a real-world impact because it helps learners to systematically develop, implement, and evaluate programs on any topic/issue, in any setting, and with any group of the population in societies around the world to bring positive changes in the lives of individuals, families, groups, and organizations. Following are five specific contributions that this book makes in SL and community engagement: (1) this book provides learners with a systematic, applied, and real-life experience of SL and community engagement through the MCEM program process; (2) this book promotes and encourage active engagement and participants of all stakeholders throughout the program lifecycle regardless of their social status in society, which results in inclusive, sustainable, and representative programs; (3) this book helps learners to address important and immediate needs and issues of individuals, families, groups, and organizations in societies around the world; (4) this book fosters engagement and collaboration among school, community, and workplace, which increases sustainability and positive outcomes locally and nationally; and (5) this book addresses existing gaps in SL and community engagement, and offers one MCEM program process globally to facilitate effective communication, collaboration, and engagement among students, instructors, researchers, practitioners, and organizations across disciplines around the world.

In sum, this book is broader enough that can be applied to and utilized by various disciplines, fields, and audiences and simultaneously, it is narrow to an extent which provides specific and step-by-step guidelines to students, instructors, researchers, and practitioners to systematically develop, implement, and evaluate their programs based on various topics, settings, and groups of the population. Due to the flexibility, adaptability, and effective operationalization of the MCEM framework, this book can be used in various ways to develop, implement, and evaluate programs of unique and distinctive scopes, lengths, and modes.

CONTEXT OF THE BOOK

As this book is grounded in the MCEM framework, which promotes SL and community engagement in school, community, and workplace by providing a systematic procedure to learners for developing, implementing, and evaluating programs, hence, it promotes and substantiates existing efforts toward SL, outreach, and community engagement. Although outreach and SL initiatives and efforts were initiated and informally carried out in the past, SL formally started in 20th century in the US (Chambers & Lavery, 2017), and since then it has been used and carried out globally (Chambers & Lavery, 2022). Different countries started community engagement and SL programs at different time periods due to different factors, such as financial resources, sufficient knowledge and expertise, supportive environment, sociocultural, and historical contexts (Davis et al., 2021; Jelinčić et al., 2022; Kusujiarti, 2011; McCarthy et al., 2005; Rusu, 2020; Xing & Ma, 2010).

For instance, SL and community engagement efforts started in 1800 through which parents' support groups and mother study groups were formed to share and discuss child-rearing approaches and practices in the US (Duncan & Goddard, 2017). Over time, the land grant university system was created through which colleges and universities formally adopted SL and community engagement practices so that students could gain practical skills along with their basic course content knowledge (Darling et al., 2022). Additionally, another purpose was to educate masses and local communities about research-based knowledge on family, social, and legal issues and provide them with appropriate skills to help them prevent important problems and function well in community and society (Duncan & Goddard, 2017). Further, a cooperative extension system was created by Congress in 1914 and the purpose was to promote the application of research knowledge, reach out to masses, and provide that knowledge in nontraditional academic settings (Darling et al., 2022). University-based outreach efforts have been carried out through which students gain experiential learning by conducting their SL projects, practicums, and internships related to their course contents (Darling et al., 2014). Students not only gain SL experiences through these projects and partnerships, but they also develop important connections with local, national, and international communities outside of the classroom (Duncan & Goddard, 2017). SL practices not only prepare students personally, academically, professionally, culturally, and ethically, students also make unique contribution in improving well-being of children and families and bring positive changes in their lives (Raza & Richey, 2021).

Family life education (FLE) also has been a part of outreach and SL efforts, which provides family life educators with essential knowledge on ten content areas of family relationship and development, such as interpersonal relationships, human sexuality, parent education, internal dynamics of families, human growth and development, etc. (Bredehoft & Cassidy, 1995; Bredehoft & Walcheski, 2011; NCFR, 2014, 2018, 2024). Students and family life educators can develop their programs on any of the ten content areas that they can offer to different groups of the population by using various modes of delivery, such as in-person and online (Ballard, 2020; Darling et al., 2020; Raza & Richey, 2021). FLE programs are primarily related to family science and human development, which also promotes interdisciplinary collaboration (NCFR, 2018, 2024). FLE contents grow and improve people's knowledge and skills on different areas of family life to strengthen family relationships and development over time (Hamon & Smith, 2014, 2017; Umberson & Thomeer, 2020).

There has been a substantial progress in outreach efforts and service delivery since its initiation; however, there is still essential need to reach out to underrepresented and underprivileged diverse groups of the population, improve school, community, and workplace collaboration, and develop culturally appropriate programs (Raza, 2022). Since the MCEM framework considers culture and diversity as the central aspects of the program process, it promotes and fosters diversity, culture, and inclusion in a collaborative and engagement program process for developing, implementing, and evaluating the MCEM programs. Essentially, the use and application of the MCEM framework may address these existing gaps, expand outreach and programming efforts, and move the field forward in the future.

SL is considered an important area for student learning and professional development around the world (Chambers & Lavery, 2022). Globally, universities and institutions have been making substantial efforts and showing improvements in integrating SL into the curriculum and creating a supportive environment and organizational structure to grow and foster SL efforts and programs (Chambers & Lavery, 2017, 2022). However, there are variations in SL among countries in terms of rigor, strengths, and challenges (Raza, 2021, 2022). For instance, SL is a relatively new area in Australian universities and institutions (Patrick et al., 2019). Although they made significant progress toward SL in terms of promoting students' interests, benefits, and academic and social awareness about it, they are still dealing with some challenges, such as a lack of consensus on a specific definition of SL, integration of SL into the curriculum, and lack of relevant policies (Patrick et al., 2019). In African, students' experience challenges on SL sites, such as clients' inappropriate behaviors, chances of getting injury or infections, lack of sufficient materials, lack of organizational structure, cultural barriers, and contusive environment (Naidoo et al., 2020). Additionally, a lack of institutional policies and arrangements and partnerships with target communities limit students' learning opportunities (Naidoo & Devnarain, 2009). Research revealed that developed SL sites fostered and increased students' positive learning experiences and successful outcomes (Camus et al., 2022). SL in Asia also showed benefits and positive learning outcomes for students such as it improved students' self-efficacy, clinical experience, and cultural competence (Davis et al., 2021). There are also problems in SL efforts and programs in this region due to lack of institutional policies and appropriate arrangements to create a suitable and supportive environment for students, faculty, and community partners (Yusof et al., 2020).

The discussion above indicates that although there have been substantial improvements and progress toward outreach, SL, and community engagement efforts, there are challenges that universities and institutions have been facing, which need additional work, collaboration, and engagement of people from various areas, disciplines, and expertise. As evident from the aforementioned review, some of the important and immediate problems are lack of institutional policies and structure conducive for SL efforts, lack of collaboration and arrangements between school and community, and challenges related to integrating SL into program curriculum. One of the advantages of the MCEM framework is that it promotes engagement and collaboration among stakeholders who are situated at different engagement levels, when learners develop and implement the MCEM program, they invite and engagement relevant program stakeholders including students, faculty, staff, and administrators from the same institutions. Learners can develop a MCEM program to foster collaboration and engagement in developing, implementing, and promoting SL policies and organizational structure for supportive and expanding SL efforts and programs in an institution. For this purpose, learners need to identify, invite, and engage all relevant stakeholders into their program. Consequently, the MCEM program may help to develop and implement effective policies conducive to SL and create a supportive organizational structure and caring environment to grow and expand SL efforts and programs within and outside of the institution. Similarly, as mentioned, when learners identify and engage all relevant program stakeholders in the program process, these stakeholders are from local communities, employers, schools, donor agencies, corporate sectors, and government institutions, which will also increase collaboration and support among different stakeholder groups and create a liaison between school, community, and workplace. Finally, due to its formation and effective operationalization, the MCEM guides instructors and students throughout the program process by providing them with a systematic procedure, which reduces pressure and burden from them. Consequently, when instructors use this framework to integrate SL into their courses, these changes and transitions may likely be smoother and successful. Hence, the MCEM framework addresses existing challenges in SL and community engagement and helps to foster and grow such efforts in an effective manner.

CASE STUDY

Karen has been thinking about developing a program that she can offer to young parents who have children between 0 and 12 years to help them foster and maintain healthy parent–child attachments. These parents belong to diverse ethnic and cultural backgrounds. Their income levels also vary and some of them are current immigrant families. Their children are of different ages who attend preschool, kindergarten, and elementary school. Karen studied existing programs and did not find sufficient programs which have been offered and implemented with such groups of the population. Most of the existing programs were based on the cultural values, beliefs, and practices of majority groups which are prevalent in mainstream society. Karen also wants to expand her program after its first phase and pilot testing after securing funds from donor agencies. Karen does not have substantial expertise in the

The Background and Context of the Book 11

areas of program development, implementation, and evaluation. She likes to have specific guidelines. She also doesn't want to limit her participants' ideas and needs because her goal is to facilitate her participants in addressing their immediate and important needs and problems for better outcomes and sustainable changes. Due to a lack of guidance and the complexity of issues discussed in the case study, Karen is concerned and eager to explore new ways of doing things through which she can develop, implement, and evaluate her program more inclusively which represents all stakeholder groups including diverse target families that she aims at focusing through her program.

DISCUSSION QUESTIONS

(1) Why are programs important for school, community, and workplace?

(2) How can programs improve individual, families, and groups' communication and teamwork within school, community, and workplace?

(3) How can programs improve individual, families, and groups' engagement and collaboration between school, community, and workplace?

(4) Why is an inclusive and collaborative process important between relevant individuals, groups, and organizations in developing, implementing, and evaluating programs?

(5) Why is a systematic process to develop, implement, and evaluate programs important for learners?

(6) Why is a good balance between scientific rigor and stakeholders' real-life experiences and relevance important for developing, implementing, and evaluating programs?

(7) How can a healthy combination of rigor and relevance make programs successful and sustainable?

(8) How can programs bring positive and impactful changes in communities and society?

(9) How can programs provide impactful learning experiences to learners and all relevant program stakeholders?

(10) What are your views and interests on program development, implementation, and evaluation?

ASSIGNMENT QUESTIONS

(1) What is your program?

(2) Why are you interested in developing, implementing, and evaluating your program?

(3) What specific areas do you want to focus on in your program?

(4) Why are you interested in those areas? What drives your interest in developing programs in those areas?

(5) How is your program important for program participants?

(6) How does your program address the immediate and important needs and issues of individuals, families, groups, and organizations in school, community, and workplace.?

(7) What did you learn from this assignment?

2

THE MULTILEVEL COMMUNITY ENGAGEMENT MODEL: A CONCEPTUAL FRAMEWORK

The objective of this chapter is to discuss the MCEM framework. The MCEM framework is used as a conceptual framework to systematically develop, implement, and evaluate programs on various topics and issues, which are implemented in different settings, and offered to diverse groups of the population in societies around the world. The author presented the fundamental principles and components of the MCEM framework. Various terms and concepts which are informed by the MCEM framework with specific definitions are also shared. A case study and discussion questions are also provided to expand readers' understanding of the MCEM framework. There is a case study provided at the end of this chapter to apply the concepts of this chapter to real-world situations. Additionally, the discussion questions are also provided for an in-depth discussion and dialog about the MCEM framework among readers.

According to the MCEM framework, there are three engagement levels (i.e. proximal, influential, and holistic level) of the MCEM. Multiple stakeholder groups are situated at each engagement level of the MCEM. At the proximal level, target families, their friends, and extended family members, support groups, schools, community-based organizations, peers, employers, coworkers, supervisors, etc. are situated. At the influential level, donor/funding agencies, electronic media (e.g. newspapers, magazine, radio, television, internet users, administrators, owners, etc.), social media (e.g., Facebook, Instagram, Twitter, TikTok, etc.), and state and federal level public institutions are situated. At the holistic level, individuals, families, and groups who belong to any area of diversity, such as socioeconomic status, disability, gender, sexual orientation, ethnicity, etc., and culture are situated.

According to the MCEM framework, stakeholder groups within and between the engagement levels have reciprocal relationships with each other. The dynamics of each stakeholder group and their reciprocal relationships with each other within and between the engagement levels change over time and are influenced by developmental, sociocultural, and historical contexts. Open areas of each engagement level signify a strong collaboration, consistent coordination, and open communication between stakeholder groups within and between the engagement levels.

It is worth mentioning that sometimes learners find similar stakeholder group(s) at more than one engagement level. Although the MCEM engagement levels are interrelated with each other, the conceptualization of each MCEM engagement level (i.e. proximal, influential, and holistic level) is unique and different from the other. Hence, it is important to differentiate the stakeholder groups and locate them at only one engagement level. Based on the focus and nature of a program, one stakeholder group may be more relevant, effective, and active at a certain engagement level compared to the other engagement level. Hence, learners need to critically examine this aspect to finally locate or associate a stakeholder group to a specific engagement level. For instance, at the first MCEM engagement level, "families" is one of the stakeholder groups. This stakeholder group refers to target families or program participants, their friends, and extended family members. At the third level, there is a different stakeholder group called "Diversity." This stakeholder group includes those individuals, groups, and families, which are different from the target families/program participants based on any areas of diversity, such as socioeconomic status, disability, gender, sexual orientation, ethnicity, family structure, immigration status etc.,. Similarly, at the same engagement level (the holistic level), there is a different stakeholder group called "Culture." This stakeholder group includes those individuals, groups, and families, which are different from the target families/program participants based on their culture. Those friends and extended family members who belong to the same culture will be identified at the proximal level (the first engagement level) and belong to the stakeholder group called "Family." Hence, it is important to differentiate the stakeholder groups and determine their location at the engagement level based on the focus and nature of the program and their relevance and influence on the program and target beneficiaries (which can be individuals, groups, families, and/or organizations). For example, if learners decide to choose single parent families for their program, then these single parent families, their friends, and extended family members will be located at the proximal level, and at the holistic level, other families which are different than the target single parent families based on any area of diversity will be located, such as two-parent families, foster care families, stepfamilies, immigrant families, same-sex families, etc.

Moreover, each term and concept associated with every engagement level has a separate definition. For instance, family and community which are located at the proximal level (the first level) have separate definitions. Similarly, diversity and culture situated at the third level (the holistic level) have separate definitions. Distinct stakeholder groups are situated at each of the MCEM engagement levels. This demonstrates that all three MCEM engagement levels are different and unique from each other. Following are the definitions of each term and concept included in the MCEM framework.

FAMILY

Family defines as two or more individuals who are in relationships of different kinds with one another and share various aspects of life, such as financially, physically, emotionally, and intellectually with common interests and goals.

Families are situated at the proximal level of the MCEM framework as it is evident from the definition of a family that all family structures are covered through this definition. Given the growing and emerging diversities in contemporary societies globally, learners may find diverse family structures in their program. Since the MCEM framework promotes diversity, culture, and inclusion as the central aspects of a program, it is important to include all families in the MCEM program, understand, and address their needs and issues regardless of their structures and social status in society.

COMMUNITY

Community defines any individuals, groups, families, organizations, schools, or local government agencies who live together, share a common place, and influence community initiatives or programs through direct or indirect ways and vice versa.

Community is also situated at the proximal level of the MCEM framework. The purpose of MCEM programs is to grow community engagement by inviting and engaging those stakeholders who belong to local communities. There are different types of individuals, families, groups, and organizations who belong to a community and are considered relevant stakeholders for a MCEM program. Hence, it is important for learners to carefully examine all stakeholders who are relevant to their programs, reach out to them, and invite them to engage and participate in their program.

MEDIA

Media defines as any kind of print, electronic, or social media, such as newspapers, magazines, television, phone, email, Twitter, Facebook, Instagram, etc., which is a source of information, communication, and dissemination for individuals, families, groups, and organizations in society and/or globally.

Media is situated at the influential level of the MCEM framework. Due to the advancement of technology all forms of media have become quite common and influential for program participants. People who use one or more forms of media can interact with target families and substantially affect their views and experiences of the program and its focus. Given the nature and scope of the program, media personnel, administrators, and owners can also become relevant stakeholders for a MCEM program. Hence, all forms of media, and media users, staff, administrators, and owners are stakeholder groups who are situated at the influential level of the MCEM framework.

DONOR AGENCY

Donor agency defines as any government or nongovernment organization which provides funds to individuals, groups, families, and/or local organizations for different purposes.

Donor agencies are situated at the influential level of the MCEM framework. Financial assistance is crucial to run any community program. Donor agencies play an important role in providing funds to local agencies to run a program. These donor agencies can collaborate with one or several local organizations to implement their programs and goals based on the focus, nature, and scope of their projects and plans. Donor agencies use different approaches, which may range from quite traditional top-down approaches in which they design their own plans and projects and invite local nongovernment organizations that work in those local target communities to implement those plans and projects to a more nontraditional and participatory approaches in which local organizations work with donor agencies and participate in the decision-making process to develop and implement their plans and projects. Sometimes, donor agencies use a mixture of traditional and nontraditional approaches to develop and implement their projects based on the context of target communities and other important factors. In addition to providing financial assistance, sometimes, these donor agencies also provide technical assistance to local organizations in the areas of research, technology, and capacity building training. Some examples of donor agencies are UNCIEF, UN Women, USAID, and OXFAM. Donor agencies are a potential and relevant stakeholder group for a MCEM program which affects the program and program participants.

INSTITUTIONS

Institutions define as any state or federal public institution which form and implement public policies and/or programs for individuals, families, groups, and/or organizations to address their needs, resolve problems, and provide them with appropriate support and assistance.

Public institutions are situated at the influential level of the MCEM framework. Public policies and programs directly or indirectly affect program participants and the MCEM program. Hence, government personnel are important stakeholder groups for the program. For instance, if a MCEM program focuses on child abuse and neglect, then policies and programs related to child and family welfare can be quite relevant to the MCEM program. Learners can collect important information from government agencies and utilize their knowledge and expertise when they engage and collaborate with government personnel through for their program. Additionally, government institutions also work and collaborate with local nongovernment organizations and donor agencies to facilitate their work and smooth implementation of their programs. Hence, public institutions, which are relevant to the program, and program participants are potential stakeholder groups for a MCEM program.

CULTURE

Culture is defined as people's relevant and meaningful ways of living life which include people's beliefs, values, and practices, and determine people's behaviors and interactions with others and their perceptions and meanings that people associate with those behaviors and interactions.

Culture is situated at the holistic level of the MCEM framework. One of the central focuses of the MCEM framework is to consider, use, and promote culture as the central aspect of and influence on program participants and the program. As it is evident from the definition, peoples' culture is an essential aspect of their lives which consists of their beliefs, values, and practices. Culture determines how people live their lives, their interactions and behaviors with others, and the perceptions and meanings that they make based on those behaviors and interactions. When programs are aligned with participants' cultural values and beliefs, participants find it more relevant, useful, and meaningful for them. Consequently, they actively participate in those programs, learn, and practice the knowledge and skills, and sustain it after the formal completion of the program because they feel it is beneficial for them and their community. One of the reasons for program failure is its ignorance or insensitivity of participants' culture. This is one of the strengths and advantages of the MCEM programs that they respect, utilize, and promote participants' culture in the program process. Moreover, due to the growing and emerging cultural plurality, individuals and families are practicing many cultures, which shape their perceptions, lives, and interactions. Below are a few cultures that program participants may choose and practice.

INDIVIDUALISTIC CULTURE

An individualistic culture promotes peoples' beliefs, values, and practices, which prioritize and value individuals' growth, well-being, and development over families and/or groups. Consequently, people's attitudes and behaviors focus on improving their own well-being and development. In this culture, those individuals who are self-relied and independent are perceived as more socially responsible, resilient, and desirable. This culture becomes more relevant and meaningful for those people who belong to it and practice this culture, which determines their behaviors and interactions with others and their perceptions and meaning that people associate with those behaviors and interactions.

COLLECTIVISTIC CULTURE

A collectivistic culture promotes peoples' beliefs, values, and practices, which prioritize and value a family and/or a group's growth, well-being, and development over individuals. Consequently, people's attitudes and behaviors focus on improving the well-being and development of their family and group. In this culture, those individuals who are family-oriented, connected, and dependent are perceived as socially responsible, resilient, and desirable. This culture becomes more relevant and meaningful for those people who belong to it and practice this culture, which determines their behaviors and interactions with others and their perceptions and meaning that people associate with those behaviors and interactions.

EVOLVED CULTURE

An evolved culture promotes peoples' beliefs, values, and practices, which simultaneously prioritize and value the growth, well-being, and development of individuals, families, and groups. Consequently, people's attitudes and behaviors focus on improving their own well-being and development as well as their family and group. In this culture, those individuals who are self-relied, independent, family oriented, connected, and dependent, are perceived more socially responsible, resilient, and desirable. This culture becomes more relevant and meaningful for those people who belong to it and practice this culture, which determines their behaviors and interactions with others and their perceptions and meaning that people associate with those behaviors and interactions.

DIVERSITY

Diversity refers to the areas of diversity, such as socioeconomic status, disability, sexual orientation, gender, religion, ethnicity, etc. which makes individuals, couples, and families unique and different from one another and shapes their experiences in society and globally.

Diversity is situated at the holistic level of the MCEM framework. As mentioned earlier, the goal of MCEM programs is to consider, use, and promote diversity in the program process. As evident from the definition, there are many different areas of diversity, which shape the experiences of individuals and families in society and globally. Similarly, these diversity areas also substantially affect program participants. The use and inclusion of diversity areas make the MCEM program more inclusive and representative. Hence, it is a strength and advantage of the MCEM program that they ensure the inclusion of all individuals and families who belong to various areas of diversity in society and globally.

DEVELOPMENTAL CONTEXT/TIME

Development is a process, which accompanies with growth, change, and stability that individuals experience during different stages, such as childhood, adolescence, youth, adulthood, middle and older age, and in various domains, such as biological, social, psychological, emotional, etc., of their life, which provides them with satisfaction and supports their survival.

The dynamics of stakeholder groups and their reciprocal relationships within and between the engagement levels are influenced by developmental context, for instance, if a MCEM program is quite long (5–10 years) and children are the primary program participants who experience continuous and substantial changes during the childhood period. Thus, during the program when they go through these developmental chances (e.g. physical, mental, social, and emotional changes), it may affect their participants, engagement, and learning process. Additionally, it may also change the nature and extent of influences they receive from other stakeholders such as their parents, friends, peers, and extended family members. Hence, the developmental context plays an important role in the MCEM program process.

SOCIOCULTURAL CONTEXT/TIME

S-Time is defined as the sociocultural context of the current society, such as social, economic, political, and/or law and order situations.

The dynamics of stakeholder groups and their reciprocal relationships within and between the engagement levels are also influenced by the current sociocultural context of society. For instance, if a MCEM program focuses on women's empowerment, but societal structures are informed by patriarchal systems, there are income disparities between men and women, and men have more access to social, economic, and political domains of live, it affects program participants and the nature, scope, and degree of influence they receive from other stakeholders who are situated at the same or different engagement level. For instance, there may be less community support for program participants, public policies and programs may not be favorable, traditional gender roles may be prevalent, and cultural support may be minimum for women. Hence, sociocultural context plays an important role in the MCEM program process.

HISTORICAL CONTEXT/TIME

H-Time is defined as the historical context of the current society, such as migration, war, and issues of justice, inclusion, and equity.

The dynamics of stakeholder groups and their reciprocal relationships within and between the engagement levels are also influenced by the historical context of society. For instance, if a MCEM program focuses on women's empowerment and even though the current sociocultural context supports and promotes women empowerment, but historically, women were marginalized and neglected in that society, it affects program participants and also the nature, scope, and degree of influence they receive from other stakeholders who are situated at the same or different engagement level. For instance, it is possible that program participants may not be supported and even face challenges from one or multiple groups of stakeholders who are situated at the same of different level due to the historical context of that society. Hence, historical context plays an important role in the MCEM program process.

The following example is provided to elaborate the reciprocal relationship between stakeholder groups within and between the engagement level and how these relationships change over time and are influenced by developmental, sociocultural, and historical contexts.

Let's assume that a learner's program focuses on early childhood education and development, based on the program, the learner includes families who have children 0–8 years old. So, these target families, their friends, and extended family members are situated at the proximal level and relate with the MCEM stakeholder group called "Families." In the community at the same proximal level, childcare center, early childhood education centers, elementary school, child advocacy centers, community organizations, support groups for parents with young children, parents' employers, etc., are also located. The experiences of parents in the workplace can affect how they raise their children in the family (Raza et al., 2023b). Parents' relationship quality with their spouse also influences their nursing and caring of children and their performance in the workplace (Raza et al., 2021). Those parents who have additional demands associated with their children due to any learning disabilities, special care needs, or any behavioral problems show symptoms of stress and become overwhelmed (Auriemma et al., 2022; Zhao et al., 2021), which also affects their parenting practices and performance in the workplace (Meral et al., 2023; Sur et al., 2021). If mothers do not have any supervision for their young children, they feel stress and anxiety during their worktime (Blocklin et al., 2012; Suarez-Morales & Harris, 2023; Suarez-Morales & Torres, 2021). Similarly, schools also play an important role in shaping the development of children in different domains, such as social, emotional, academic, etc., (Flack et al., 2023; Goldberg & Iruka, 2023; Lin et al., 2023), and children bring their cultures and unique background, and needs in schools, which also influence schools' functioning, approaches, and strategies toward educating those children (Harkness et al., 2020; Peplak et al., 2023). Hence, families and community reciprocally influence each other.

Moreover, donor agencies, public institutions, and media also have reciprocal relationships with each other (Raza, 2020a). For instance, donor agencies fund public institutions or vice versa. Public institutions facilitate donor agencies to ensure a smooth implementation of their projects/programs in local and remote communities. On the other hand, donor agencies abide by the laws and policies of public institutions (Raza, 2022). Media provides important information for donor agencies to learn about their community partners, target beneficiaries, and mainstream societal culture and norms. On the other hand, donor agencies and public institutions also utilize different forms of media to promote and share their vision and agenda with citizens at the macrolevel (Raza, 2020b). Hence, donor agencies, public institutions, and media reciprocally influence each other. With respect to the example provided above, young children learn certain behaviors from the media (Hamilton & Dynes, 2023; Lu et al., 2022). They likely idealize certain entertainers or characters, which influence how children think, feel, and behave (Vanderbilt & Andreason, 2023). Screen time also affects children's social and emotional development (Kracht et al., 2023; Sundqvist et al., 2024). Similarly, children are directly or indirectly affected by the programs of donor agencies and/or the policies of public institutions (Aranbarri et al., 2021). For instance, the child welfare and financial assistance programs offered by the government play an important role in raising children for single mothers in the US (Riser et al., 2023; Rodriguez et al., 2022).

Furthermore, diversity and culture also have reciprocal relationships. For instance, culture informs gender roles for men and women, which shapes the behaviors, expectations, and experiences of men and women in society (Kaynak et al., 2022; Raza et al., 2023b). Since individuals are an active agent of their change, they also bring changes in their culture regarding gender norms, which may change their behaviors, expectations, and experiences of men and women within in that culture and society (Mendenhall et al., 2019).

Similarly, racial/ethnic groups are unique and different from each other who also practice their culture. For instance, different racial and ethnic groups (White, African America, Hispanic, Asian, and Native Americans) in the US have unique culture, which informs their family practices and interactions with one another within and outside the cultural group (Olson et al., 2021). For instance, African American, Hispanic, Asian, and Native American practice collectivistic culture in general, whereas White racial/ethnic group practice individualistic culture. Though there are some variabilities within each racial/ethnic group in terms of their cultural practices such that families also practice evolved culture particularly if they are multigenerational, such as their children are born in the US, whereas their parents came from a foreign country. Additionally, the values, beliefs, and worldviews of these racial/ethnic groups are quite different and unique from one another. It is worth mentioning that there are differences as well as commonalities among these racial/ethnic groups. Hence, diversity and culture reciprocally influence each other.

Moreover, the MCEM engagement levels also have reciprocal relationships with each other. For instance, diversity can affect target beneficiaries/program participants. For instance, with respect to the example provided above, children learn gender roles during their socialization process, which determine their behaviors, attitudes, and perception toward themselves and others. Children's socialization may vary based on the cultural context. For instance, some cultures promote nontraditional gender roles compared to others. There may also be variabilities within cultures, such that some parents promote traditional gender roles even though the culture promotes nontraditional gender roles particularly if they were socialized in traditional families during their childhood. Hence, family structure (an area of diversity), gender, and culture reciprocally influence each other.

Further, if the target beneficiaries are families of young children, those families who went through this phase can provide support and share important information and strategies with program participants who are currently going through these phases. These expert families are situated at the holistic level (diversity). Similarly, target beneficiaries can connect with social media groups for social and emotional support, they can also attend any program in their local communities funded by a donor agency, government personnel can also provide them with any financial support and these stakeholder groups are situated at the influential level. Hence, there are reciprocal relationships between the MCEM engagement levels.

According to the MCEM framework, the dynamics of each stakeholder group and their reciprocal relationships with each other within and between the engagement levels change over time due to developmental, sociocultural, and historical contexts. For instance, target families developmentally change over time. With respect to the example provided above, young children go through age specific changes, which are important for them to grow and develop. If there is support at the societal level for target families, it trickles down and benefit these families. For instance, due to laws and policies regarding same-sex, interracial marriages, adoption, same-sex and interracial families with young children are receiving more support, recognition, and assistance at the community level compared to the past. Although, there was less support and more hostility for same-sex and interracial families/couples in the past before 1960s, the current societal efforts brought about changes and the current sociocultural context shows a different picture though there are still historical effects on these families and their experiences in the current society. This indicates how the dynamics of this stakeholder group (target diverse families) and their relationship with other stakeholder groups (public institutions, local organizations' support, community acceptance, etc.) have been changed over time due to developmental, sociocultural, and historical contexts.

Sometimes, it is also possible that due to a specific focus and certain nature of a MCEM program, learners may not find any relevant stakeholder groups that they can associate with any of the engagement level or a group (i.e. families and community) at the engagement level. For instance, if learners decide to choose target families for all family structures and areas of diversity for their program, such as single parent families, two-parent families, step-families, etc. These families, their friends, and extended family members are located at the proximal level, then learners may not find any stakeholder groups that they locate at the holistic level or associate it with the stakeholder group called "Diversity" because learners identify those stakeholders at the holistic level who differ from the program participants based on any area of diversity. Similarly, those stakeholders who differ from target beneficiaries/program participants based on their culture belong to the stakeholder group called "Culture," which is satiated at the holistic level. However, due to the substantially growing and increasing diversity among individuals, families, and groups, it is quite a rare situation for learners. For instance, if learners offer a program to families of children ages between 0 and 12 years with special care needs and include all family structures, then families who have children 13 years of age and above are located at the holistic level because they are considered different from target beneficiaries based on their children's age who can share important information, strategies, real-life experiences, and personal success stories with program participants. Hence, learners need to

The Multilevel Community Engagement Model

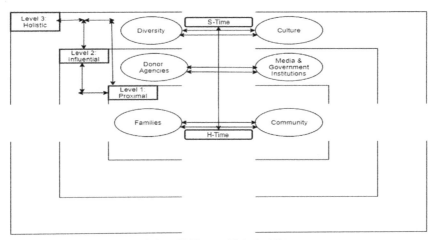

Note: S-Time = sociocultural time; H-Time = historical time.

Fig. 1. The Multilevel Community Engagement Model (MCEM).

critically think and examine who can benefit the program and program participants and identify them with respect to the engagement level they belong to.

As it is displayed on the MCEM (please see Fig. 1) and it is explained above that different groups of stakeholders are located at each engagement level. For example, the proximal level includes families (This stakeholder group refers to target families or program participants, their friends, and extended family members) and community (This stakeholder group refers to schools, support groups, organization, activists, employers etc.). Those groups which are situated at each engagement level are relatively proximal to one another, quite similar to one another, perform quite similar roles and responsibilities, and also match with one another in terms of their degree of influence on the program and program participants. For instance, at the proximal level, target families/program participants, their friends, and extended members are more proximal to local schools, support groups, community organizations, activities, employers, etc. compared to when we examine the proximity and influence of target families with state and federal public institutions or personnel. These groups are likely to perform quite similar roles and responsibilities. For instance, parents in the family and teachers in schools help children to attain their education, become productive citizens, and show positive moral values, etc. Similarly, parents and teachers have equally important influence on children and sometimes children listen to their teachers and idealize them more than their parents, especially when they are in their middle childhood period. Hence, these stakeholder groups (parents and teachers) are located at the same engagement level (i.e. the proximal level).

Moreover, donor agencies, media owners, and government/public institutions' personnel are relatively proximal to one another. Donor agencies and public institutions need to collaborate with each other to ensure a smooth functioning and implementation of projects in local and remote communities, which are funded by any donor agencies. Public institutions also provide funds to local nongovernment organizations for research, advocacy, and practice purposes. On the other hand, donor agencies also make sure that they follow the public rules, protocols, and policies and abide by them when they work with local community organizations to design, implement, and evaluate different projects that they provide funds for. Similarly, both donor agencies and public institutions have a substantial influence on media advertisement and messages delivered to general public regarding their programs/projects and policies. These stakeholder groups usually situate and function at the influential level and their influence on target beneficiaries is quite strong and large in scope and coverage. There are several examples of it, such as the advertisement of contraception use and promotion of family planning programs, incentives for young children, and single parents, etc. Furthermore, if we examine the third engagement level (the holistic level), diversity and culture are situated at this level. Diversity includes areas of diversity, such as socioeconomic status, disability, gender, sexual orientation, ethnicity, etc., and culture refers to different cultures, such as individualistic culture, collectivistic culture, and evolved culture. These stakeholder groups are also quite similar in many ways. For instance, women are a diverse stakeholder group in society whose experiences are unique and different from men based on gender, which are informed and perpetuated by their culture. If learners include women of one ethnic group in their program, then other women who belong to the other ethnic groups and different from the target beneficiaries based on the area of diversity (ethnicity) and cultural group (s) are the stakeholder groups situated at the holistic level. Hence, diversity and cultural groups are relatively proximal to one another, quite similar to one another, perform quite similar roles and responsibilities, and also match with one another in terms of their degree of influence on the program and program participants.

According to the MCEM framework, the dynamics of each stakeholder group and their reciprocal relationships with each other within and between the engagement levels change over time due to developmental, sociocultural, and historical context. Those stakeholder groups which are situated at the same engagement level are influenced by developmental, sociocultural and historical context quite similarly compared to those stakeholder groups which are situated at a different engagement level. For example, target beneficiaries, their friends, and extended family members are likely to seek additional support from community organizations and support groups in their community. Schools provide additional support (counseling, financial assistance, and extracurricular programs) to children and families and promote school–home engagement, which benefits children compared to the past. Employers also offer more flexibility (work from home) to parents, which facilitates and supports parents in managing their household and childcare responsibilities. Supportive workplace policies, environment, and programs are offered to employees to help them maintain a healthy work-family balance. Similarly, public institutions formed and implemented policies (the law passed in 2015, which allowed same-sex couples to legally get married), which are more supportive to diverse couples and families. Media also promotes nontraditional gender images, which helps children to learn nontraditional gender roles, positively changes their perceptions and attitudes towards gender expectations and roles and decreases disparities between men and women. Donor agencies are formed (UN Women) to explicitly work on the issues of women (i.e. intimate partner violence, gender equality). More institutional support and employment opportunities are available for women to earn economic resources and take leadership roles compared to the past before 1960s. Hence, the influence of sociocultural and historical contexts on the stakeholder groups situated at the influential level are quite similar, which also shape their roles and responsibilities in society. Further, women were considered and labeled as idealized mothers who stayed home and raised their children, whereas men's roles were to make economic resources in the past before 1960s. In the current sociocultural context, women are outperforming men at all educational levels who make considerable economic resources and take leadership roles. Consequently, there is a substantial change in the division of household labor between men and women in the family. Cultural changes are also happening particularly in multigenerational families whose children are born in the US. Parents are acculturating into society such that they are integrating mainstream culture with their culture they brought from the family/country of origin to successfully raise their children. Hence, the influence of developmental, sociocultural, and historical contexts is quite similar on these stakeholder groups (diversity and culture) situated at the holistic level.

In conclusion, the MCEM framework is a complex, multilevel, and multifaceted framework, which offers a systematic procedure to develop, implement, and evaluate programs on different topics/issues to implement in various settings, and work with diverse groups of the population in societies around the world. It is worth mentioning that the MCEM framework is broader enough to apply to diverse societies and cultures globally, and simultaneously, it is narrow to an extent that can be operationalized and measured. The following chapters provide a step-by-step operationalization of the MCEM framework to systematically develop, implement, and evaluate programs. The MCEM is the first scientific and global framework in SL and community engagement, which provides a healthy balance between rigor (systematic procedure) and relevance (stakeholders' real-life experiences and active engagement and participation) throughout the program process in different settings, such as school, community, and workplace.

CASE STUDY

After identifying her program topic and potential program participants, Karen is not sure who else she needs to consult with and include it in her program. She also does not know what makes an inclusive program. What should be the timing to reach out, engage, and collaborate with other people? How would she know who is relevant and who is not quite relevant to her program. Since her goal is to make her program inclusive and representative of all groups in her local community and those who can play an important role for a longer period of time for program successful outcomes and sustainability, she is interested in learning, discovering, identifying, and reaching out to those people. She is also not sure who is considered a stakeholder for her program and where these individuals, families, groups, and/or organizations are situated in society. She also wants to learn whether program participants are different from or a part of relevant stakeholders. Her friends told her about the MCEM framework that answers all these questions. Her friends told Karen that the MCEM framework provides learners with an appropriate balance between rigor (systematic procedure) and relevance (stakeholders' real-life experience) in the process of systematically develop, implement, and evaluate the MCEM program inclusively. Karen explored and found a book "The Multilevel Community Engagement Model: School, Community, Workplace Engagement and Service-Learning." After purchasing and reading the book briefly, she is very happy, excited, and confident that she would be able to successfully develop, implement, and evaluate her program according to her needs, interests, and desires. She also feels that she doesn't need any substantial training or prior knowledge since this book will be her mentor and guide throughout the program process. She is thinking of reaching out to the expert in these areas if she needs any specific help regarding the use of the MCEM framework.

DISCUSSION QUESTIONS

(1) Discuss the role of MCEM framework in fostering stakeholders' engagement and collaboration in the program process?

(2) Which program topics/issues can be addressed through the MCEM programs?

(3) Which stakeholders are more influential than the others in a program?

(4) How does the MCEM framework recognize the voices of all stakeholder groups regardless of their social status in society?

(5) How does the MCEM framework acknowledge and utilize the knowledge, skills, and expertise of all relevant stakeholder groups in the program process?

(6) How are the MCEM programs more inclusive, engaged, and representative of all stakeholder groups?

(7) How are the MCEM programs likely to show successful program outcomes and ensure sustainability?

(8) Why is the MCEM program more relevant and meaningful for stakeholders including target beneficiaries?

(9) Share your reflections on the topic.

ASSIGNMENT QUESTIONS

(1) Describe the fundamental principles and components of the MCEM framework.

(2) What is the purpose and function of the MCEM framework?

(3) Describe the proximal level. Which stakeholder groups are situated at the proximal level?

(4) Describe the influential level. Which stakeholder groups are situated at the influential level?

(5) Describe the holistic level. Which stakeholder groups are situated at the holistic level?

(6) Discuss the role of developmental, sociocultural, and historical contexts in the MCEM framework.

(7) Discuss the reciprocal relationships between the stakeholder groups within and between the engagement levels.

(8) How do the reciprocal relationships between the stakeholder groups within and between the engagement levels change over time and influenced by developmental, sociocultural, and historical contexts.

(9) How does the MCEM provide learners with a systematic framework to develop, implement, and evaluate programs?

(10) What did you learn from this assignment?

3

THE PROCESS OF MCEM FRAMEWORK DEVELOPMENT, OPERATIONALIZATION, AND EMPIRICAL TESTING

The chapter discusses the process of development, operationalization, and empirical testing of the MCEM framework with specific information, details, and description. The author also shared his background, experience, and expertise, which led and guided him to work on the MCEM framework and develop it successfully. The author also included his personal reflections, which contributed to the development of the MCEM framework along with a specific scientific procedure that he used to develop this framework.

    I (the author) developed the MCEM framework after my decade long work on it. In this section, I share a process of its development with readers. The MCEM framework is a product of my background, work experience, and expertise. I worked with many different nongovernment local, national, and international organizations in Pakistan. I started my work as a community mobilizer and training facilitator for education. I was directly interacting with individuals, families, groups, and organizations who were partners with us to implement our projects. Then I joined another organization and worked with them as a program officer where I used to analyze data, conduct surveys, and write reports. It was also quite a useful experience as I was documenting all the work that my colleagues were performing in the field. After that, I joined an international organization and worked with them as a consultant. My role was to coordinate with field offices, visit them, build professional and technical capacities, and maintain organizational records. I also worked to create consistencies in terms, codes, and concepts to increase communication between organizational offices. It was comprehensive experience of both field and office work. Then I worked with a research organization as a program coordinator/

research associate. My role was to write proposals, design and conduct surveys, provide training to surveyors, field monitoring, data management, and report writing. It was also quite an extensive and useful learning experience for me. During this work with these different organizations, I was also working as a private consultant with other local organizations as a part-time job. My work was to provide them with technical support on proposal writing, survey design, research, and evaluation. It was also a quite beneficial experience for me professionally during which I was interacting and collaborating with these organizations and also other community stakeholders including individuals, families, groups, and community-based organizations.

Prior to starting my doctorate degree in the US, I had a few scholarly publications and presentations. I had methodological and theoretical experience and expertise at that time that I expanded during my PhD studies. I extensively worked on my theoretical knowledge and expertise and relate it with my applied knowledge and expertise that I gained while working with those local, national, and international organizations. Since I was extensively involved in doing research during my studies. I started using secondary data collected by a couple of nongovernment organizations in Pakistan (I requested them to provide me with their data and received an IRB approval for using it) that I worked with and also reflecting on my past work experiences and observations with these different organizations. In addition to analyzing data, I was also documenting my observations retrospectively when I was working with these organizations. My primary focus was to critically examine and review the approaches that these organizations used to work with local families and communities while carrying out their projects. Simultaneously, I was reviewing relevant literature to learn about other community development approaches, strategies, and perspectives that practitioners used with local communities around the world and how the approaches I observed during my work with nongovernment organizations in Pakistan were directly or indirectly related to them.

After an extensive review, examination, and documentation of various approaches, strategies, and perspectives, I found that traditional top-down, nontraditional bottom-up and participatory, and a mixture of these approaches were used by donor agencies, researchers, and practitioners when they worked with local communities. I also learned the advantages and disadvantages of these approaches and how these approaches produced distinctive outcomes and community sustainability. I kept publishing additional papers in scholarly journals, writing my reflections, and reviewing existing theoretical frameworks. Over time, I gained additional theoretical knowledge and expertise through my work, practice, and reflection, which substantiated my methodological and practical expertise. Then I started creating and documenting questions and insightful information based on the issues I was noticing through my research, data analysis, review, and reflection. For instance, why were some groups of the population underrepresented in community programs? Why were there gender and age disparities among program participation? How were different diversity areas affecting community people? Community people were not quite aware of public policies and programs which were directly or indirectly impacting their lives. There was a prevalent of traditional top-down approaches in community programs. There was a lack of communication, coordination, and collaboration between partners including donor agencies, local nongovernment organizations, and community target families. There was a lack of representation and participation in the decision-making process by target local families and communities. Each community individual, family, group, and organization had some strengths that could have improved and utilized for the success of community projects. Communities had important local knowledge, expertise that could have utilized for the success and sustainability of community projects. Communities were motivated, and they had wisdom who were willing to work hard, collaborate, and participate in community programs to bring positive changes in their lives. Due to the sociocultural and historical contexts of society, some communities were more vulnerable, poor, and deprived compared to the others. Children and women were more vulnerable in local communities compared to other groups. Due to their dependency and developmental changes, children were at a greater risk of experiencing physical, mental, and social emotional issues. These were some of questions and insightful information that I wanted to explore and discover the answers for (Raza, 2017, 2018, 2020a).

For this purpose, I used my own self-reflections that I had been recording continuously and extensively, and different theoretical frameworks, such as family systems theory (Goldenberg et al., 2017; Smith & Hamon, 2022; von Bertalanffy, 1968; White et al., 2019), participatory action research (Herr, 1999; Herr & Anderson, 2015), and ecological systems theory (Bronfenbrenner, 1978, 1979) and consulted with them to get my answers to these questions and insightful information. For instance, I learned from family systems theory that it is important to include all family members in a program to adequately address a problem even though only one family member is experiencing that issue. From participatory action research perspective, I learned that when power hierarchies are removed or minimized between program participants and practitioners, it fosters collaboration and engagement of all partners in a program and provide each member with an opportunity to actively participate in the decision-making process. Such a participatory and empowering approach produces successful project outcomes and ensures sustainability. I learned from ecological systems theory that it is important to consider and examine the influences of different ecological systems on community individuals and families because they play an important role in shaping their experiences in society to gain insightful information about community needs, experiences, and issues. Moreover, the issues of diversity, culture, and inclusion were also prevalent in community programs, such that some individuals and groups who belonged to high socioeconomic status had more power and influence in the decision-making process of community program, whereas poor individuals and families were marginalized and isolated. Hence, through my direct observations and reflections, I learned the importance of carrying out an inclusive process which respects and appreciate all areas of diversity, such as education, gender, age, disability, race, socioeconomic status, etc., recognize the voices of all individuals, families, groups, and organizations regardless of their social status in society, and provide them with fair and equal opportunities to participate in decision-making process over the course of a project lifecycle. Finally, through my self-reflection and review, I learned that for the success and sustainability of community programs, open communication, consistent coordination, and strong collaboration among all partners are essential.

In order to address the aforementioned gaps based on the answered that I learned and discovered from these theoretical frameworks and perspectives along with my personal reflections, I developed the MCEM (Raza, 2020a, 2021, 2022) as a potential framework to use in programs on various topics and issues, which can be implemented in various settings, and with diverse groups of the population in societies around the world. The MCEM framework promotes active participation and engagement of all relevant program stakeholder groups who are situated at different engagement levels of society throughout the program process regardless of their knowledge, skills, and social status in society. Such an inclusive process, which recognizes the voices and utilizes expertise of all relevant program stakeholders, results in programs which are culturally appropriate, comprehensive, representative, successful, and sustainable. Consequently, the MCEM programs are likely to show successful outcomes and sustainability.

After developing the MCEM framework, it was quite challenging to operationalize it because it is a comprehensive and multilevel framework. I used many ways to explore and discover an accurate and realistic operationalization of the MCEM framework. For this purpose. I used existing programs and developed multiple operationalization to use, review, and assess those programs. I also developed hypothetical programs based on these operationalizations. I recorded my steps, practices, and processes of the MCEM operationalization. When I felt confident about the operationalization of the MCEM framework, I started using it in my classrooms. First, I used it in my seated undergraduate classrooms, then I used it in online courses. I then used it in my graduate level course. Over time, I started developing specific assignments which were demonstrating the operationalization of the MCEM framework. I was also using assignments, discussions, and lectures, of different degrees, sizes, and complexities to test the reliability and generalizability of the MCEM framework.

After obtaining successful results from multiple courses, consolidating, and critically reviewing them, I planned on conducting a formal empirical study to examine and assess the effectiveness of the MCEM framework, its operationalization, and the MCEM programs. For this purpose, I submitted an IRB application and got my study approved. I conducted this study in my seated and online undergraduate and graduate level classes and found successful results. I also assessed the validity and reliability of the MCEM framework by changing the assignments description, moving the assignments into different modules for different courses, increasing and decreasing the number of assignments per course and found consistent, supportive, and successful results. Below are a few responses from the students from that study that illustrate the effective operationalization, empirical testing of the MCEM framework, and the success of the MCEM programs.

UNDERGRADUATE STUDENT

"Developing my MCEM program with my partners was really interesting and helped me understand some of the topics we learned in this class on a deeper level."

The above response from an undergraduate student is evident that the process of MCEM program, which was informed by the MCEM framework provided them with valuable opportunities to learn the course contents on a deeper level by developing the MCEM programs. Students developed the MCEM programs for their SL projects, which is the core purpose of SL to apply and practice classroom learning in real-world settings. This happened when students used the course knowledge and skills and applied it to real-world settings, work with individuals, families, groups, and organizations, and resolve real-life problems. Consequently, this practice also fostered positive SL experiences and promoted community engagement among students. Moreover, students worked in their small groups on their SL projects throughout the semester, which also provided them with an important experience teamwork, learn about each other, practice problem solving, and work collaboratively for a specific purpose. This learning experience was quite applied and practical, and students found it quite meaningful and valuable.

GRADUATE STUDENT

"This was a wonderful class project to enhance diversity in ECE and apply it in a real-world way. The timing of each week was perfect."

The above student response indicates the significance of developing, implementing, and evaluating the MCEM programs for students' SL projects to promote diversity in early childhood education classrooms. The advantage of using the MCEM framework in developing the MCEM programs is that it provides learners with systematic guidelines and fit with their schedule and timelines to successfully complete it. Those learners who do not have any prior experience in this area can easily follow the step-by-step guidelines and work on their SL projects. It is worth mentioning that although the MCEM framework provides systematic guidelines, these guidelines do not limit learners' abilities to choose and explore their own interests and apply their personal ideas. The MCEM framework facilitates learners in the MCEM program process who make their own decisions and choices and work with program relevant stakeholders including the program participants as a team member throughout the program process, which increases their motivation, efficiency, and productivity in SL projects.

GRADUATE STUDENT

"Overall, my experience with my MCEM program was great! I appreciated all the assignments that helped me to build my program and stay on track with it. I felt prepared and successful when executing my program."

The above response from a graduate student shares another success story regarding the MCEM program. It is worth mentioning that students can either work on their MCEM programs in small groups; they can also work individually particularly when they are taking online classes and not physically closer to one another. This is due to the flexibility on the MCEM framework and its operationalization that makes it applicable to all modes of learning and delivery to successfully help, guide, and facilitate learners in completing their SL projects.

UNDERGRADUATE STUDENT

"Overall, my experience in developing, implementing, and assessing my MCEM program was successful and beneficial. I think that the development process was well thought through and helped my group develop teamwork skills. The implementation process helped us to understand why all of the work we had been putting in truly mattered. After assessing our program, I think the outcome and process itself taught us valuable lessons both pertaining directly to our subject and also in unrelated ways."

As it is evident from the above student response, the MCEM program process is a valuable, continuous, and complex process. Although it can be quite challenging and exhaustive for learners, it pays off when learners reflect on their learning and gains; they receive from the MCEM program process. It is worth mentioning that at the beginning of the MCEM program, learners may not be quite sure or clear about what the process will look like. Hence, it is important for instructors to provide learners as much information as possible and learners should have time and opportunities to share and discuss their project ideas and strategies with their small group members and the instructor. Even though learners work individually on their MCEM program, instructors need to create their small groups from the beginning of their class (for each mode of delivery, such as seated, hybrid, synchronized and non-synchronized online) so that they are engaged with their small group members throughout the process, share ideas and strategies to help and facilitate each other's learning. Moreover, when students work in their communities with diverse groups of population to address their needs and resolve immediate and important problems, it provides them with valuable opportunities to learn about different cultures and interact with those who look different from them. Students also take a lead in developing their programs, engaging with program stakeholders, and planning to implement it with program participants, which increases their leadership skills. Students also make social connections with different stakeholders' groups in local communities. Students also discover and explore their passion and interest in different professional areas which they might not have thought about. When students reach out and bring all relevant program stakeholder groups together who work collaboratively to develop, implement, and evaluate the MCEM program for addressing the needs of their local individuals, families, and groups or resolving their important or immediate problems, it fosters community engagement and grow positive citizenship behaviors among all stakeholders. Hence, the MCEM program not only provides students with essential experiences of SL and community engagement, but it also benefits them in other nonacademic, personal, social, and professional ways.

The above empirical evidence in support of the MCEM framework, its operationalization, and the MCEM programs shows the flexibility, adaptability, effective operationalization of this framework in developing, implementing, and evaluating programs on different topics/issues, with diverse groups of the population, and in various settings, such as school, community, and workplace in societies around the world. It is worth mentioning that the MCEM framework has been developed and tested through a complex and cyclical process of induction and deduction. It was tested in various classroom settings including undergraduate seated classes, undergraduate online class, graduate online classes, school, community, and workplace settings, and with various individuals, families, groups, and organizations. After such a complex testing, empirical evidence in support of the MCEM framework and its validity and reliability were obtained and recorded, which showed a success and positive outcomes. Similarly, I developed all definitions of the terms are concepts related to the MCEM framework and programs included in this book, which are inclusive, comprehensive, and relevant to the MCEM framework and programs.

In sum, the MCEM framework is a global framework to systematically develop, implement, and evaluate programs on any topic, work with any group of the population, and in any settings in culturally diverse societies around the world. The MCEM framework is broad enough that can be used and applied globally, and simultaneously, it is specific and precise to a certain degree that can be implemented, assessed, and measured. It provides a paradigm shift in SLand community engagement by offering an appropriate and useful balance between scientific procedure and real-life experiences of stakeholders. The MCEM framework addressed the existing gaps and weakness which have been prevalent in the field of SL and community engagement and provided new ways to develop, implement, and evaluate programs for SL and community engagement, which makes the MCEM programs successful and sustainable.

CASE STUDY

Karen has been learning the challenges and struggles of researchers and practitioners to operationalize theoretical frameworks for their use, application, and empirical testing. She is not aware of what she needs to look at to examine the effectiveness and accuracy of the operationalization of a theoretical framework. She understands that due to a lack of effective operationalization, the utility of any theoretical framework can be limited and suffered in real-world situations. After reviewing the MCEM framework and its effective operationalization, she is very glad and quite confident that she does not require any additional skills to learn, apply, and understand the operationalization of the MCEM framework to use it for her program. Each assignment is a part of the MCEM operationalization, which is backed and supposed by prior empirical testing through research and practice. She knows that she just needs to follow each chapter to complete each step of the program process to successfully develop, implement, and evaluate her programs, which reduced her substantial pressure, stress, and burden.

DISCUSSION QUESTIONS

(1) Discuss the role of direct observation and prior relevant experience in developing the MCEM framework.

(2) Which theoretical framework and perspectives were used in the development process of the MCEM framework?

(3) Discuss the role of reflective process in developing the MCEM framework?

(4) How did the development of the MCEM framework address the existing gaps and make a unique contribution in the field?

(5) Discuss the process of operationalization and empirical testing of the MCEM framework?

(6) Why was the operationalization and empirical testing of the MCEM framework important?

(7) In which settings the MCEM framework can be used and applied?

(8) How does the MCEM framework produce program success and sustainability?

(9) How does the MCEM framework provide a useful balance between rigor and relevance?

(10) How does the MCEM framework provide a paradigm shift in SL and community engagement?

ASSIGNMENT QUESTIONS

(1) How is the MCEM framework operationalized? Provide some examples.

(2) How do the SL assignments demonstrate the operationalization of the MCEM framework?

(3) How do you see a consistency between the theory and application in the MCEM framework?

(4) How is the operationalization of the MCEM framework to make the MCEM programs more flexible, adaptable, and effective?

(5) Discuss the strengths and challenges of the MCEM operationalization.

(6) What did you learn from this assignment?

4

THE ROLE OF MCEM FRAMEWORK IN SCHOOL, COMMUNITY, WORKPLACE ENGAGEMENT AND SERVICE-LEARNING

The objective of this chapter is to present the benefits and challenges of SL for students, instructors, institutions, and communities to grow and sustain SL and community engagement in school, community, and workplace around the world. Based on a critical examination of the existing literature of SL and community engagement, the author developed a few important themes and concepts on the benefits and challenges of SL and community engagement and discussed the role of MCEM framework in addressing those challenges and expanding the benefits to foster positive student learning experiences in their SL projects, facilitate instructors to integrate SL into their courses, guide institutions to develop and implement supportive policies and conducive environment for SL, and engage and benefit local communities in SL projects. This chapter also shares how the MCEM framework makes SL projects more inclusive and sustainable.

SERVICE-LEARNING

The author defines SL is a meaningful and action-oriented practice of using relevant classroom knowledge and skills and applying it to real-life situations for the purpose of providing students, researchers, and practitioners with applied, experiential, and authentic experiences in a reflective and transformative manner for addressing the needs and issues of individuals, families, groups, and organizations to strengthen them and bring positive changes in communities and society.

The above definition of SL demonstrates its many benefits. One of the fundamental purposes of SL is to provide learners with opportunities to use and apply the knowledge, information, and skills that they learn in the classroom when they study course contents, complete assignments, participate in discussions, and write reflections in real-life situations. When learners work with individuals, families, groups, and organizations in real-world settings to address their needs and issues, they practice theoretical knowledge and gain applied and experiential learning experience. When learners work with diverse individuals and families and partner with different groups and organizations to carry out their SL projects, they come across several challenges. In order to deal with those real-world problems, learners take concrete actions, design specific plans, and develop useful strategies. This process not only fosters learners positive learning experiences but it also prepares learners professionally because they are likely to face similar problems, work with individuals, families, groups, and organizations, manage projects and run programs in their professional career. In addition to preparing learners academically and professionally, SL also prepares learners personally and ethically. This can be achieved by promoting critical thinking, positive attitude, and reflective process among learners. When learners examine their biases, values, and beliefs, and reflect upon them to find out how they impact learners' thinking, approaches, and working with others, such a reflective process brings positive changes in their lives because learners can overcome some or all their self-biases, which hinders their positive interactions or attitudes toward others. Consequently, they become more authentic and prepared to deal with any ethical and personal challenges when they work with local schools, communities, and/or workplaces. When learners work in real-world settings, they learn from actual problems and work collaboratively with others to resolve them, which brings positive changes in the lives of learners and all other stakeholders including program participants. Additionally, when learners find SL projects relevant to their personal, academic, and professional lives, it becomes meaningful for them, which motivates them to work diligently and collaboratively for bringing positive changes in local communities and society. As it is evident from the definition, SL carries many benefits for learners, communities, and society. The author shares important themes on the benefits and challenges of SL which emerged based on his critical review of literature on SL and community engagement in the following sections.

BENEFITS AND CHALLENGES OF SERVICE-LEARNING

SL offers many benefits for students, instructors, institutions, and communities (Cress et al., 2023), but it also brings some challenges for them. The following are a few themes which demonstrate the benefits and challenges of SL. The role of MCEM framework is also discussed in expanding SL benefits and addressing its challenges to provide students with applied and experiential learning experiences, facilitate instructors in integrating SL into their courses, and guide institutions to create and sustain a conducive environment to support and grow SL efforts and work.

Student Level SL Benefits and Challenges

SL provides students with impactful and high-quality learning experiences (Garner & Parker, 2016; Halsell & Gallant, 2022; Tatkin, 2016). It develops and fosters students' positive attitudes and perceptions about community service and makes them better citizens (Cress et al., 2023). SL provides students with opportunities to apply disciplinary knowledge to real-world situations for addressing immediate and important community needs and problems (Cress et al., 2023). In education, when students carry out their SL learning projects in classrooms and schools, it not only provides students with useful opportunities to take a lead and collaborate with teachers, staff, and leadership team for their SL projects, but it also creates liaison and connection between educational institutions and educators (Heras-Colàs et al., 2023; Deng et al., 2021; Herr & Anderson, 2015). Research shows that when preservice teachers successfully implement and complete their SL projects, it grows their knowledge and skills, practical experience, and increases the likelihood of their success when they start their professional career in teaching and education (Anderson, 2000; Barth et al., 2024; Herr, 2017; Kinsella, & Hollins, 2022). Innovative SL projects transform ideas, thinking, and approaches of early career teachers towards teaching and learning, and shows positive impacts on them as teachers (Anderson et al., 2022). When preservice teachers carry out their SL projects in teacher education programs, they also gain opportunities to work with culturally diverse population, which prepares them for their early career to work with diverse student population (Clark & Andreasen, 2021). Preservice teachers also work with participants who have a disability or special care needs, which provides them with opportunities to deal with students' special needs and demands and professionally develop them for their teaching career (An, 2021). Preservice teachers work with in-service teachers during their SL projects and learn to develop syllabi, curricula, course assignments, activities, and participate in decision-making process, which is also quite a beneficial practice and learning experience for them during their studies (Ayton & Capraro, 2021). Effective instructions and guidance including clarity, feedback, and support in the areas of learning fosters pre-service teachers' motivation and self-efficacy and shows positive outcomes (Chan et al., 2023; Gonzalez-DeHass et al., 2021; Herr & Anderson, 2015).

Moreover, research illustrates that there are gaps in students' expectations to meet school and community needs through their SL projects and the actual needs in real-world situations, which can trigger students' stress and frustration but it also promotes a critical thinking and reflective process among students (Herr & Anderson, 2015; Herr, 1999; One, 2022). For instance, the dynamics, problems, and needs in schools, communities, and workplaces are more complex and multifaceted than they apparently look (Herr & Anderson, 2015; Raza, 2020a). Such a reflective process transforms students' thinking and approaches towards their SL projects and brings changes in their lives personally and professionally (Herr, 2017; Raza, 2020a). Consequently, students are well prepared for their professional careers by going through these situations and experiences and implementing their SL projects (Heras-Colàs et al., 2023; Herr, 2017).

SL also promotes students' discussions and collaboration and increases teacher–student interactions on the topic, who work together to design and implement SL projects, share ideas, and discuss challenges, which also provides them with opportunities to learn about each other and build positive interpersonal relationships (Young, 2024). When students work in communities, they discover and explore their professional interest and identity; it further guides them for their professional career (Bolger & Murphy, 2024; Gallop et al., 2023; Valdez & Lovell, 2022). SL increases students' professional portfolio and makes them more marketable in the job market because employers value candidates' prior applied experience relevant to the role and position (Jung, 2021; Rego et al., 2022; Riepe et al., 2011; Samad, 2022). When students partner with community organizations for their SL projects, they also learn workplace communication, professional behaviors, teamwork, and interpersonal skills (Goodman et al., 2023; Karasik, 2020). Consequently, students learn the importance of social and civic responsibilities and engagement and feel pride to perform a valuable and compassionate service for schools, communities, and workplaces to address immediate and important needs and problems and bring positive changes in their lives (Terry & Qi, 2024; Jin & Bierma, 2023; Patterson, 2020; Raza, 2022).

Further, in international SL, students are exposed to various cultures, languages, and traditions, which enriches their cultural knowledge and understanding about diverse cultural groups even though they experience some language barriers in performing their SL projects (One, 2022). Students learn new things about communities, their family life, and culture, and while collaborating with diverse community groups for their SL projects, they become comfortable working with those who are different from them in terms of cultures, ethnicity, and/or language, which increases their cultural competence (Robinson, 2021; Torres et al., 2022). International SL experience also provides students with opportunities to reflect on their self-biases and preconceived notions and evaluate their capacities and comfort level, which strengthens their leadership skills and improves students' abilities to make the best decisions regarding their SL projects to adequately address community problems internationally (Berman, 2015; One, 2022). Hence, SL contains many benefits for students.

Despite these benefits, SL accompanies with challenges. Research shows that students have distinctive learning styles, abilities, and needs (Kinsella & Hollins, 2022). If SL projects are not aligned or matched with students' learning needs, students may not take interest in SL projects, perform poorly, and likely get frustrated while doing SL projects (Ewa Domagala-Zyśk, 2021). Additionally, if SL projects do not offer an appropriate application of course contents to real-life situations and lack to provide students with and experiential learning and applied experience, students may not find SL projects useful and relevant to them personally, academically, and professional, which may affect their motivation, participation, and learning outcomes (Garwood et al., 2023). Students with special educational needs who have learning disabilities need additional assistance and support in traditional classrooms. When SL is integrated into the course, SL projects need to be modified and aligned with their learning needs and abilities (Garwood et al., 2023). When SL projects help to foster their daily functioning skills and are consistent with their special learning needs, it may increase student learning outcomes (Garwood et al., 2023; Moore, 2024). Moreover, students learn theoretical knowledge in classrooms settings, and the purpose of SL projects is to provide students with an opportunity to use and practice that theoretical knowledge in real-world situations (Raza, 2022). When there is a disconnection between theory and application due to poor operationalization, students get confused and lost, which affects their learning outcomes (Raza, 2022). Sometimes, SL projects are controlled and directed entirely by the instructor, which limits students to test, explore, and use their cognitive abilities, autonomy, and ideas, and increases their frustration and anxiety (Yusof et al., 2020). When SL projects lack appropriate guidance, details, and advice, students get lost and frustrated, and due to the complexity of SL, students perform poorly in their SL projects (Hoeh et al., 2023; Sundberg & Koehler, 2023). In international community settings, when students perform their service and implement their SL projects, if there is a lack of communication, consensus, and inclusive participation of all stakeholders in the decision-making process, interpersonal conflicts are likely to arise during or after the formal completion of the project between students and local communities in SL projects (Crabtree, 2013). The evidence indicates that SL contains many challenges and complexities, and students, faculty, institutions, and community partners need to work together to successfully deal with them.

Instructor Level SL Benefits and Challenges

SL facilitates instructors to explore, discover, and reflect on their personal strengths and weaknesses and adopt different teaching styles to foster student SL experiences (Feuerherm et al., 2022). Instructors expand student learning of the course contents when they effectively structure, organize, integrate, and align SL projects with course contents and learning objectives, which also results in positive learning outcomes of the course (Davis et al., 2021; Kumar et al., 2022). SL experience and expertise increases the marketability of instructors and increases professional opportunities for them (Raza, 2022). It also provides instructors with inner satisfaction and pride as they promote positive citizenship behaviors and civic engagement among students (Herr, 2017; Raza, 2017). Instructors make direct and/or indirect contributions in sustainable community efforts to bring positive changes in the lives of community individuals, families, groups, and organizations (Raza, 2022). They interact with students to learn about their projects' experiences and local communities they work with. Sometimes, instructors also coordinate, review, and visit community partners and may interact with other groups of community stakeholders who belong to different cultures, ethnicities, and languages, which also increases their cultural competence (Raza, 2018). As SL is beneficial with all individuals and groups who are involved in SL projects, instructors facilitate and guide students in their SL projects and provide students with useful advice and suggestions to deal with real-world challenges and problems students might face while implementing their projects and working with target families, which provides instructors with opportunities to learn and practice leadership skills (Raza, 2020a). Since SL is also a reflective process for all partners, when instructors reflect on their ongoing experiences with students and other stakeholders who they interact with, it may validate or question some of their values, believes, and/or preconceived notions and helps them to overcome their self-biases toward others (Herr & Anderson, 2015; Raza, 2022). Hence, SL contains many benefits for instructors.

Instructors play an integral role in carrying out and sustaining SL efforts in their institutions, who also face challenges when they integrate and implement SL in their courses (Egan et al., 2024; Herr, 2017; Raza, 2022). For instance, the integration of SL consumes substantial time of instructors and requires a time commitment, and if instructors do not receive appropriate support from their institutions, colleagues, and/or department, it can create additional challenges for them (Cooper, 2014; Egan et al., 2024; Lau et al., 2023). Instructors complete their course contents in a limited time, and if SL projects are not effectively integrated into their course contents, it may consume their additional time to make appropriate adjustments and guide students about them which takes the time away from teaching students specific course contents (Jin & Bierma, 2023; Lalloo et al., 2021; Leftwich et al., 2022; Lewis, 2021). Due to misalignment between SL projects and course learning objectives, instructors as well as students experience frustration, confusion, and anxiety in completing their SL projects (Lalloo et al., 2021; Wyche-Jonas, 2022). Since SL requires additional knowledge and skills from instructors and collaboration among stakeholder groups, such as school, community, workplace, inexperienced instructors avoid taking additional risk particularly if they don't receive any capacity building trainings or resources from their institutions (Cress et al., 2022; Chung, 2020; Neeper & Dymond, 2020). Instructors also feel reluctant in implementing SL if there is a lack of institutional support and resources for them in integrating SL into their courses because it creates additional barriers for them (Feuerherm et al., 2022; Garvin & Acosta Lewis, 2022; Lewis, 2021). Instructors with less or no experience in SL are less likely to continue SL courses particularly if there are additional challenges and changes in course delivery, such as the recent Pandemic because they already deal with additional work and challenges due to having less or no experience and expertise and any additional pressure or burden can create hurdles in their SL efforts (Garvin et al., 2022; Sartor-Harada et al., 2022). It is evident that instructors can get demotivated to integrate SL into their courses if there is no recognition or appreciation of their SL work and efforts from their institution (Faulconer & Kam, 2023; Kong et al., 2024). Instructors perceive that they may lose control over students or their learning because SL projects are implemented outside of classrooms, which also decreases their intent or motivation to integrate SL into their courses (Cooper & Kotys-Schwartz, 2022; Miller, 2020; Wetzl & Lieske, 2020). Since SL is carried out outside of the classroom and this is the purpose of SL which is to provide students with opportunities to use classroom knowledge and apply it real-world settings, it becomes difficult for instructors to assess students' performance and learning outcomes (Casquero et al., 2022; Cecilia, 2022; García, 2023; Hou & Wilder, 2015b). Additionally, if there is a lack of common language or examples on SL projects for instructors with no or less experience, it becomes difficult for them to understand, apply, and integrate SL principles into the courses (Hoeh et al., 2023). SL opens many doors for students who explore and discover their interests and professional careers while performing their SL projects, sometimes, instructors do not have sufficient knowledge and skills in all areas, and if there is no transdisciplinary partnerships and collaboration, it can limit instructors' abilities to facilitate students in their SL projects and hinder their SL efforts (Sundberg & Koehler, 2023).

Institutional Level SL Benefits and Challenges

Institutions also benefit from SL. For instance, SL expertise and practices have become important and useful for institutions to improve the quality of their educational programs (Kandakatla et al., 2023). It enhances the popularity and marketability of institutions among their competitors and improves their accreditation (Angel, 2021; Kandakatla et al., 2023; Malone et al., 2023). SL expands universities' outreach efforts and prepares their students to work with local communities outside of traditional classrooms (Darling et al., 2022). SL also increases state and federal funding opportunities for institutions, which generate additional reviews and profits for them (Duncan & Goddard, 2017; Raza, 2022). SL learning helps institutions to create connections and good reputation in local communities, reach out to historically underrepresented groups of the population, and provide scientific knowledge outside of academic settings in remote and rural areas (Raza, 2022; Raza & Richey, 2021). Due to offering SL courses, institutions attract more students particularly those who are interested in gaining hands-on experiences and prefer experiential learning, which increases enrollment and generates additional revenues for them (Raza, 2022). Institutions provides their students with unique community engagement exposure and valuable SL experience locally, nationally, and/or internationally that students like to have, and they find it engaging and interesting, which increases student retention in that institution (Crabtree, 2013; Raza, 2022). Hence, SL contains many benefits for institutions.

SL also brings challenges for institutions that they need to deal with to successfully grow and implement SL. Although institutions have policies that recognize SL courses and support its implementation, a lack of application and practice of such policies decreases faculty's morale and motivation to implement SL (Dholakia & Hartman, 2023; Markaki et al., 2021; Novak et al., 2020). Instructors are usually self-motivated due to having personal beliefs and values regarding civic and social responsibilities, and they see SL as a potential way to implement and foster these values among their students and local communities; due to the lack of institutional support and external barriers, they feel reluctant to adopt or integrate SL in their courses (Abell et al., 2023; Hou & Wilder, 2015a; Smith et al., 2020; Weakley et al., 2021). If institutions don't facilitate instructors or fail to provide appropriate resources and support to determine and use straightforward and culturally appropriate evaluation methods and techniques for assessing SL projects, it can also create barriers in growing SL efforts and work in those institutions (Chan, 2022; Finley, 2021; Kanan et al., 2023). Therefore, it is essential for institutions to promote interdisciplinary partnerships and collaboration among their faculty, which helps to foster SL efforts, and a lack of such partnerships and conducive environment may hinder these efforts (Hoeh et al., 2023; Sundberg & Koehler, 2023). Additionally, due to inefficient documentation and dissemination of SL projects, principles, rules, and policies from the institutions, faculty are discouraged and demotivated to use and integrate SL into their courses (Camus et al., 2023; Carpenter et al., 2022; Johnston, 2022; Schneider et al., 2018). Finally, community partners are imperative for implementing SL; hence, it is essential for institutions to develop and maintain effective communication and coordination with local communities and organizations to form and sustain community partnerships because if there is no connection, collaboration, partnership between formal institutions and local communities, the implementation of SL for students can be quite challenges and time consuming (Compare et al., 2022; Kimiecik et al., 2023; Tyndall et al., 2020; Walker et al., 2021).

Community Level SL Benefits and Challenges

SL offers many benefits for local or target communities, which is also accompanied by some challenges (Raza, 2020a, 2022). Due to income disparities, growing mental health problems, mass shooting, substance abuse, child abuse, intimate partner violence, special needs, pandemic, and other social and environmental issues, individuals and families living local communities are facing many problems, which are important and immediate because they affect the well-being and development of these individuals and families (Herr, 1999; Raza, 2020a). Consequently, these communities show their needs, which are essential to be addressed to ensure their smooth functioning and optimal development (Herr, 2017; Raza, 2022). Many communities are culturally diverse, which brings additional demands and challenges for practitioners to effectively work with them (Herr, 1995). A lack of communication between practitioners and community families and insensitivity to community culture hinder the successful implementation of community programs, which limits sustainability and positive outcomes (Zorondo-Rodriguez et al., 2014). For instance, when programs do not resonate community cultural values, beliefs, and practices, target families do not find such programs relevant, useful, and meaningful for them, and consequently, they lose interest, motivation, and participation in these programs (Herr, 1999; Raza, 2021). The use of traditional and top-down approaches limits collaborations and coalitions between practitioners and target communities and fails to adequately understand and address community issues (Dirix et al., 2013; Raza, 2017). Through top-down approaches, practitioners and organizations have their predetermined plans and goals that they implement without gaining insights about the target families and communities and having inputs from them (Herr & Anderson, 2015; Raza, 2020b). There have been substantial improvements in practitioners/organizations' communication, strategies, and approaches to work with culturally diverse communities; however, the prevalence of traditional and top-down approaches, which lack to consider community context, dialog, and actual needs, and provide no or less opportunities to community families to participate in the decision-making process are still quite prevalent (Herr, 1999; Paquette et al., 2015; Raza, 2022).

Researchers and practitioners have been doing wonderful work and carrying out participatory and action-orientated projects to understand and address community needs and issues (Herr & Anderson, 2015). Although these efforts have been making considerable differences and bringing important and positive changes in the lives of these individuals and families, there is essential need to sustain these efforts and ensure that such efforts are continued so that these communities receive an adequate dosage and amount of information, knowledge, skills, and treatment to be able resolve their serious issues (Herr, 1999; Herr & Anderson, 1993; Raza, 2018). For this purpose, an effective and consistent collaboration and engagement between school, work, and community is needed. SL plays an important role in creating a liaison between school, community, and workplace when students from universities partner with nongovernmental organizations and work with local communities (Herr & Anderson, 2015; Raza, 2022). Even though student SL projects are completed in short time periods, students who come later can continue these efforts and projects with the same local communities to sustain these efforts. Additionally, when people from school, community, and workplace engage and work together on SL projects, they can also integrate and sustain those efforts through their programs, services, and organizational platforms. Hence, the integration of SL learning into the institutional curriculum becomes quite fruitful not only for students, instructors, and institutions but also for community families.

THE ROLE OF MCEM FRAMEWORK IN ADDRESSING SL CHALLENGES

This section discusses the role of the MCEM framework in expanding SL benefits and addressing challenges which are examined and discussed above. There are three themes/concepts that emerged from the above discussion, each from students, instructors, and institutions, which are primarily important. First, SL is important for students because it provides students with applied and experimental learning experience, which develops students personally, academically, ethically, and professionally. Instructors are self-motivated to carry out SL efforts and integrate SL into their courses, but they become reluctant to integrate SL into their courses due to a lack of expertise, no prior experience, inadequate institutional support, fewer resources, and unconducive environment. Third, although institutions develop policies and procedures in favor of SL, these policies and procedures are not effectively implemented at the institutional level; consequently, instructors face challenges to integrate and implement SL in their courses.

The MCEM framework provides a step-by-step guideline to all groups of learners including students, instructors, and institutions that they can follow to integrate SL into their courses. All assignments related to each step and in-depth discussions are provided in this book that makes the integration of SL quite easier, smoother, and less time-consuming for learners. When instructors are well-organized and prepared in terms of integrating SL into their courses by using the MCEM framework, they feel more confident, communicate more effectively with colleagues and department administrators, and provide required information or evidence to the relevant authority to demonstrate the integration of all requirements of SL if necessary. When instructors are clear and confident in their approaches and guidelines, it also facilitates students' SL experiences and promotes SL in that institution. The MCEM framework naturally integrates SL into a course. For instance, students choose a topic for their program from their course contents and all steps are integrated into the course contents, which makes it quite a seamless process. There are several suggestions for the MCEM program topics provided in this book, cases studies, discussions, and reflection questions, which facilitate students and instructors to expand the course content knowledge and apply it to real-life situations by using the MCEM framework for their SL projects. As discussed earlier, the use of MCEM framework for SL projects creates an alignment between SL project and course contents, which are usually aligned with the course learning objectives. Consequently, the SL projects are aligned with the course learning objectives. Instructors can also modify any course objectives and develop one specific objective for their SL projects if they think it is necessary for that course. Otherwise, if the course contents are aligned with the learning objectives, then the integration of the MCEM framework for SL projects is much smoother and easier because the SL assignments grounded in the MCEM framework naturally embedded in the course contents. Due to such a seamless and smooth integration of SL into the course, the MCEM framework helps and guides instructors and institutions to provide students with positive, effective, and meaningful SL experiences as it is a useful and important experience for them, which develops them in many areas of their live.

The use of the MCEM framework does not require any additional or specialized knowledge about SL. Instructors need to familiarize themselves with the book and guidelines provided for each step. These guidelines provide instructors with some control over students' learning regarding their SL projects and also empower students to pursue their interest and choices in their SL projects. Students carry out most of their SL projects, the role of instructors is to provide appropriate information and guidelines to students for their projects to facilitate their learning and those guidelines are provided in this book. For instance, if students are facing any difficulties in finding community partners, then instructors can coordinate with the relevant SL office, attain a list of potential/approved partners, and share it with students. Instructors can also explore and find potential community partners, provide additional information on the relevant community partner, and work with students to review and approve their community partner for their SL projects. Similarly, if students struggle with any step of developing, implementing, or evaluating their MCEM program, instructors can provide them with additional information, explanation, and examples to improve their understanding of that particular step or procedure.

Moreover, this book guides instructors to integrate SL into their seated, online, and hybrid courses. Students can also work remotely and complete all steps online like they do in seated or traditional on-campus classes due to the flexibility of the MCEM framework and the use of technology. For instance, students can reach out and meet with relevant stakeholders online, by phone, or email and learn about them through their websites. The implementation can also be held online through Zoom meetings. Students can conduct as many workshops/educational sessions as they like with their program participants on Zoom or through any other online platforms. Hence, this book is a guide and mentor for those instructors who have no prior experience of SL to successfully integrate and implement SL into their courses based on the type of course and its mode of delivery.

Instructors neither need to substantially showcase their work nor quite concerned about the recognition of it, when they use the MCEM framework in their classrooms and their students develop, implement, and evaluate different programs on various topics and work with diverse groups on campus, schools, communities, and workplaces, instructors' work is automatically recognized and appreciated. The MCEM program are sustainable and transformational; hence, due to the positive and sustainable changes among relevant stakeholders including program participants, it is likely that these groups who are involved in the program process share their positive experience directly or indirectly with the administration and leadership team of the institution. Because institutions also work with schools, communities, and workplaces, carrying out their outreach efforts, and develop partnerships, they may also likely learn about instructors' efforts and SL projects. The MCEM programs bring stakeholder groups together and connect them with the university administrators and leadership team, who work together to develop, implement, and evaluate SL projects with students. Consequently, external barriers are minimized because stakeholder groups including schools, communities, and workplaces from multiple engagement levels who are external to the institutions are engaged throughout the program process. These stakeholders can provide a solution to any problem and collaborate to resolve it particularly if they find a program more relevant and meaningful for themselves and their communities. Consequently, the use of MCEM framework minimizes many barriers for instructors, which hinders the integration of SL into their courses.

Additionally, there are several assessments provided in this book that students and instructors can use to evaluate students' or program performance throughout the SL project lifecycle. Hence, instructors guide, facilitate, and supervise students to make sure that SL projects are implemented smoothly, accurately, and in a timely manner. Instructors can use ongoing assessments, methods, and/or carry out discussions provided in this book to assess the learning and performance of students on their SL projects. The MCEM program process itself demonstrates the accuracy and progression of learners regarding their projects. If students are following the guidelines and applying them accurately, they are more likely to show progress in developing, implementing, and evaluating their SL projects. Since the MCEM programs foster collaboration, engagement, and coordination among all relevant program stakeholders including students, instructors, and institutions, which makes the program process inclusive, trustworthy, and representative, the evaluation of the MCEM programs is quite relevant, easier, and ongoing throughout the program lifecycle. There is a specific chapter in this book, which provides a step-by-step and extensive procedure, methods, and tools to continuously assess the MCEM programs in an inclusive, accurate, culturally appropriate, and collaborative manner. Therefore, the use of MCEM framework and its evaluation also address instructors' concerns about their control and supervision on students' learning and assessment.

One of the advantages of the MCEM framework is that it provides instructors with specific, clear, and straightforward operationalization, which connects theoretical knowledge with application and practice. Each chapter discusses a step/stage of the MCEM programs with specific examples and case studies. Instructors and students do not need prior expertise or background knowledge to follow the steps to successfully develop, implement, and evaluate their programs. Although the MCEM framework provides specific guidelines for instructors and students, it also facilitates them in making their own choices and decisions throughout the program process. Consequently, it empowers students and helps them to maintain their autonomy, use cognitive skills, and make appropriate decisions to achieve program success. When instructors and students have clarity in terms of what they are going to do, it helps them to bring other stakeholders including institutional administrators, staff, faculty, and community partners into a loop. Therefore, the MCEM process and its effective operationalization promote and encourage SL among students, instructors, and institutions by removing important barriers.

Additionally, the MCEM framework provides a common language and specific procedure to students and instructors to systematically develop, implement, and evaluate their program. Additionally, instructors from various disciplines who have relevant knowledge and expertise collaborate and work together throughout the program process to facilitate students in their SL projects, which promotes interdisciplinary partnerships and foster engagement between scholarly communities and groups. Institutions can also create a supportive environment and system to promote transdisciplinary collaboration and engagement for their students and faculty due to the use of a common language and specific procedure used in the MCEM program process because it improves communication between institutions and instructors and helps them to collaborate and work together on students' SL projects.

The MCEM programs create a liaison between schools, communities, and workplaces. When students identify and involve stakeholder groups from multiple engagement levels, they are more likely to engage campus organizations, colleagues, and administrators in addition to other community groups including the community partners, schools, support groups, etc., which encourage and promotes a collaborative environment and engagement between them and minimize the gap between schools, communities, and workplaces. Hence, a systematic and engaged MCEM program process bring all relevant program stakeholders together, makes the process more inclusive and representative, recognize the voices of all groups, decreases challenges, and struggles for instructors, students, and institutions, and foster collaboration and engagement among all stakeholders to work together and achieve successful outcomes and sustainability. Further, there is a specific chapter on program share and review which discusses the importance of recording, documenting, and disseminating the program's findings, success stories, and lessons learned among program stakeholders and those who may be interested in participating in the future. There are different approaches and strategies which are shared with learners to maintain and carry out proper and effective documentation and dissemination for their program as these efforts also contribute to program sustainability. Hence, the MCEM program process develops and fosters engagement and collaboration among all relevant stakeholders including school, community, and workplace.

The process of developing and implementing SL policies is quite complex, lengthy, and systematic, which takes time, effort, and requires collaboration of all relevant stakeholders including students, instructors, staff, and administrators. Due to other businesses or important tasks, such collaboration is usually neglected. The use of MCEM programs fosters such collaboration. For instance, every student engages stakeholders for their SL project when they use the MCEM framework to develop their program. People from their own institutions are essential stakeholders for their program success. For instance, if their program focuses on improving workplace communication, faculty, administrators, staff, IT personnels, and campus organizations are all their partners and stakeholders. When such systematic efforts are carried out, which brings these people from an institution together, they may acknowledge the importance of SL, observe its challenges, and realize the role of developing and implementing policies and procedures to promote SL in their institution. If SL is consistently integrated and implemented into the courses, it may help to continuously invite and engage these stakeholders who can discuss, review SL policies, its challenges, and effectiveness and explore additional measures and actions to improve them in collaboration with other stakeholders including students and instructors. Therefore, instructors need to be proactive and mindful of that and encourage students to invite and engage people from their own institution in their SL projects. Hence, the MCEM program process helps to strengthen existing policies, improve collaboration and engagement within the institutions, and create a conducive environment to implement, review, and improve SL policies. When SL policies are effectively developed and implemented, instructors are more comfortable integrating SL into their courses, which helps them to provide students with such applied and impactful learning experiences.

The above discussion illustrates the significance of the MCEM framework and its important role in expanding SL benefits and addressing challenges for students, instructors, institutions, and communities. The MCEM is a unique framework, which finds a good balance between rigor (scientific and systematic procedure) and relevance (real-life experiences of stakeholders). Given the current complexities of SL and community engagement and issues of inclusion and justice, the MCEM framework addresses contemporary issues of SL and community engagement and provides a roadmap to all students, instructors, and institutions for successfully carrying out SL projects and working with culturally diverse communities around the world. For instance, the MCEM framework decreases power hierarchies among stakeholders which are created due to their social status in society because it allows everyone to participate and actively engage in the program process, particularly in decision-making. It recognizes the voices of historically underprivileged and underrepresented groups of the population because people share and learn from each other during the program process. When all stakeholders participate in the program process, share their experience and expertise, and learn from each other, it ensures program sustainability and improves outcomes for students' SL projects. The MCEM acknowledges the issues of diversity, inclusion, and cultural plurality, and it is developed to minimize these power differences so that the MCEM programs can become engaged, inclusive, relevant, and meaningful. Consequently, the MCEM programs address community needs, grow ethical leadership among all partners including students, and promote positive student SL experiences. The MCEM also acknowledges and appreciates the differences and similarities among stakeholders and encourages them to engage and utilize each other's resources and strengths for the purpose of program successful outcomes and sustainability. The process of MCEM programs is engaged and inclusive, and simultaneously, it is a systematic process, which also accounts for rigor and scientific standards. Therefore, the MCEM programs are likely to be more successful and sustainable, which may help to effectively address community needs and improve students' learning outcomes.

The above description indicates that the MCEM framework can be used for SL and community engagement in institutions and communities around the world to systematically develop, implement, and evaluate the MCEM programs. When the MCEM framework is used globally, it may improve communication and promote a common language among students, instructors, and institutions. When students, instructors, and institutions learn, use, and apply similar concepts and procedures in developing, implementing, and evaluating their MCEM programs for SL projects, it may increase efficiency, productivity, and learning outcomes. This is a uniqueness of the MCEM framework that it is broader enough that can be used and applied globally, and simultaneously, it is narrow to a certain extent due to its effective operationalization to be successfully implemented, assessed, and measured in SL projects.

CASE STUDY

Karen's overall purpose is not only to help parents with young children 0–12 years, but she wants to develop a program that brings different community groups together. She also likes to grow and increase community engagement and sustainability through her program. Hence, she plans on learning which groups are more relevant to and important for her program. Her purpose is also to foster collaboration and engagement among school, community, and workplace because she knows that most of the parents are working parents who also have school-aged children. These parents also are concerned about neighborhood factors which can affect how they raise their children and directly impact the development of their children. She understands that continuous and effective collaboration and engagement between people who belong to school, community, and workplace is crucial for the success and sustainability of her program. Since she is developing her program herself and lacks any institutional or organizational supports, she believes that when different groups from these domains of life will come together and work as a team with her to develop, implement, and evaluate her program, their support will be essential for her program's success and positive outcomes. She wants to make her program a highly impactful learning experience for all groups including herself and program participants. Although she is inexperienced in SL and community engagement, she believes that if she could find a multilevel framework that provides her with step-by-step guidelines and foster stakeholder engagement throughout the program process that will be quite beneficial for her. She has been reviewing various programs and SL projects; these programs showed substantial progress and achieved successful outcomes. However, some programs are overly scientific and follow advanced designs and methods, whereas other programs are less structured and takes control away from the facilitator/learner, Hence, she aims at using a framework, which provides her with a good balance between scientific procedure and active engagement, participation, and inclusion of all groups who are relevant to the program.

DISCUSSION QUESTIONS

(1) What is SL?

(2) How does SL provide learners with experiential learning and applied experiences?

(3) How does it provide learners with opportunities to use and apply course contents to resolve real-world problems?

(4) Discuss a few important strengths and challenges of SL?

(5) How does the MCEM framework address existing gaps and challenges of SL?

(6) How does SL foster stakeholder collaboration and teamwork?

(7) How does SL increase community engagement and communication?

(8) How does the MCEM framework grow collaboration and engagement between schools, communities, and workplaces?

(9) How does SL address community needs and issues?

(10) How does SL bring positive and sustainable changes in community and society?

(11) Why is SL important in classrooms?

ASSIGNMENT QUESTIONS

(1) Describe the role of SL in students' academic and learning outcomes.

(2) Why is SL important in classrooms?

(3) How does SL prepare students for their profession?

(4) How does it provide learners with opportunities to use and apply course contents to resolve real-world problems?

(5) How does SL learning experience increase learners' marketability and chances to secure a potential job?

(6) How does SL increase school, community, and workplace engagement and communication?

(7) How does SL address immediate and important needs and issues of school, community, and workplace?

(8) What did you learn from this assignment?

5

THE MCEM PROGRAMS

The learning objective of this chapter for learners is to learn about the definition of a program and its different components. Learners will also be exposed to many different programs topics from which they can choose their program topic.

Following is the definition of a program:

A program is a culturally and developmentally appropriate plan of engaged, organized, and related instructions, activities, resources, and/or services grounded in theory, research, and practice which are offered in various modes and carried out in continuously reflective, transformative, and collaborative manners with target audiences/beneficiaries to achieve particular short- and long-term goals and objectives.

One of the purposes of using the MCEM framework is to guide learners to systematically develop, implement, and evaluate programs, which is shared and discussed in this book. It is worth mentioning that this book guides learners to develop their programs from scratch. Hence, the use of MCEM framework for existing programs, their modification and refinement, review, and assessment are topics for different editions of this book. Therefore, the above definition is provided which is grounded in and consistent with the MCEM framework. Non-MCEM programs may or may not have these components, but in order to develop a MCEM program, it is essential for learners to follow and stick to this definition of a program, which provides them with a consistency and guide them systematically throughout the program process. As mentioned in Chapter 3, the author developed all these definitions, refined, and tested them over time through empirical and reflective processes.

According to this definition, a program consists of four components, which includes instructions, activities, resources, and/or services. The first component of a program is instructions. Learners can develop presentations and posters to educate participants about the program. They can also use charts, white boards, or any other modes of instruction to conduct/implement their program. A variety of modes of instruction can be useful based on participants' various preferences and learning styles. Hence, given the background of participants, learners need to determine which modes of instruction they can use to effectively deliver or implement their program. Therefore, it is important for learners to learn about their participants before they conduct their educational sessions or work with program participants to implement their program. For instance, if learners' program focuses on parent–child attachment, they can first educate their participants about the attachment theory, different childhood attachment styles, and their impacts on children's social emotional development (Bowlby, 1958, 1960). Learners can also provide participants with an assessment before, during, or after their instructions to help them learn about their children's attachment. Parents can also learn about their own attachment styles, relate it to their childhood experiences, and examine different aspects of their attachments, such their childhood attachment styles, the linkages between their childhood and adult attachment styles, and how it affects their attachment and parenting practices with their children. Learners can decide which topics/contents they want to cover and how they want to carry out and implement their instructions to make it more impactful for participants to improve participants' learning of the topic. Another example can be the use of posters, charts, or whiteboards for instructions on the topic. Learners can ask children to write their feelings and views about the parents' responsiveness and sensitivity of their needs. Children can write about it on either posters, charts, or whiteboards and share it with each other. Learners can then teach children about qualities and characteristics of different attachment styles. Children can relate their descriptions and expressions with any of the attachment styles and provide a justification for it. There can be many forms, modes, and techniques that learners can use for instructions.

The second component of the program consists of activities. Activities can be of many different kinds. For instance, learners can conduct large or small group discussions, online games or surveys, debates, role plays, storytelling, and reflective journals, which provide participants with opportunities to share, apply, and express their personal and real-life experiences relevant to the topic of discussion. Participants can also demonstrate a real-life application of knowledge and skills they learned through the program by performing role plays, playing games, and/or carrying out small group discussions. Learners can facilitate participants' small and large group discussions by providing them with some prompts and guidelines (e.g. rules, expectations, ethics, and inclusiveness). Participants can learn important lessons and strategies from those who have prior real-life experiences on the topic or issues. When participants have opportunities to share their real-life experiences and relate it with the topic, they find the program and contents more relevant and meaningful for them, which further increases their participation, retention, and motivation in the program. Hence, given participants' background and the nature of program, learners can decide which activities they want to use that can improve participants' understanding of the topic and they find it more relevant, engaged, and interesting. The activity component of the program helps to engage participants and apply the contents that participants learn through instructions. Hence, learners need to determine which activity is more effective and aligned with the instructions for participants to apply and practice the contents to real-life situations and their personal experiences when learners include these two components in their program.

The third component of a program is resources. Learners can develop different kinds of informational resources for their program, such as manuals, pamphlets, and brochures, and provide these resources to participants. Learners can also share online resources, such as assessments, websites, YouTube videos, Podcasts, Ted Talks, interviews, journals, curriculum, contact information of experts, groups, or organizations, or any other relevant resources that participants can use during and after the program to expand their understanding of the program. A resource is an important component of the program. Sometimes, due to limited time, finances, or any other circumstances, learners do not carry out and implement their program directly with the program participants. In that case, they can develop an informational resource and distribute it among their participants. Moreover, there is usually a variety of course contents that instructors include in their courses, and students also explore and find many important information and resources to complete their assignments. Hence, it is essential for instructors to suggest and advise their students to primarily use the course contents and materials that they learn and use in the classroom and include them in their program. This practice further enhances students understanding of course contents when they use and apply them for their program as this is the purpose of SL which is to apply the course contents to real-life situations to resolve problems and address needs of individuals, families, groups, and organizations. It is worth mentioning that students can expand on the classroom contents and materials and find additional information, materials, and resources for their program and instructors should facilitate students in doing so but the primary source needs to be the course contents and materials that students learn in the course, which helps instructors to ensure a consistency, rigor, and supervision in students' SL projects and facilitates students to stick to a specific program they chose to work on. Learners need to make sure that the resource they disseminate among program participants is simple, self-explanatory, and straightforward based on participants' educational backgrounds, knowledge, and skills about the topic because learners may not have an opportunity to educate participants about it or explain it to them. If learners feel that recording a short video about the resource is effective and beneficial for participants, they can also record a video and include a link of that video on the resource. Hence, there can be many forms of a resource and learners can use various ways and strategies to develop a useful resource and make it beneficial for program participants to achieve positive outcomes of their program.

The fourth component of a program is service. A program can provide different types of services to its participants. For instance, participants can receive counseling and therapeutic services through the program. A program can also offer legal (e.g. legal procedures in case of abuse) and social (social emotional support from support groups or those who also were the victims of abuse) services and support to its participants. Additionally, a program can also offer tutoring, teacher education and preparation, and/or mentoring services to participants to help and support them on the topic or issue that the program intends to focus. Therefore, the MCEM program can be preventative, intervention-based, or a mixture of both. Sometimes, programs have limited scope, budget, and expertise. Consequently, it becomes difficult for learners to offer actual professional services to program participants especially if the service needs any specialized professional knowledge and expertise, such as therapy, mental health expertise, or any medical treatment. In this case, learners can provide participants with information on those services and advise participants to reach out to relevant organizations, groups, or individuals to receive those services. Learners can also help participants by making appropriate arrangements to support and facilitate them to receive those services. For instance, learners can offer their space, schedule appointments, write emails, and do follow-ups to ensure a smooth, effective, and safer delivery of specific services for program participants. Usually, the MCEM programs increase the likelihood of engaging such individuals and/or organization in the program who provide such services since the program process is quite thorough, which takes time, and encourages learners to identify, reach out, and invite all relevant program stakeholders. Additionally, learners can also collaborate with nongovernment organizations, health facility, doctors, social workers, and hospitals, who provide that service because they are potential stakeholder groups for the program. Sometimes, learners can collaborate with such organizations through those organizations or individuals who already partnered with learners for their program because it is possible that those organizations, agencies, or professionals who provide such specialized services may be out of the target communities where learners implement their program. Hence, learners need to consider all options and maximize their opportunities through stakeholders' engagement and collaboration to support and address the needs of program participants.

A program can have all four components or a few of these components. There are many factors which determine the selection of these MCEM program components, such as the program purpose, scope, human and financial resources, context of participants, community, and society, nature of program, duration of the program, sustainability, etc. Hence, it is important for learners to learn about and examine contextual factors related to participants and target communities carefully and collaborate with all relevant stakeholders to determine which components they want to include in the program. Learners can choose from many different options. For instance, if they have sufficient time, money, expertise, and human resources, they can include all four components in their program. If they have limited resources, then they can choose one, two, or three components for their program. Learners can also focus on one to two components extensively to foster participants' learning and understanding of the program, or they can include all four components but keep a small quantity and intensity of each of the components. The main focus and concern of learners is to consider participants' learning and engagement of the program, positive outcomes, and program sustainability.

It is worth mentioning that a program needs to be specific and appropriate according to the age of participants. For instance, the program might be different when program participants are children compared to when participants are adults. Therefore, it is important for learners to determine which age group they would like to offer their program to. The determination of specific age group for the program may also affect which components learners want to include in their program and how learners will implement these components when they work with program participants. For example, if program participants are elementary school children, learners may choose instructions and activities in their program. Moreover, when learners develop their lesson plans, they need to choose those modes of delivery, teaching methods, and techniques which foster children's learning experiences, such as book reading, role plays, drawing and painting, discussion and sharing, etc. On the other hand, when learners choose to offer their program to adults, they might include activities and resources (if they cannot include all four components). Learners engage participants in small and large group discussions, encourage them to share their real-life stories and experiences, and foster engagement and reciprocity in the learning process. Additionally, learners can develop and disseminate printed or online resources among participants which may be more convenient due to their schedules and responsibilities. If the program focuses on couple relationships and their partner is not present, they can use those printed and online informational resources at home at their convenience with their partners and other family members. For instance, if learners provide them with links to an assessment that guide and explain to couples about their relationship quality, participants can also take it with their partners at their convenience. Hence, resources can be quite an effective component to include in the MCEM program.

It is also important for learners to develop a culturally appropriate and relevant program for their participants. If apparently participants look quite similar in terms of their race and ethnicity, they must be different based on their gender, class, culture, religion, values and beliefs, family background, rituals, and practices, and other diversity areas. Hence, it is essential for learners to consider the culture and diversity of their participants and make their program culturally appropriate and inclusive. If participants are substantially different in terms of their culture and diversity, then it may require additional work on learners' end to make their program more inclusive and respectful to the cultures of all participants. They need to be ready to deal with any cultural and ethical challenges when they work with participants. When the program is appropriate and consistent with participants' cultural values, beliefs, and practices, participants usually find it more relevant and useful for themselves, which increases their participation, engagement, and retention in the program.

Furthermore, effective programs are grounded in theory, research, and best practices. Given the amount of information available on the Internet, learners need to make sure that the knowledge, skills, and information they offer and provide to program participants through their program are informed by empirical research and theories. Learners can also review existing programs and best practices and take some information from those programs and practices for their program. The primary purpose of learners is to make sure that their program provides scientific, reliable, and valid information to participants.

Learners can offer and deliver their programs in various modes and settings. For instance, they can offer in-person programs, online programs, or make them hybrid based on the needs of their participants. Therefore, it is important for learners to identify their program participants, learn about their demographics, context, and needs to make the program accessible and convenient for them. Such approaches increase participants' enrollment, retention, and engagement in the program. Consequently, learners achieve success and sustainability of their program. The advantage of MCEM programs is that learners spend extensive time to identify all relevant program stakeholders and then collaboratively share, discuss, and reflect on different aspects of the program with them. During such an extensive and thorough process, stakeholders and program participants share their needs and concerns, which helps learners to identify and choose the most appropriate, useful, and effective approaches for the program to address the needs and issues of program participants. Hence, learners need to acknowledge this opportunity and phase and best utilize it to strengthen their program.

Moreover, learners need to be reflective throughout the program lifecycle. They need to critically examine and reflect on their own beliefs, values, practices, worldview, and biases and how their personal qualities and biases affect the program and their interactions with program participants. It is also important for learners to learn about their program participants as much as they can. In addition, they need to carry out a collaborative process with all relevant stakeholders including their program participants throughout the program lifecycle to make their program inclusive, comprehensive, relevant, and appropriate to their program participants and their needs. When learners' program process is reflective and collaborative, it recognizes the voices of all stakeholders including the program participants, and brings positive changes in the lives, expertise, and experiences of learners and all relevant stakeholders including their program participants who are engaged in the program.

Finally, learners' purpose of offering a program is to achieve specific program goals and objectives. These goals and/or objectives can be either short- or long-term depending upon the scope of a program and other many factors, such as participants' needs and funds, human resources, learners' expertise, etc. A program may consist of one or more goals and/or objectives. A program can only have objectives, which are more specific and short-term if the duration and scope of a program is quite small. Therefore, learners need to identify and discuss all relevant and contextual factors based on which they develop program goals and objectives with program stakeholders including program participants. Chapter 9 specifically discusses the goals and objectives of the MCEM programs and provides learners with specific and detailed guidelines and examples on developing them.

When a program achieves its particular goals and objectives, it shows positive outcomes. If learners' program goals and/or objectives are to bring positive changes in parent–child relationships, and their program demonstrates these changes among program participants; consequently, learners' achieve their program goals and/or objectives, which shows positive outcomes. It is worth mentioning that an effective program shows positive and sustainable changes among program stakeholders and participants. Sustainability is an essential element of successful MCEM programs. When all relevant stakeholders, including program participants, are actively engaged throughout the program, their voices are heard, their input and feedback are taken and utilized during the program process, they feel empowered, appreciated, and welcomed and consequently, they find the program beneficial and useful for them. As a result, they not only engage and actively participate during the program lifecycle but continue the program after its formal completion. Hence, learners need to consider sustainability as an important element of the MCEM programs when they develop their program. They need to explore and share different ideas and strategies with program stakeholders that they can utilize during the program lifecycle to ensure the sustainability of their program. Successful MCEM programs are more likely sustainable.

In conclusion, the MCEM program components provide a foundation of the program to learners and guide them for the next steps. Learners need to critically examine, share, and discuss these components, their strengths, and potential outcomes with all relevant program stakeholders including program participants to decide which of the components they want to include in their program. Once learners choose the program components, it is essential for them to develop program contents/curriculum based on relevant scientific research, theory, and best practices to implement and deliver these program components, which makes the program reliable, valid, and impactful. When programs are culturally and developmentally appropriate, participants are likely to find them more beneficial and useful for themselves, which increases their participation, engagement, and retention. Consequently, learners achieve their program goals and/or objectives, and their program shows successful outcomes and sustainability.

CASE STUDY

Karen has been developing a program to raise awareness on the importance of parent–child attachment for families who have children aged between 0 and 12 years old. She reviewed extensive research on this topic and found important information that she decided to include in her program. She plans to create some posters, share online websites for additional information on the topic, and distribute brochures containing information of the relevant organizations that provide free of charge services, such as counseling and therapy to families on this topic/issue. Additionally, she plans on doing a small group discussion, role plays, and games during her educational sessions. She is working hard to make sure that her program is appropriate to the age, needs, and developmental trajectories of her program participants. Additionally, she also has been learning different cultures of her participants through multiple sources and ways, such as online, books, articles, libraries, and by meeting with the program participants. She has been writing about her challenges and biases during this process and has plans on continuing it throughout the program to make the program process more transparent and trustworthy. Her teaching approaches focus on facilitating her participants and carrying out a collaborative learning environment to ensure respect, inclusion, and participation of all stakeholders, including program participants during her educational sessions. Since she hasn't secured any funds yet for her program, her program consists of six months; therefore, she plans on developing a few objectives for her program. However, she aims to secure funds in the future and expand her program by adding additional goals and objectives and increasing its scope.

DISCUSSION QUESTIONS

(1) What are the different components of a MCEM program?

(2) Discuss the pros and cons of each program component.

(3) How can a program become culturally relevant for program participants?

(4) What are the essential qualities of a developmentally appropriate program?

(5) What are the different modes of program delivery?

(6) How can the program be scientifically informed?

(7) What should learners do to learn about their program participants?

(8) How does collaboration in a program look like?

(9) Describe learners' reflective process, challenges, and experiences during a program?

(10) What are the qualities of a successful program?

(11) How can a program achieve sustainability?

ASSIGNMENT DESCRIPTION

(1) What is the topic of your program?

(2) Describe your program based on the definition discussed in this chapter. For instance, what comprises your program? Choose at least two or more components for your program discussed in the definition.

(3) What is the purpose of your program?

(4) Describe the demographic characteristics of your potential program participants, such as age, gender, race, income, family structure, etc.

(5) How is your program important in addressing the issue and needs of your program participants? Provide a rationale for your program?

(6) What did you learn from this assignment?

The MCEM Programs

Table 1. Potential Topics for the MCEM Programs According to the Subject Area.

Subject Area	Potential Topics
Child and family development	What is intimacy?
	Love styles
	Ways to learn intimacy?
	Attachment styles
	Gender socialization
	Authenticity
	Intimacy killers
	Intimacy healers
	Love languages
	Budgeting
	Cultural awareness
	Long-lived relationships
	Money and happiness
	Couple communication skills
	Family support and intimate relationships
	Infidelity
	Social support and intimate relationships
	Jealousy
	Interracial relationships
	Motivations of learning intimacy
	Divorce and breakups
	Cohabitation among college students
	Couple and family map
	Stepfamilies
	Cohabitation among elderly couple
	Stress and coping in couple relationships
	Child abuse and neglect
	Marriage, happiness, and challenges
	Intimate partner violence
	Single parenting
	Sibling relationships
	Media and gender roles
	Parent-child relationships
	Coparenting
	Individualistic culture versus collectivistic culture
	Child custody between divorced parents
	Couple income and happiness
	Same-sex couples challenges and strengths
	Strengths among ethnic groups

(Continued)

Table 1. *(Continued)*

Subject Area	Potential Topics
	Middle aged couples
	Parenting styles
	Intimacy among older couples (65+)
Early childhood, elementary, middle, and high school education	Promoting gender equality in classrooms
	Making classrooms inclusive for of students
	Reflecting on self-biases, experiences, and privileges and plan actions for the future
	Acceptance and appreciation of all
	Exploring racial and cultural identity with elementary students
	Teaching race and gender as a social construct in middle schools
	Educate children to show pride and delightfulness in their identities and background
	Importance of diversity and the role of teacher in fostering it high school classrooms
	Parents' engagement in promoting diverse cultures in classrooms
	Addressing the issue of disability and bullying in classroom settings
	Fostering school-home collaboration among minority families
	Effects of poverty on children's education and development
	Promoting diversity literature and curriculum in classroom settings
	Educating children about stereotypes and prejudices and their impacts on peoples' lives
	Engaging families of children with disability in classrooms
	Understanding self-advantages and privileges and how they can negatively affect others
	Encouraging activities in classrooms that promote diversity and celebrate differences
	Awareness about whiteness and white privileges in the US society
	Discovering and exploring true histories and developing authentic identities
	Promoting home-school collaboration to stimulate

Table 1. (*Continued*)

Subject Area	Potential Topics
	multiculturalism in classrooms
	Learning to understand, communicate, and accommodate diverse students and their needs
	Educating LGBTQ issues and exploring resources to support them
	Promoting inclusion of all children in classrooms regardless of their areas of diversity
	Welcoming, sharing, and promoting family traditions to foster learning on diversity in classrooms
	Self-reflection and collaboration to think, reflect, and act on diversity issues in education
Family stress and functioning	Daily stressors and family functioning
	Parenting stressors and family functioning
	Relationship problems and family functioning
	Enduring vulnerability and family functioning
	Diverse families, challenges, and functioning
	Divorce children and parents and their family functioning
	Immigrant families, their experiences, and family functioning
	Adaptive process and family functioning
	Relationship conflict and family stress
	Maltreated children, challenges and experiences, and functioning
	Family violence, abuse, and functioning
	Impacts of mass violence and family functioning
	Family stress and coping with mindfulness
	Transitions and changes in family size, relationships, and functioning
	Physical and mental health problems and family functioning
	Substance abuse, stress, and family functioning
	Economic stress and family functioning
	Daily stressors among college students
Child life and medicine	Children with special needs and family functioning
	Wait-time and patients' satisfaction in hospitals
	Pain and Stress Management in Hospital Settings
	Patient, family, and hospital experiences
	Hospital professional, support, and family experience in hospitals

(*Continued*)

Table 1. *(Continued)*

Subject Area	Potential Topics
	Understanding patients' needs in hospital
	Educating about pros and cons of hospital experiences
	Navigating hospital procedures and treatment
	Supporting children with illness in hospitals
Family life education	Growing healthy family relationships
	Improving child-parent quality time
	Parent's engagement in a child's life
	Effects of social media on a child's well-being
	Helping families to deal with life challenges
	Preparing couples who want to be parents
	Caring for a foster child
	Importance of family and friends' support for families
	Dealing with a chronic illness in the family
	Parent-child attachment
	Significance of rituals for families
	Helping families to deal with economic challenges
	Sibling relationships and rivalry
	Diverse families, challenges, and strengths
	Effective use of electronic media
	Preparing families to deal with transitions
Workplace and business	Work-family balance
	Workplace policies
	Employees' retention and satisfaction
	Business improvement
	Stress free workplace
	Schedule flexibility
	Friendly workplace environment
	Promoting healthy practices in the workplace
	Supervisors and coworkers' support
	Clients' experiences, challenges, and satisfaction
	Workplace collaboration and engagement
	Facilitating employees and increasing efficiency
	Employees and employer's productivity
Interpersonal and workplace communication	Types of listening in communication
	Types of communication
	Positive and negative communication
	Self-esteem and communication

Table 1. (*Continued*)

Subject Area	Potential Topics
	Personality traits and communication
	Effects of emotions on communication
	Positive listening and speaking in communication
	Influences of personal values on communication
	What to say and how to say
	Communication and the workplace goals
	The role of self-disclosure in communication
	Positive communication and health relationships
	Communication and the workplace needs
	Communication in different settings
	Impacts of emotional intelligence on communication
	Communication and conflict resolution
	Patterns of communication in contemporary workplaces
	Communication and relationship problems
	Workplace and interpersonal relationships
	Technology and workplace communication

6

THE MCEM STAKEHOLDERS

The objective of this chapter for learners is to learn about the definition and the role of stakeholders in the process of program development, implementation, and evaluation. Learners will also identify relevant stakeholders for their program from each of the MCEM engagement levels based on the given definition, and the influences these stakeholders create for program participants.

One of the uniqueness and a fundamental focus of the MCEM framework is that it promotes active participation, collaboration, and engagement of all relevant program stakeholders who are situated at each of the MCEM engagement levels. When stakeholders participate in all decisions throughout the program process, their voices are recognized, local knowledge is utilized, and valuable and relevant experience is shared. Consequently, the program becomes more inclusive, relevant, and representative of the needs and issues of all stakeholders, including the program participants.

Following is the definition of stakeholders:

Stakeholders refer to individuals, families, groups, and/or organizations who are engaged in a collaborative process during which they identify, utilize, and/or strengthen each other's resources and efforts and minimize vulnerabilities to achieve shared and relevant goals and objectives, positive outcomes, and ensure community sustainability.

Stakeholders play an important role in any program. These are individuals, families, groups, and/or organizations who can either affect the program or are affected by the program. Stakeholders are unique and different from one another. For instance, if there are different family structures, such as two-parent families, single-parent families, stepfamilies, foster care families, or LGBTQ families who have a stake in a program, they bring unique experience, expertise, resources, and strengths, as well as vulnerabilities and risks for the program. Similarly, some stakeholder groups may be more useful and stronger than others based on the focus and nature of the program. For instance, if a program focuses on advocating for a policy change, then policymakers and government institutions' personal will be more important and influential stakeholders compared to community support groups, families, or local schools.

According to the MCEM framework, it is important for the program to identify all relevant stakeholders, which include individuals, families, groups, and/or organizations who can play an important role throughout the program cycle. Sometimes, it happens that some stakeholders are ignored due to their lack of education or skills or low social status in society. However, they can offer valuable social skills, local knowledge, and experience for the program. For instance, research shows that those stakeholders who do not have higher levels of education or any technical skills, but they have social skills and vast networks in local communities are quite valuable because it is an important resource and skills that helps learners in a smooth implementation of a program (Raza, 2017, 2020a). Hence, it is essential for learners to identify, reach out, and collaborate with all relevant stakeholders who are situated at different engagement levels of the MCEM framework.

The purpose of such collaboration among different stakeholder groups is to support each other's efforts, identify and utilize each other resources and strengths, and minimize each other's risk and vulnerabilities. Therefore, it is important for learners to respect and recognize individuals, families, groups, and/or organizations who are their program stakeholders. It is essential for learners to encourage and promote continuous collaboration, communication, and engagement among all stakeholders throughout the program lifecycle. When these stakeholders work together to focus on specific issues and simultaneously support each other to identify and utilize their resources and strengths, and minimize vulnerabilities, the program will be a shared product of all stakeholders including program participants. When it is a shared product, everyone will likely be engaged in the program process because they will feel the ownership of their program. These stakeholders will perceive the program more relevant and beneficial for their families and local communities. Consequently, it will increase participation, engagement, and retention of stakeholders in the program. Stakeholders will work hard and support each other in the program development, implementation, and evaluation process. Consequently, their program will show positive outcomes. After learning from each other throughout the program process and engaging in the program while acknowledging and observing the benefits of the program for themselves, target families, and local communities, these stakeholders are likely to continue program efforts even after the formal completion of the program, which ensures the sustainability of the program (Raza, 2018, 2021). The uniqueness of MCEM framework is that it considers stakeholders' and their active engagement as central to the success and sustainability of a program. Stakeholders' engagement not only ensures program success and positive outcomes, but it also brings people from different engagement levels of society together which helps to address other community needs and issues of equity, inclusion, and justice. Hence, learners need to make sure that they actively identify and engage all relevant stakeholders in their program. It is worth mentioning that the degree and nature of stakeholders' engagement may vary based on the focus, scope, and purpose of the program.

Moreover, based on their age, developmental stage, and transitions that they experience during the program process, their influence and contribution in the program may be different from one another. For instance, if the program focuses on building a secure parent–child attachment, then those parents who currently have young children may vary in terms of their influence on program participants and contribution compared to those who have teenagers. Similarly, if the program focuses on children with disabilities, parents, and siblings of children with disabilities may vary from others in terms of their influence on program participants and contribution to the program. Likewise, if the program consists of several years, these stakeholders including program participants may go through different developmental changes and stages and experience various events, which can also affect their influence on the program participants and contribution to the program over time. Hence, it is important for learners to carry out a continuous reflective process, which may help them to identify and discuss these changes with program stakeholders and make appropriate changes throughout the program lifecycle.

Further, stakeholders' influences on program participants and participation/contribution to the program can also be shaped by societal factors. For instance, if a program focuses on women's empowerment, and the program is carried out in a society, which promotes gender equality and nontraditional gender roles, then women's influence on program participants and their participation/contribution may look quite different compared to societies where patriarchal systems are prevent and there are disparities between men and women based on gender. Likewise, if a society supports LGBTQ individuals and families, and a program focuses on supporting diverse LGBTQ families, then the extent of LGBTQ stakeholders' influence on program participants and their participation/contribution to the program look different than those societies where there are restrictions and lack of support for these diverse individuals and families.

In addition, stakeholders' influences on the program and program participants may also be influenced by the historical context of society. For instance, if a program focuses on supporting minority groups in the workplace, and those minority groups were historically underrepresented, less supported, and underserved, stakeholders' influence on program participants and their participation/contribution to the program may look different compared to those societies where these minority groups gained relatively more support historically.

Lastly, it is worth mentioning that developmental, current sociocultural, and past historical contexts can reciprocally influence each other and consequently, there reciprocal relationships shape stakeholders' influence on program participants and their participation/contribution to the program. For example, gender roles were prevalent in most societies around the world before the 1960s. During that time, men were more likely to work outside the household who were making economic resources, whereas women were staying at home and caring and nurturing children (Raza et al., 2023a, 2023b). Consequently, men had more access to social, economic, and political resources. Therefore, they had more power, influence, and control in their relationship with women (Raza et al., 2021, 2023a). Hence, there were more disparities between men and women in many domains of life including the family life. These circumstances also affect women's social, emotional, and professional development. For instance, women were lacking greater degrees of self-esteem, self-efficacy, and social networks (Mendenhall et al., 2019; Raza et al., 2023b). Due to industrialization, feminist movements, and other different factors, women started to make progress in many areas of lives since 1960s (Raza et al., 2023b). They have been attaining higher educational levels, securing highly paid and leadership jobs, and outperforming men in social, political, and economic domains of life (Olson et al., 2021). Women's employment not only produced economic resources for them, but it also increased women's satisfaction, self-esteem, and social networking, which improved women's well-being and development (Raza et al., 2023a). Although, past societal context is supporting these gender disparities between men and women as women are likely to perform a second shift at home and even men and women divide the household work, women are more likely to carry out labor intensive, childcare, emotional, and mental labor in the family, the current sociocultural context motivates and encourages men to support women and take their influence in the relationship (Mendenhall et al., 2019). For instance, gender roles have been changing and, in many families, women are making economic resources and men are raising children at home (Marsh et al., 2020). The division of labor is also becoming less equal and the intimate relationship between men and women are becoming egalitarian because those couples, which are happy and successful, they believe in an egalitarian intimate and family relationship (Olson et al., 2021). Hence, it is evident how developmental, sociocultural, and historical contexts influence each other, which affects program participants, stakeholders' influences on the program and participants, and the nature and degree of stakeholders' participation and contribution to the program.

It is worth mentioning that due to the flexibility of the MCEM framework and effective operationalization, learners find various options and alternatives in terms of step-by-step guidelines informed by this framework. For instance, given the scope, time, and purpose of the program, after identifying program stakeholders with reference to research literature, learners reach out to these stakeholder groups including program participants and learn about their experiences, views, and influences they create for program participants. This process and practice help learners to relate relevant research to real-life experiences, consequently, they find a good balance between rigor (scientific procedure) and relevance (stakeholders' real-life experiences). Additionally, it develops and maintains engagement among learners, program participants, and other relevant stakeholder groups. It also uncovers insightful information for learners about program participants in relation to the program which they can validate later through research. This process also shows a reciprocal relationship between research and real-life experience, which is one of the advantages of using the MCEM framework because it helps learners to stay between these two ends of a continuum (rigor—relevance) and provides a unique balance to learners for their program.

Sometimes, it happens that learners find no or fewer research on a specific program, participants, and any or all stakeholder groups. So, when learners identify and reach out to these stakeholders, they may help to inform other stakeholders (snowball), which are either hidden or not highlighted by research. Hence, this cyclical process between research and stakeholders may help learners to identify gaps in research, which can lead to future studies. This process is also quite useful to understand additional stakeholders, their context, and real-life experiences.

Hence, it is important for learners to not only identify the stakeholders who are situated at different engagement levels of the MCEM framework but also examine how their influence on program participants and their participation/contribution to the program may change over time and is influenced by developmental, sociocultural, and historical contexts. It is worth mentioning that the MCEM program process can be quite complex, dynamic, and challenging for learners, but it pays off because this process fosters culture, diversity, and inclusion, and provides fair ownership to all program stakeholders. This process increases stakeholder engagement, participation, and retention throughout the program lifecycle during which stakeholders create, share, and transform new knowledge through a continuous collaborative and reflective process. Therefore, the MCEM program process helps learners, stakeholders, and program participants achieve their program goals and objectives, positive outcomes, and ensure the sustainability of schools, communities, and workplaces in society.

CASE STUDY

Since Karen is using the MCEM framework to systematically develop, implement, and evaluate her program, she is reading about different individuals, families, groups, and organizations, who are situated at each of the engagement levels (i.e. the proximal level, the influential level, and the holistic level) of the MCEM framework. She learned that her target families (i.e. families who have children aged 0–12 years), their friends, and extended family members are situated at the proximal level. Additionally, childcare, preschools and elementary school teachers, staff, and employers who interact with these children and families are also her program stakeholders who are also situated at the proximal level. She also found out that one support group and nongovernmental organization have also been working in the same community on building a healthy parent–child attachment which also become a part of her stakeholder groups at the proximal level.

Further, Karen identified a social media (Facebook group), which provides these families with a platform to share their experiences and strategies in building a secure parent–child attachment. She also learned the negative effects of screen time on children's behaviors. She studied different programs for low socioeconomic families, which provide financial assistance to these families. Karen also learned how diverse families (e.g. families which are different from the target families based on ethnicity, socioeconomic status, religion, education, family structure, etc.) socialize their children differently, which also impacts how they form and develop a parent–child attachment. Additionally, since family practices are informed by their culture, it is also important to invite and engage families from different cultures who can share their experiences, strengths, and strategies with program participants/target families. Karen also discovered how parent–child attachment dynamics and the influences that these stakeholder groups who are situated at different engagement levels create for program participants change over time and are influenced by developmental, sociocultural, and historical contexts.

DISCUSSION QUESTIONS

(1) Who are the stakeholders?

(2) Discuss the role of stakeholders in a program process?

(3) Why are stakeholders important for the success and sustainability of a program?

(4) Why is stakeholders' collaboration and engagement important for a program?

(5) Discuss the stakeholder groups situated at the proximal level of the MCEM framework.

(6) How do stakeholders at the proximal level influence program participants and the program?

(7) Discuss the stakeholder groups situated at the influential level of the MCEM framework.

(8) How do stakeholders at the influential level influence program participants and the program?

(9) Discuss the stakeholder groups situated at the holistic level of the MCEM framework.

(10) How do stakeholders at the holistic level influence program participants and the program?

(11) Why are some stakeholders more important and stronger for a program compared to the others?

(12) How does stakeholders' influence on program participants and their participation change over time?

(13) How do developmental, sociocultural, and historical contexts affect the influence and participation of stakeholders?

(14) Discuss the importance of stakeholders' engagement in ensuring the sustainability of schools, communities, and workplaces in society.

ASSIGNMENT QUESTIONS

(1) Identify all relevant stakeholders who belong to the proximal level. How are these stakeholders influencing your program participants at the proximal level (the first level) of the MCEM in relation to your program? For instance, your participants may be influenced by their family members, friends, community support groups, schools, local organizations, employers, etc.

(2) Identify all relevant stakeholders who belong to the influential level. How are these stakeholders influencing your program participants at the influential level (the second level) of the MCEM in relation to your program? For instance, your participants may be influenced by social media, the internet, television, phones, magazines, donor agencies, public institutions, etc.

(3) Identify all relevant stakeholders who belong to the holistic level. How are these stakeholders influencing your program participants at the holistic level (the third level) of the MCEM in relation to your program? For instance, your participants may be influenced by any diversity areas, socioeconomic status, disability, gender, sexual orientation, ethnicity, etc., or culture.

(4) Discuss your participants' developmental, sociocultural, and historical experiences in relation to your program. For instance, if your program focuses on cohabitation among college students, then discuss the cohabitation trends and patterns among college students in the current society and how they were before the 1960s. Describe the changes over time.

(5) How are the influences of these stakeholders you identified at the three engagement levels on your program participants changed over time and are shaped by developmental, sociocultural, and historical contexts?

(6) What did you learn from this assignment?

Table 2. The MCEM Stakeholders.

The MCEM Engagement Levels	Groups	Stakeholders	Citations
The proximal level	Families	Program participants, their friends, and families.	Raza (2024c)
	Community	Schools, workplace, support groups, community organizations, volunteers, etc.	
The influential level	Donor agencies	Any public or private funding agencies.	
	Media	Print, electronic, social media, and users.	
	Public institutions	Government institutions responsible to form policies and programs.	
The holistic level	Culture	Any cultural group which is different from program participants based on their culture.	
	Diversity	Any individual, family, or group which is different from program participants based on any area of diversity.	
Developmental context/time	Age-specific changes and developmental needs over time.	Children grow and change over time. Children with any developmental delays or disabilities.	
	Developmental transitions at the individual and family levels.	Any normative or nonnormative changes or events. Individuals and families' transitions from one stage to another developmental stage.	
Sociocultural context/time	Society, environment, law, and order, and macrolevel level context.	Current societal situation which relates to the program and topic. For instance, societal attitudes and support toward women and/or single parents.	

(Continued)

Table 2. (Continued)

The MCEM Engagement Levels	Groups	Stakeholders	Citations
Historical context/time	Issues of war, immigration, inclusion, equity, and justice.	Historical changes that have been happening which are affecting the program participants in relation to the program.	
Sociocultural and historical contexts	Effects of historical context on current sociocultural context.	How have the historical views or situations been affecting the current views or situations of program participants in relation to the program.	
	Effects of current sociocultural context on historical context.	How have the current views or situations been affecting or changing the past views or situations of program participants in relation to the program.	
Developmental, sociocultural, and historical contexts	Linkages between developmental, sociocultural, and historical contexts.	Program participants are children of same-sex families who are going through important developmental changes during childhood, due to the current societal support, these diverse families are recognized, which positive affect their children's development, however, these families still face challenges because there were fewer or no support in the past and changings have been happening steadily, which affect these children and their families' development and functioning.	

7

THE MCEM STAKEHOLDERS' RESOURCES AND VULNERABILITIES

The objective of this chapter for learners is to learn the definitions of resources and vulnerabilities and use these definitions to identify the resources and vulnerabilities that stakeholders (who they already identified) create for their program and participants from each of the MCEM engagement levels. Learners will also critically examine how these resources and vulnerabilities change over time and are influenced by developmental, sociocultural, and historical contexts. Following is a definition of resources:

Resources define as any tangible or intangible means, strengths, and/or support including the personal, interpersonal, and/or group-level resources, which maintain and improve the well-being and development of individuals, couples, families, and/or groups in society.

The purpose of developing and offering a MCEM program to a particular group (s) of participants is to address their problems, needs, and/or build their strengths and capacities. It is worth mentioning that participants always have some existing resources including any tangible or intangible resources related to the problem that the program intends to address. Participants can use their existing resources to deal with their issue/problem. For instance, if participants are experiencing economic or money-related issues in their marital relationship, they must be making some income and may have any assets that they can learn to effectively use along with new resources they receive through the program. Thus, if participants already have resources and they receive additional new resources (i.e. gain appropriate skills and knowledge) through the program on how to create a simple, straightforward but effective budget based on their income and expenses and stick to it for efficiently managing their debt or expenses, it helps them to address their financial problems in their marital relationship.

Sometimes it happens that program participants have useful resources to address their problem, but they do not identify those resources, or they haven't thought about it. For instance, social and emotional support from extended family members, friends, and community support groups are useful resources for program participants (Ermer & Proulx, 2020; Zhaoyang & Martire, 2021), which is usually ignored when participants experience any problem. Therefore, it is important for learners to critically think and examine the resources that program participants have from each of the MCEM engagement levels and the resources that program stakeholders who they identified create for program participants. These resources for program participants can be from personal, interpersonal, and/or group-level. For instance, participants' personal income, physical health, emotional and psychological well-being, any assets, property, inheritance are the personal level resources for them (Smith & Wesselbaum, 2023; Ye et al., 2023). Similarly, from the interpersonal level, participants experience or gain resources through effective couple communication skills, cohesion, flexibility, joint income and saving, etc. (Bannon et al., 2020; Carlson et al., 2022; Olson et al., 2021). Likewise, program participants can experience and receive resources from group level, such as social and instrumental support from each partner's family members, friends, community support groups, etc. (Brewster et al., 2021; Fahmy, 2021; Stuhlsatz et al., 2021). Hence, in order to develop a comprehensive MCEM program, achieve successful outcomes, and ensure program sustainability, learners need to collaboratively work with all relevant stakeholders including program participants and identify these resources that participants already have and those which stakeholders create for participants from each of the engagement levels. This also helps learners to identify, explore, and include those new resources in their program, which substantiate and support participants' existing resources.

Following is a definition of vulnerabilities: vulnerabilities define as any situations, exposure, and/or experiences, such as exposure to hardships, tough life situations, and/or negative experiences, including personal, interpersonal, and/or group-level vulnerabilities, which increase the risks of lowering the well-being and development of individuals, couples, families, and/or groups in society.

Program participants also experience or receive vulnerabilities from each of the engagement levels and program stakeholders also create vulnerabilities for participants. For instance, if participants genetic disposition increases the risk of negative experiences (al'Absi et al., 2021), their assessments or responses to any stressful situation (Peter et al., 2023), it is a vulnerability for them because it increases the risks of lowering the well-being and development of participants (Bush & Price, 2020). Additionally, if participants had adverse childhood experience, it is

The MCEM Stakeholders' Resources and Vulnerabilities   89

a vulnerability for them (Brown et al., 2023; Duffy et al., 2024). Likewise, if participants have any disability, it can be a vulnerability for them (Vetri et al., 2021), and they are struggling to meet their basic needs and living in poverty, it is a vulnerability for them because it is lowering their well-being and development (Troller-Renfree et al., 2023; Wang & McLeroy, 2023). Hence, given the focus of a problem, learners need to collaboratively work with program stakeholders including program participants and identify those vulnerabilities, which program participants experience as well as those that stakeholders create for them from each of the engagement levels. Likewise, the interpersonal level vulnerabilities can be a high frequency of conflicts between a couple (Flanagan et al., 2020; Gong et al., 2023), poor communication skills between couples or children and their primary caregivers (Murphy et al., 2021; Shrout et al., 2023), high debt or lack of budgeting in a family (Liu et al., 2024). Similarly, group-level vulnerabilities can be a lack of support from friends and families. For instance, interracial or interethnic couples are less likely to receive sufficient support from their family members and friends (Brummett & Afifi, 2019; Mendenhall et al., 2019). Since interracial couples are more likely to face additional challenges in their relationship due to having two different backgrounds (Kim et al., 2021; Olson et al., 2021), fewer or no support from their families and friends can increase the risk of lowering their well-being and development, which ultimately affect their relationship quality and marital satisfaction (Calderon et al., 2022). Such situations create quite similar or even additional vulnerabilities for same-sex couples (Newcomb, 2020; Rosenthal, et al., 2019). Additionally, if a MCEM program includes single parents who substantially need support from their families and friends but do not receive it, can experience risks of lowering their and their children's well-being and development (Choi et al., 2020; Nunes et al., 2021). For instance, single parents need to make additional money to manage their expenses for housing, food, clothing, transportation, etc. because they lack a partner/spouse who could share these expenses with them (Radey et al., 2021; Raza et al., 2023b). These single parents usefully receive childcare support from their parents such that grandparents supervise their children when they are at work, which saves childcare cost for single parents (Radey et al., 2022). Additionally, grandparents also provide financial, social, and emotional support to their adult and grandchildren (Lee et al., 2021). Thus, a lack of support from family and friends can increase the risk of lowering the well-being and development of these single parent families and their children and become a vulnerability for them (Baker & O'Connell, 2022; Kim et al., 2023). Therefore, it is important for learners to collaboratively work with program stakeholders including program participants and carefully identify those vulnerabilities which program participants face or experience relevant to the program and those vulnerabilities, which program stakeholders create for participants from each of the engagement levels.

It is worth mentioning that developmental, sociocultural, and historical contexts play an important role in shaping the influence of these resources and vulnerabilities on participants, and participants' meaning and value that they associate with these resources and vulnerabilities. For instance, at the personal level, age-specific changes create a risk of lowering the well-being and development for program participants if a MCEM program includes elderly population ages 65 and older (Ji & Fu, 2021; Ma et al., 2023). Similarly, children who are raised in single-parent families have relatively higher risk of having a teen pregnancy or substance abuse issues in their youth (Harding et al., 2022; Yoon et al., 2024). Single parents, particularly mothers, have fewer economic resources to address basic family and children's needs (Hastings & Schneider, 2020; Lee & Allen, 2021; Wu et al., 2020). Single mothers are more likely to work additional hours, nonstandard work schedule, and shift work (Coba-Rodriguez & Lleras, 2022; Hwang & Jung, 2020), which also affect parent–child relationship and impact their children's development (Coba-Rodriguez & Lleras, 2022; Walther & Pilarz, 2024). Likewise, at the interpersonal level, those children who either experience abuse or neglect or observe any domestic abuse or violence between their parents are far more likely to either abuse their partner/spouse or experience abuse in their adult relationship (Costanzo et al., 2023; Pakdaman et al., 2021; Tapia et al., 2024; Voith et al., 2022). At the group level, same-sex couples are likely to experience a lack of support or hostility in their local communities, which not only affect their couple relationship but it also impacts their children's well-being and development (Kennedy & Dalla, 2020; Snyder & Henry, 2023; Webb et al., 2020). If families don't have money, which limits their options, and increases the likelihood of living in less supportive and low socioeconomic neighborhoods (Zhou et al., 2024). High-income couples and families have more opportunities and options and consequently, they can choose to live in more supportive and resourceful communities (Boye & Evertsson, 2021; Olson et al., 2021). Hence, participants' resources and vulnerabilities change over time based on the developmental context.

Moreover, participants' resources and vulnerabilities are also influenced by sociocultural context. For example, ethnically diverse and same-sex couples face legal and social difficulties in adopting children in some countries than the other (Frame, 2021; Gato et al., 2021). Their children are at a greater risk of experiencing identity-related issues in their childhood and adolescence (Aubry, 2023; Messina & Brodzinsky, 2020). They are also more likely to face bullying and prejudice in schools (Lessard et al., 2020). Similarly, ethnically diverse and immigrant children experience discrimination and additional challenges in schools, communities, and workplaces (Barajas-Gonzalez et al., 2022; Basilici et al., 2022; Caravita et al., 2020;

Palladino et al., 2020; Rodgers et al., 2023), which affect their growth and development (Gong et al., 2021; Koyanagi et al., 2020). Additionally, in some countries like the United States, there is more support for same-sex couples and marriages (Colistra & Johnson, 2021; Kaufman et al., 2022) compared to those countries where same-sex marriages are legally prohibited (Ojilere, 2024). In the United States and globally, women are outperforming men in education (Bibbo et al., 2015), taking leadership roles (Jones, 2022; Olson et al., 2021), experiencing a better division of household work (Carlson, 2022), and in many cases, making more economic resources compared to their male counterpart though there is still a wage gap between men and women (Connors et al., 2021; Olson et al., 2021). On the other hand, in South Asian countries, such as India, Pakistan, Bangladesh, and Middle East countries, such Kuwait, Qatar, Dubai, and Saudi Arabia, and African Countries, such as Senegal, Sudan, Chad, Central Africa Republic, Mali, Liberia, Niger, and Gambia. Within African, due to religion, culture, and societal norms, support for women and men may vary (Raza, 2022). Similarly, many Muslim countries do not allow same-sex relationships or marriages and gender equality also vary among them (Çakın et al., 2024; Nordin et al., 2023; Pritchard et al., 2023; Sheen et al., 2023). So, if a society favors diversity, inclusion, gender equality and expression of sexuality and institutional structures support and implement it, participants resources and vulnerabilities may look different compared to other societies.

Similarly, sociocultural context also influences how and what resources and vulnerabilities stakeholders create from each engagement level for program participants. For instance, if there is a lack of societal support for diverse and same-sex families in a society, and they are at a greater risk in terms of their health, security, and environment, their roles in terms of creating resources and vulnerabilities for program would be different compared to those societies where these families experience friendly and supportive environments. Similarly, institutions work differently as stakeholders in terms of creating resources and vulnerabilities for program participants in friendly and supportive societies than nonsuppurative or hostile societies. Hence, stakeholders' resources and vulnerabilities that they create for program participants are influenced by sociocultural context.

Similarly, historical context also can influence participants' resources and vulnerabilities. For instance, if women faced disparities or certain racial/ethnic groups were marginalized historically, it influences how women as participants experience resources and vulnerabilities, participants' meaning and value of these resources and vulnerabilities, and the resources and vulnerabilities that women as program stakeholders create for program participants. For instance, women were oppressed and marginalized globally before 1960s and their situations started to change due to industrialization, feminist movements, and women's workplace participation (Raza et al., 2023b; Smith & Hamon, 2022). Although, there have been many substantial changes in women's lives but still due to these historical realities, women look different as program participants as well as a stakeholder group in traditional societies in terms of creating and experiencing resources and vulnerabilities for the MCEM program compared to those women who live in nontraditional societies. Hence, the resources and vulnerabilities that program participants experience, and stakeholders create for program participants are also influenced by historical context.

It is worth mentioning that the developmental, sociocultural, and historical contexts also reciprocally influence each other and affect the resources and vulnerabilities that participants experience, and stakeholders create for program participants from each engagement level. For example, societies which were historically patriarchal have been changed, and the current societal environments are challenging and changing the influence of the past on people and families (Eagly et al., 2020; Raza et al., 2023b). For instance, South Asian, Middle East, and African regions, gender norms are changing and disparities between men and women are decreasing, consequently, women have more access to social, economic, and political resources, which are improving women's self-esteem, well-being, and development (Raza, 2022). Before 1960s, men were more likely to work outside the home and make economic resources in the United States, whereas women's roles were to raise and nurture their children (Mendenhall et al., 2019; Olson et al., 2021). Due to feminist women, gender norms have changed and, consequently, gender roles are becoming more egalitarian and there is more social and workplace support for women compared to the past (Charlesworth & Banaji, 2022; Friedman & Rodríguez Gustá, 2023). Additionally, the United States passed a law in 2015, which legalized same-sex marriage in all states, which increased support and acceptance for LGBTQ individuals and couples at the macrolevel as well as the microlevel (Colistra & Johnson, 2021; DiGregorio, 2021). Due to the acceptance, legal recognition, and additional support, LGBTQ children and families are experiencing positive well-being and development (Chen & van Ours, 2022; Huang & Hang, 2024). Moreover, when diverse individuals and families experience positive attitudes, interactions, and environments, they also make their efforts towards bringing positive changes in society and minimizing the negative effects of past historical context (Mendenhall et al., 2019; Olson et al., 2021). Hence, developmental, sociocultural, and historical contexts reciprocally influence each other, which also determine the resources and vulnerabilities that program participants experience, and stakeholders create for program participants from each engagement level.

Therefore, learners need to collaboratively carry out this process with relevant stakeholders including program participants which is accompanied with critically thinking, sharing, reflecting, communicating, and recording during which they identify the resources and vulnerabilities that their program participants experience and the resources and vulnerabilities that program stakeholders create for program participants. Additionally, how these resources and vulnerabilities change over time and are influenced by developmental, sociocultural, and historical contexts.

Further, learners conduct extensive literature reviews to learn about program participants and stakeholders' resources and vulnerabilities for their program. After conducting a literature review and learning about the resources and vulnerabilities that program participants experience and relevant stakeholders create for program participants from each engagement level, learners share this information with program stakeholders. Stakeholders including program participants may validate the knowledge that learners share with them about the resources and vulnerabilities and provide learners with additional knowledge and information on it. Consequently, learners have rich and extensive information based on research and stakeholders' real-life experiences which inform the next steps of the program.

In conclusion, the goal of MCEM programs is to support and help relevant stakeholders including program participants in addressing their important and immediate problems, needs, and strengthen their knowledge and skills to make them resilient and ensure their healthy functioning in different areas of life. Therefore, the focus of learners and a MCEM program is to learn about the resources and vulnerabilities from stakeholders and program participants, and then educate them based on research by providing them with additional knowledge, skills and services through their program, which expands their existing resources and minimize/decrease their vulnerabilities to ensure successful program outcomes and sustainability.

CASE STUDY

After identifying families, extended family members, and/or friends as potential stakeholders for her program, Karen learned that they provide program participants with social, emotional, and financial support which is a useful resource for program participants, whereas a lack of such support and assistance can create vulnerabilities for program participants.

Local schools, their teachers, staff, and administrators offer important programs to foster parent–child attachment. They also work with parents to discuss children's social and emotional problems which are linked to parent–child attachment. Schools also provide free breakfast and lunch to needy children which positively affects their mood, behavior, and performance in school. Educators are also trained to form a positive/secured attachment with children while they study with them. These programs and efforts are a great resource for program participants, whereas a lack of these supports and assistance become a vulnerability for program participants. Additionally, local support group and a nongovernmental organization are raising awareness and funds for these families, whereas a lack of awareness and access to these community resource can lower the well-being of program participants.

Social media platforms, such as a Facebook group is a resource as parents and children share their positive experiences and effective coping strategies with young parents who currently go through those situations, whereas unrealistic expectations from young parents and unnecessary comparisons with these successful parents can lower the well-being and development of these families. Government financial assistance decreases the stress of parents and help them to form and maintain a secure attachment with their children, whereas a lack of knowledge and access of program participants to these programs can create vulnerabilities for them.

Diverse families share important knowledge, information, and strategies with program participants. Families from different cultures can also share their strengths and strategies on parent–child attachment. Learning about the experiences and coping strategies from diverse and culturally unique families can enhance the knowledge and information of program participants and become a resource, whereas an unwillingness to learn and share, biases, and prejudices create vulnerabilities for program participants. Children's developmental needs change over time between 0 and 12. Parents have more access to education, information, professional services on parent–child attachment compared to the past. Research has been growing over time on parent–child attachment. Currently, society demands and expects more from young parents but there is a lack of formal support and assistance for parents to be well-prepared for raising their children and forming and maintaining secured attachments with them over time.

DISCUSSION QUESTIONS

(1) What are the resources and vulnerabilities of program participants at the personal level?

(2) What are the resources and vulnerabilities of program participants at the interpersonal level?

(3) What are the resources and vulnerabilities of program participants at the group level?

(4) Which resources and vulnerabilities do participants experience from the three engagement levels (the proximal, influential, and holistic levels)?

(5) Which resources and vulnerabilities do program stakeholders create for program participants from the three engagement levels (the proximal, influential, and holistic levels)?

(6) How do these resources and vulnerabilities change over time?

(7) How are these resources and vulnerabilities affected by developmental, sociocultural, and historical contexts?

(8) How do participants' meaning and value for these resources and vulnerabilities change over time and are shaped by developmental, sociocultural, and historical contexts?

(9) Why is identifying participants' resources and vulnerabilities that program stakeholders create for them important to develop a MCEM program?

(10) What did you learn from this assignment?

ASSIGNMENT QUESTIONS

(1) Based on the stakeholders you identified and the influences they create for your program participants at the proximal level (the first level) of the MCEM, identify the resources and vulnerabilities that the program participants experience, and these stakeholders create for your program participants at the proximal level in relation to your program. For instance, your participants (e.g. children or adolescents) may experience a resource of positive parenting practices and a vulnerability of lack of peer support at the proximal level.

(2) Based on the stakeholders you identified and the influences they create for your program participants at the influential level (the second level) of the MCEM, identify the resources and vulnerabilities that the program participants experience, and these stakeholders create for your program participants at the influential level in relation to your program. For instance, your participants (e.g. children or adolescents) may experience a resource of social media platforms and a vulnerability due to high students' loan-related policies/programs at the influential level.

(3) Based on the stakeholders you identified and the influences they create for your program participants at the holistic level (the third level) of the MCEM, identify the resources and vulnerabilities that the program participants experience, and these stakeholders create for your program participants at the holistic level in relation to your program. For instance, your participants (e.g. children or adolescents) may experience a resource of cultural belonging and a vulnerability due to their race and/or family structure at the holistic level.

(4) How are these resources and vulnerabilities of your participants changed over time and affected by developmental, sociocultural, and historical contexts in relation to your program? For instance, your participants (e.g. children or adolescents) currently use social media as a resource more actively compared to 1960s. Describe the changes over time.

(5) What did you learn from this assignment?

Table 3. The MCEM Stakeholders' Resources and Vulnerabilities.

The MCEM Engagement Levels	Groups	Stakeholders	Resources/Strengths	Vulnerabilities/Risks	Citations
The proximal level	Families	Participants, their families, friends, and extended family members.	Social, emotional, financial, and instrumental support.	Conflicts, lack of communication, no cohesion, lack of multigenerational relationships and support.	Raza (2024c)
	Community	Schools, support groups, local organization.	School counselling, parent–teacher communication, classroom inclusion.	Lack of community support, fewer or no support groups, poor neighbourhood, negative peer influence.	
The influential level	Donor agencies				
	Media				
	Public/Private institutions				
The holistic level	Culture				
	Diversity				
Developmental context/time	Age-specific time				
	Developmental transitions at the individual and family levels.				

(Continued)

Table 3. *(Continued)*

The MCEM Engagement Levels	Groups	Stakeholders	Resources/Strengths	Vulnerabilities/Risks	Citations
Sociocultural context/time	Society, environment, law, and order, and macrolevel context.				
Historical context/time	Issues of gender, inclusion, equity, and justice.				
Developmental, sociocultural, and historical contexts	Reciprocal influences between developmental, sociocultural, and historical contexts.				

8

THE REVIEW OF LITERATURE

The objective of this chapter for learners is to review and effectively utilize the existing literature related to the program to learn more about their program, stakeholders, resources, vulnerabilities, and the influences of developmental, sociocultural, and historical contexts on the program and its participants. The author shares why an extensive review of literature is essential to gain insightful information about the program, its participants, and context. The integration of scholarly literature in all steps of a program throughout the program lifecycle substantially improves a program and increases its trustworthiness among program stakeholders and other groups of audience.

Following is a definition of a literature review:

A literature review is a process of searching, identifying, reviewing, examining, assessing, and synthesizing existing, relevant, and recent research, which includes peer-reviewed articles, books, theses, dissertations, or any scholarly/reliable sources to learn about a topic, identify existing gaps, and inform the current research and practice.

The MCEM programs have several different steps that learners need to successfully complete to move forward in the program. For instance, choosing a program topic, describing the program, identifying stakeholders and their influences, highlighting resources and vulnerabilities that program participants experience, and stakeholders create for them, and how they change over time and are influenced by developmental, sociocultural, and historical contexts are the steps, which are discussed/covered in the earlier chapters. Learners need to critically review the existing research and best practices to expand their understanding of each step of the program throughout the program lifecycle. Learners also learn more about their program participants, stakeholders, and the resources and strengths and vulnerabilities and risks that their program participants experience, and the stakeholders create for them at the three engagement levels. Additionally, learners also study about the developmental and age-specific changes that their program participants and program experience, and the current sociocultural and past historical context in relation to their topic, program, program participants, stakeholders, resources, and vulnerabilities. Learners need to study and learn the facts and figures about their participants in relation to their program. For instance, if the program focuses on parents with young children, then learners need to know how many families have recently become parents in that area, their ages, socioeconomic status, race, family structure, ethnicity, etc. They also need to know the seriousness, intensity, and/or prevalence of the problem that their program aims to address. It is also important for learners to know whether program participants already participated in any program in the past or they are currently participating in any other relevant program, and/or government/nongovernment programs, which relate to the learners' program.

Moreover, the purpose of developing and offering a program to participants is to resolve their problems, minimize challenges, address their needs, strengthen them, and improve their lives. Hence, learners need to develop and offer a program, which minimizes participants' vulnerabilities and maximizes their resources so that participants can meet their needs and/or address their immediate problems they experience and that the program focuses on. For instance, if a program focuses on parent–child attachment. At the proximal level, families including children, parents, their friends, and extended family members are a part of stakeholder groups called "Families." Then learners need to review the relevant literature about this topic, which may include attachment theory (Bowlby, 1958, 1960; Dugan et al., 2024; Twohig et al., 2024), childhood attachment styles (Castellini et al., 2022; Donadio et al., 2021; Mays et al., 2021; Türk et al., 2021), adult attachment styles (Marchlewska et al., 2024; Pepping et al., 2024; Samraj et al., 2023), and qualities of a healthy parent–child attachment (Tao et al., 2020; Temelturk et al., 2021; Walsh & Zadurian, 2022). When learners review the relevant literature and learn about these topics, they find out what aspects and factors of parent–child attachment support a healthy parent–child attachment and relationship, and which ones hinder it or create challenges for a healthy parent–child attachment and relationship. Since the general focus of a MCEM program is to increase participants' resources, strengths, and capacities, and minimize vulnerabilities, risks, and challenges, learners educate participants about both aspects (e.g. vulnerabilities and resources) of parent–child attachment and all participants including learners can further discuss, explore, and share how they can deal with vulnerabilities and expand their resources to foster and grow a healthy parent–child attachment and relationship.

As discussed in Chapter 7, resources and vulnerabilities can be tangible or intangible. For instance, if participants learned communication skills and sensitivity to children's emotional needs through a program, it is a resource for them, which they can keep using after completing the program to maintain a healthy attachment with their child. On the other hand, if participants have a family member with a disability, which increases family vulnerability and lowers their well-being and development (Bennett Murphy et al., 2022; Greenberg et al., 2021). Hence, learners need to study and review both tangible or intangible resources and vulnerabilities for their participants. This is only one of the steps of a MCEM program process. At every step, learners need to review the relevant literature to inform themselves about the work already done, what research says about that particular step or aspects related to it, and what is important that learners need to educate their participants about. It is worth mentioning that some resources are useful for one group of participants, but they may not be quite useful or effective for another group. Hence, learners need to continuously share and consult with their program stakeholders and participants to determine which information, knowledge, and skills are useful, beneficial, and meaningful for them in addressing their needs, resolving their problems, and then include it into their program (Herr, 2017; Raza, 2020a). When learners conduct a comprehensive literature review, they also come across best practices related to their program, contextual challenges, and important strategies, which they can also utilize in their program (Raza, 2022). Learners also find and record important information about services and organizations that they can share with their program participants or reach out to these organizations, service providers, and/or professionals to collaborate with and engage them in their program. In addition to scholarly sources, other potential sources for learners to review are websites, Google searches, newspapers, magazines, social media, libraries, etc. to learn about their program, participants, and relevant stakeholders. Learners can also attend any community events, webinars, and/conferences to meet with and learn about their program participants. Hence, it is important for learners to explore and utilize all useful and effective sources of information and share it with their program stakeholders including program participants to maximize the utility and effectiveness of their program as the primary purpose of the learners' program is to provide participants with a comprehensive education, knowledge, and skills on the topic, which addresses participants' needs and issues and strengthen their capacities to effectively deal with it during and after the program.

It is worth mentioning that the MCEM programs can be preventative, intervention-based, or a mixture of both prevention and intervention. As the

MCEM framework continuously promotes and guides stakeholders' engagement throughout the program lifecycle, even though learners do not have any specialized expertise, certification, or formal education to provide program participants with any professional or specialized services, such as counselling, therapy, or mental health treatment, learners can collaborate with these professionals and engage them in their program who can offer their services to program participants. Hence, due to the uniqueness of MCEM framework, its flexibility, and effective operationalization, learners can maximize its utility in fostering stakeholders' engagement, addressing participants' needs and problems, and achieving positive program outcomes.

Moreover, an effective and comprehensive program needs to be grounded in research, theory, and best practices. Therefore, learners need to extensively read and review scholarly and reliable sources for their program, its different aspects, and all relevant stakeholders including program participants and their relationship dynamics. When learners conduct a critical review of existing research, theories, and practices, they learn about important factors, strategies, and approaches to strengthen a program which they can replicate for their program if possible or integrate it with their existing approaches to achieve the best outcomes of their programs. Learners also review various cultural and ethical issues that previous programs faced and learn potential strategies to overcome these challenges, which helps them to make the current program successful and sustainable. Learners can also choose and include any relevant part from the previous program (s), which they consider relevant and suitable for their program to strengthen it. However, it is worth mentioning that if the participants, stakeholders, and the context of the program is different from those programs which were previously implemented, then learners may need to modify those parts or specific elements that they take from the best practices/previous programs and conduct some pilot testing, review and/or discussion with their program participants and stakeholders to make sure they are effective, relevant, and aligned with their own program and all relevant stakeholders including the program participants. Therefore, it is imperative for learners to find an appropriate balance between rigor (scientific knowledge and procedure) and relevance (stakeholders' inputs and real-life experiences) when they conduct literature review for their program. Learners need to make sure that they include the information and materials which are informed by valid and reliable research and sources and simultaneously it is also equally important for learners to engage stakeholders including program participants in that process, share and consult these contents with them and choose those which are most effective and useful for their program and participants.

Since the MCEM programs vary in terms of their time, scope, and allocated resources, learners need to determine the amount of information they would like to offer through their program, the degree and frequency of stakeholders' engagement, and the extent of complexity and rigor they want to use and apply for their program so that they can complete their program on time. For instance, if students are using the MCEM framework to complete their SL projects in one semester period, then instructors need to guide students about these aspects, provide specific guidelines, and determine the boundaries so that students work within the scope and focus of their program and complete it within a due course of time. On the other, a MCEM program may look different in terms of rigor, engagement, and the amount of contents when learners develop, implement, and evaluate it for their practicum or internship projects and experiences because students have a lot more time to complete their program/project. Since the MCEM framework can be used in many ways, modes, situations, and for several purposes, instructors need to determine in consultant with students and relevant personnel the extent, scope, and nature of the MCEM program to meet students' SL requirements, needs, and foster students' positive experiences.

Further, the literature review is a continuous task that learners need to perform throughout the program lifecycle to foster their learning of the topic, stakeholders, and program participants and enrich their program. Learners need to share and discuss the contents, materials, and information they research and find for their program with all relevant stakeholders including program participants, invite and welcome their inputs and feedback, and make appropriate revisions and modification into their program with a consensus and agreement to strengthen their program and make it effective and meaningful for program participants.

(1) Articles which expand learners' understanding of the topic, program, and its different components.

(2) Articles which provide contextual information about the program participants, such as age, ethnicity, prevalence and intensity of the problem, education, culture, income, family structure, and participants' learning styles and needs.

(3) Articles which highlight and describe program stakeholders, their dynamics, and specific influences on program participants and the program.

(4) Articles on how the dynamics of stakeholders, their reciprocal relationships, and the influences on the program participants and program change over time and are influenced by developmental, sociocultural, and historical contexts.

(5) Articles which describe and explain the resources and vulnerabilities that program participants experience at the three MCEM engagement levels.

(6) Articles which describe and explain the resources and vulnerabilities that stakeholders create for program participants at the three MCEM engagement levels.

(7) Articles on how the resources and vulnerabilities that program participants experience, and stakeholders create for them change over time and are influenced by developmental, sociocultural, and historical contexts.

(8) Articles on ethical and cultural challenges and opportunities that learners can face during the program process.

(9) Articles on program curriculum, delivery, and participants' engagement.

(10) Articles on program evaluation, share, and dissemination.

It is worth mentioning that these are only some suggestions that the author provided to learners as examples to highlight important aspects of the program that learners need to focus on when they conduct a literature review for their program. Learners can expand the review of literature on other aspects of their program in addition to the ones mentioned above if they need to. However, learners need to be precise and specific with respect to the scope of their program. The process of MCEM programs is systematic, but it also dynamics, multilevel, and complex, consequently, each step or stage of the program relates to one another. Hence, consistency among all steps of the program is important to make the program more rigorous, effective, and specific to the needs of program participants. Sometimes, covering too many things/aspects in a program can be overwhelming for learners, program stakeholders, and participants and may deviate the focus of the program, which affects program efficiency, effectiveness, and outcomes.

Moreover, it is worth mentioning that this chapter provides an overview of the literature review, its role in MCEM programs, recording, management, synthesis, and effective use of a literature review to strengthen a MCEM program. The literature review is essentially a part of every chapter. The case study included in each chapter better guides learners on different aspects and needs for conducting a literature review at each stage/step of the MCEM program.

For instance, a case study included in Chapter 4 highlights the components and many other aspects of a program that learners need to learn about and focus on in their MCEM program process. Learners achieve this goal by conducting extensive and critical reviews of existing and current literature by using techniques, methods, and strategies shared in this chapter. Learners also synthesize, record, and manage the information in the table shared at the end of this chapter to effectively utilize literature reviews for the development, implementation, and evaluation of the MCEM programs.

As discussed earlier, since learners need to conduct a continuous review of literature at each stage of their program process, literature reviews should not be conducted at only one specific time point or stage of a MCEM program. Learners cannot ignore the importance of conducting literature reviews over time through the program lifecycle. A continuously literature review keeps learners up to date, refresh their knowledge, and provide them and other program stakeholders with opportunities to discuss, reflect, and effectively use the information, knowledge, and lessons learned they collect by reviewing the existing literature for their program. However, the frequency, degree, and intensity of literature reviews may vary based on many factors, such as time, scope, nature of the program, learners' expertise, etc. Hence, learners need to examine these aspects in consultation with relevant stakeholders and determine specific boundaries and parameters to efficiently utilize their time, resources and efforts for conducting an effective, comprehensive, and meaningful review of relevant literature for their program.

CASE STUDY

Karen has been following the step-by-step systematic process informed by the MCEM framework in the development of her program. Most of the information she collected through Google searches, magazines, and libraries. She also reached out, met, and spoke with potential program stakeholders and participants. She still feels a need to extensively read about her program and its various aspects and components. Her friends told her about different online databases and libraries, which offer many relevant peer-reviewed journals from which they can search, find, read, and review relevant research, developments, and information about her topic. She decided to take that route and contacted a librarian to gain additional information, skills, and insights about the use of these databases to find and review relevant articles on her topic. After a few days of having hands-on experience with the librarian, she felt confident in searching for, reviewing, and recording these articles. She has been using the template provided at the end of this chapter to record and maintain her information, which helps them to come back and rereview the information to use it for her program. She also shares the template with all relevant stakeholders including program participants. Some expert stakeholders requested additional information. Since she successfully saved and maintained in this template, she just looked at the full citation, find the article in a folder in which she saved all her articles and found that information requested by the stakeholders, and included in the same chart for their review and further discussion. She also has been also recording this entire literature review process, her experience, challenges, biases, stakeholders' engagement, and lessons learned in her reflective journals.

DISCUSSION QUESTIONS

(1) What is a review of literature for a MCEM program?

(2) Why is a literature review process important for a program?

(3) How does a critical review of literature improve the program?

(4) What are the different aspects of a program that you learn through the literature review?

(5) Why is choosing facts, information, and resources from a scholarly/reliable source important for a program?

(6) What specific information do you plan on finding by conducting a literature review?

(7) What other sources are important to find information about a MCEM program other than peer-reviewed/scholarly articles and why?

(8) What did you learn from this assignment?

ASSIGNMENT QUESTIONS

Based on your reading of the chapter, find scholarly/peer-reviewed articles for each component of your MCEM program and fill out the information asked in Table 4. It is important for learners to spend extensive time in conducting the literature review of the program. After completing the table, synthesize your information and write a 2–3 pages paper to describe your review of existing research, findings, gaps, learning, and how you would use it for your program.

(1) Describe your program, program participants, and stakeholders.

(2) How did the articles you chose by reviewing relevant literature expand your understanding of different aspects of your program?

(3) What other sources of information that you also found useful for your program and why?

(4) What did you learn about different aspects of your program after reviewing the relevant research and practice of your program?

(5) Describe your process of engaging program stakeholders in your literature review process. What challenges and opportunities did you experience?

(6) What do you want to focus on in your program to address your participant's needs and issues, decrease their vulnerabilities, and improve their resources?

(7) How would you use the information you collected through the literature review for your program?

(8) Share your personal reflections, biases, and lessons learned of the literature review process.

(9) What did you learn from this assignment?

Table 4. A Review of Literature for MCEM Programs.

APA Citation with a Direct Weblink to the Article	Aspects of the MCEM Program	Research Question/ Purpose of the Study	Research Methodology (Qualitative, Quantitative, Mixed Methods)	Sample Characteristics (Participants' Age, Race, Gender, and/or Other Demographic Characteristics)	Data Collection Instruments (Quantitative Surveys, Qualitative Interviews, etc.)	Main Findings of the Study	Your Overall Impression/ Evaluation of the Study in Relation to the Program	How Does This Article Relate to Your Program and Expand Your Understanding on Specific Aspects of Your Program?
Article 1	The proximal level							
Article 2	The influential level							
Article 3	The holistic level							
Article 4	Developmental context/time							
Article 5	Sociocultural context/time							
Article 6	Historical context/time							
Article 7	Developmental, sociocultural, and historical context							

Note: This is a sample table/template, and learners can modify and expand this table and make it as complex and lengthy as they like. For instance, they can also add additional rows to include articles which help them to understand stakeholders' reciprocal relationships between the engagement levels, how these relationships change over time, and are influenced by developmental, sociocultural, and historical contexts, etc.

9

THE MCEM PROGRAM VISION, SAMREEN GOALS, AND OBJECTIVES

The objective of this chapter for learners is to learn the definitions of SAMREEN vision, goals, and objectives. The author developed SAMREEN goals and objectives for the MCEM programs, which can also be used in non-MCEM programs. SAMREEN goals and objectives take program goals and objectives to the next level as they guide and facilitate program stakeholders for a multilevel, inclusive, and meaningful development, implement, and evaluation of the MCEM programs. Additionally, SAMREEN goals and objectives also strengthen the assessment of a MCEM program because it enables learners and program stakeholders to carry out multilevel, engaged, and continuous evaluations of their program throughout its lifecycle, which increases program transparency and trustworthiness of the MCEM programs. A description of each element of SAMREEN goals and objectives with details and specific examples is also provided in this chapter.

Following is a definition of a program vision.

A program vision is a broad statement composed of a general and long-term idea about achieving ultimate conditions and bringing positive changes for program stakeholders and broader community, which lays a foundation to design certain goals and objectives and carry out concrete actions to bring about those desirable conditions and changes in the lives of target groups of the population.

A program vision plays a critical role for learners, program stakeholders, and broader community. One of the advantages of the MCEM framework is that it guides, encourages, and promotes sustainable programs. Hence, for a program to be sustainable, it needs to be continued and produce positive changes in the lives of target population and for broader community. Learners and stakeholder groups may change over time as more and more communities are engaged and take over the program, but the program focus may not be substantially changed because the program works toward its vision, which is a long-term idea and roadmap and beneficial for broader community and society. Therefore, developing a broader, relevant, and appropriate program vision is crucial for learners and program stakeholders as it provides them with a clear view and roadmap that they need to follow for an extended period of time to produce desirable conditions and changes among target families in their communities and society. It is worth mentioning that program vision may be different than the organizational vision or they can be alike based on the scope, focus, and nature of the organization. If a program is short-term like students develop and complete a SL project in a semester, then they may not need to develop a vision, or they can develop a vision for their program that they can carry in the future. Hence, learners may or may not develop their program vision depending upon many factors, such as time, scope, and the purpose of their MCEM program. Below are a few examples of program vision.

Example 1: Supporting families in developing secure parent–child attachments for successful and sustainable families, communities, and society.

Example 2: Making global families resilient by developing and promoting healthy parent–child attachments.

Example 3: Producing healthy citizens by supporting families in developing secure attachments with children during childhood and adolescence.

Example 4: Our vision is to help parents and children to form secure and healthy attachments to experience optimal development in society.

Example 5: We envision a healthy parenthood for producing successful citizens, families, and communities in society.

As the above examples demonstrate that vision statements are quite general, broad, and long-term because the purpose is to develop it for a longer period of time so that continuous efforts can be directed and guided for the future. A vision provides continuity to organizations and programs because it motivates organizational leadership and learners to make continuous efforts and carry out actions to achieve desired outcomes and conditions in communities and societies. Since contemporary health, social, and economic problems that individuals and families experience are quite complex and dynamic and the prevalence of some problems are also quite high such as substance abuse (Anona et al., 2024; Joseph et al., 2024; Okoyo et al., 2022), child abuse and neglect (Esparza-Del Villar et al., 2022; Fatemi et al., 2022; McMullan et al., 2023), and intimate partner violence (Dai et al., 2024; Juwono et al., 2024; Zhang Kudon et al., 2023), organizations and learners keep making efforts for bringing positive changes in the lives of target population, and this process continues.

Moreover, a SAMREEN vision guides organizations and learners to develop and establish an inclusive, engaged, and successful vision statement with relevant stakeholders. A SAMREEN vision also provides organizations and learners with a lens to review and examine a vision after they develop it. A SAMREEN vision has seven different elements, such as Sustainable, Attainable, Meaningful, Related, Engaged, Evaluative, and Neat. Since organizations continue their functioning over time and successful programs are sustainable, it is important for stakeholders (whether they develop a vision for an organization or for a program) to consider and include the element of sustainability in their vision or assess their vision by using the lens of sustainability. Although a vision is a broader and long-term statement, it should be attainable and realistic, which helps organizations and learners to attract target population, engage stakeholders, and efficiently direct efforts. If stakeholders are not clear about the vision and they are confused regarding its specificity, authenticity, and attainability, it limits their engagement and participation in organizational and program activities. Additionally, if a vision is meaningful for organizations, learners, and other relevant stakeholders, all partners work together towards the vision because they feel it useful and relevant to their lives and beneficial for their people and communities. A vision needs to be aligned with organizations and learners' values, backgrounds, and priorities. If an organization or learners value education, then the vision needs to resonate with such values. Such a consistency increases the efficiency and motivation of organizations, learners, and stakeholders. Hence, it is important for organizations and learners to reflect upon their values when they develop and establish a vision. A vision is a lifelong roadmap for organizations and learners. Hence, it is imperative for them to engage all relevant stakeholders in the development of a vision. An engaged and inclusive process results in the development of a vision which all partners can relate to. Therefore, an active engagement in developing a vision for an organization or a program from all relevant stakeholders is essential to successfully complete this task. Although a vision is broad, general, and vague statement because it is developed for a long-term future and most of the time, the final outcomes and conditions do not happen and this process continues, it is also important to develop a vision in such a manner that organizations, learners, and stakeholders can revisit, review, and examine it to assess their overall efforts and progress towards it.

Sometimes, organizations and learners' priorities are changed, and they need to focus on more important and new problems and tasks. Consequently, they revise and modify their vision statement to reflect their new paths, ideas, and plans and share it with the audiences. When their current vision statement is evaluative that they can revisit, review, and examine, it saves time, efforts, and bring all stakeholders together because all partners are likely to be clear about the current vision, they effectively inspect and examine it, discuss new plans and ideas, and make appropriate revisions and modifications to their vision statement. Finally, a vision statement should be well-written, organized, and straightforward so that it makes sense to all partners. A complex or confused vision statement disengages stakeholders and creates confusion among them because when stakeholders are not clear about it, they think and perceive it differently, which leads to disagreements and conflicts among them. Hence, a simple, clean, and orderly vision statement brings all partners together. The above discussion demonstrates that the SAMREEN vision and lens guide and facilitate organizations, learners, and relevant stakeholders to develop an inclusive, meaningful, and appropriate vision statement, which they can revisit, review, and examine to evaluate their efforts and progress towards it and make revisions and modifications in case their priorities and paths are changed in future.

Following is a definition of the SAMREEN goal:

A SAMREEN goal is a broader and long-term statement which is comprised of an idea or general roadmap of various types, lengths, and degrees that groups and/or organizations develop for achieving positive long-term outcomes in future.

A MCEM program has one or more goals and/or objectives. Some programs have multiple goals, whereas other programs have only one goal depending upon time, scope, and resources allocated for that program. For each goal, learners can develop multiple objectives because objectives are more brief, short-term, and specific, whereas goals are broader and long-term. It is worth mentioning that a program can also have objectives only due to its limited time and scope. A program can only have a single objective if learners are developing a MCEM program for their SL project over the course of a semester or the time allocated for the program is quite limited. If a program has only one objective, then there is no need to develop program goals. If a program has multiple objectives, then one or more goals can be developed. It is important to keep a consistency between program goals and objectives because the program objectives are different pieces of a program goal. Hence, when the assessment is conducted to evaluate the effectiveness of a program, program objectives are usually measured, and if a program meets its objectives,

The MCEM Program Vision, SAMREEN Goals, and Objectives 113

ultimately the program goals are also met. Therefore, greater consistency and alignment between program goals and objectives increases the rigor of a program and make the evaluation straightforward, valid, and accurate.

As mentioned in the definition of a SAMREEN goal, a program goal is a broader and long-term statement, which provides a roadmap to learners and stakeholders including program participants about the program. A program may be of different types and focuses. For instance, some programs focus only on education and prevention, some programs focus on intervention, whereas other programs combine both intervention and prevention. Additionally, some programs only offer services, consultancy, financial counseling, and/or assistance, whereas other programs also offer hands-on activities. Hence, programs can be of different types. Therefore, the goal of a program indicates the type and nature of the program. It is worth mentioning that the program goals are consistent with program description and all other steps that learners accomplish before developing the program goals and/or objectives. For instance, there are steps discussed in each of the previous chapters that learners need to complete before they get to this chapter and develop their SAMREEN goals and objectives. Hence, learners need to review the previous work before they start working on and complete the current step, which is to develop the SAMREEN goals and objectives for their program. The MCEM framework guides learners to systematically develop, implement, and evaluate their MCEM programs. Therefore, each step of the program is connected and interrelated with each other.

It is worth mentioning that the program evaluation can be conducted at any time over the course of a program's lifecycle. In that case, program objectives can be quite useful because they are brief, specific, and short-term. Therefore, an evaluation can be conducted to examine the progress of the program in relation to the program objectives. If the program needs any improvements, which can be done before investing additional resources in the program. Hence, program objectives facilitate learners and relevant stakeholders including the program participants to review and assess the progress and effectiveness of their program in different areas and engagement levels at any given time over the program lifecycle.

Similarly, the programs may vary based on their length, degree, and intensity. For instance, if programs are developed by donor agencies, which aim to partner with local organizations to implement their programs, such programs are usually quite longer, lengthy, and intensive. On the other hand, if a program is developed by a local support group to increase awareness about an important community issue, such as parenting practices or human sexuality, then the program likely stays short, simple, and less intensive. Likewise, if students are developing, implementing, and evaluating their programs for their SL projects for a semester, their program would be quite shorter, simpler, limited in scope, whereas the MCEM programs which are developed for students' practicums and/or internships are relatively longer because students have more time to complete those programs/projects. Additionally, some programs are more intense than others because participants are usually more vulnerable or at a greater risk. For instance, programs that focus on child abuse and neglect, substance abuse, mass violence, or intimate partner violence are usually intensive, complex, and dynamic because participants need more dosage and support from the program to recover from the problem or trauma they have been experiencing.

Moreover, the program's purpose is to address participants' needs and issues. Those programs which effectively address participants' needs and issues are considered successful. The intent of successful outcomes is included in the program goal. Hence, learners develop and implement their program to achieve their program goals (and objectives) and when they successfully achieve their programs goals, consequently, the program shows positive outcomes. Hence, one of the purposes of conducting program evaluation is to find out whether the program outcomes demonstrate that the program achieved its goals (and/or objectives), which learners and relevant stakeholders including program participants collaboratively developed for the program.

Following are different components of a SAMREEN program goal:
SAMREEN Goals.

(1) Sustainable

(2) Attainable

(3) Meaningful

(4) Related

(5) Engaged

(6) Evaluative

(7) Neat

Program goals should be SAMREEN (Sustainable, Attainable, Meaningful, Related, Engaged, Evaluative, and Neat).

An example of SAMREEN goal is as follows:

Parents of young children 0–8 years will work together to learn and practice useful parenting practice for effectively raising their children in a local community over the next 3–5 years.

As mentioned in the definition of a SAMREEN goal, it is a long-term idea, so, 3–5 years is a long-term idea or plan, which is attainable for any group or organization. Parents also have sufficient capacities/abilities to learn parenting knowledge and skills. It is also meaningful for young parents because this is their primary purpose to effectively raise their children. If the program focuses on promoting positive parenting practices, then this goal is also consistent with all other components of the program. For instance, positive parenting practices are a resource for parents and children, which increases their well-being and development. Thus, it also contains the "Related" component of a SAMREEN objective. All parent participants work together in the program, which makes the program an engaged and a collaborative learning experience for them. The goal can also be assessed by observing parenting practices of parent participants. The goal statement is clear, simple, and well-written, which can be understood by all program stakeholders. When parent participants practice the knowledge and skills they learn through the program, they are likely to practice them after the formal completion of the program because it is quite useful, relevant, and beneficial for them. Consequently, the program goal also shows sustainability component. Hence, the above example of a SAMREEN goal demonstrates all components of a SAMREEN goal.

Following is the definition of a SAMREEN objective:

A SAMREEN objective is a specific and short-term statement which is comprised of certain actions, strategies, and/or activities of various types, lengths, and degrees that groups and/or organizations develop for achieving current and/or future short-term positive outcomes.

As discussed earlier in this chapter, that program objectives are different pieces of one or more program goals. A program's goal may have one or more objectives. Hence, a program objective is brief, short-term, and specific. Program objectives can focus on various areas of a program, such as program staff, stakeholders, participants, implementation strategies, actions, policies, and/or activities, which can be assessed at any time over the course of a program lifecycle to examine the progress of a program in one or more areas. Like program goals, program objectives also have various types, durations, complexity, and intensity. Since the program objectives are brief and short-term, which helps learners to evaluate program goals, their implementation, and/or the effectiveness of a program, and learners can also assess the program objectives anytime. Consequently, the assessment of program objectives demonstrates the current progress of a program. Learners can also design and carry out continuous assessments to evaluate their program objectives over time. For instance, after every module, learners can ask participants to rate the module and ask a few questions to share their learning experiences, and the extent they were able to meet the module objective. Each module helps participants to pursue one or more program objectives. Thus, such evaluations facilitate learners, relevant stakeholders, and program participants to examine the extent to which they are achieving their program objectives, which will ultimately get them closer to the program goals if they developed any goals for the program. It is worth mentioning that some assessment methods and techniques are more useful and effective for certain programs than the others. Since evaluations take time, money, effort, and require expertise and people who can accurately conduct it, therefore, it is important for learners to collaboratively discuss program evaluation methods and techniques and other aspects related to it with all relevant stakeholders including program participants and determine the most effective, suitable, and relevant method and technique to conduct it. It is worth mentioning that since the components of SAMREEN goals and objectives expand the program to many areas and increase clarity in program evaluation for learners, it is essential for learners to assess all components of SAMREEN goals and objectives or at least some important and relevant ones if they cannot assess all of them due to limited time, scope, resources, and expertise.

Following are different components of a SAMREEN program objective.

(1) Sustainable

(2) Attainable

(3) Meaningful

(4) Related

(5) Engaged

(6) Evaluative

(7) Neat

Program objectives should be SAMREEN (Sustainable, Attainable, Meaningful, Related, Engaged, Evaluative, and Neat).

An example of SAMREEN objective is as follows:

Young parents who need additional support (e.g., counseling, therapy, and financial assistance) will receive it from program stakeholders who are partnered in the program.

This is one of the SAMREEN objectives which is aligned with the SAMREEN goal discussed above. Additional examples on SAMREEN goals and objectives are provided in the tables after this chapter. The objective is quite specific and short-term compared to the SAMREEN goal as mentioned in the definition of a SAMREEN objective. The statement of this objective also shows certain actions, which is to provide additional support to those young parents who need it. It is attainable because it is assumed that counselors, therapists, and financial experts are partnered in the program. Parents also have the capacity and willingness to receive these services. These services improve parenting practices and positive parent–child interactions; hence, it is quite meaningful and relevant for parents. These professionals are engaged in the program with parent participants who receive professional services from these experts, which shows collaboration and engagement of relevant stakeholders including program participants in the program. Since the program focuses on promoting positive parenting practices, this objective is also consistent with all other components of the program. It is written in a simple, organized, and orderly manner so that all stakeholders can understand it. Parents can be observed, and their parenting skills and financial problems can be assessed once they receive counseling and financial services from professionals who are partnered in the program. Finally, when parents receive counseling and financial services, they are more likely to improve their parenting skills and practices that they use after the formal completion of the program, which shows the sustainability component of the SAMREEN objective. Hence, the above SAMREEN objective contains all components of a SAMREEN objective.

The section below provides a detailed description of each component of SAMREEN program goals and objectives. Both SAMREEN goals and objectives have quite similar components, hence, one description for each component of SAMREEN goal and objective is provided.

(1) Sustainable (Transformational, reciprocal exchange of knowledge, skills, and experiences among all relevant stakeholders including program participants, adaptability and continuity).

The MCEM framework promotes an active engagement and collaboration among learners and all relevant stakeholders including program participants in the process of developing, implementing, and evaluating a program. When all stakeholder groups participate in the program process regardless of their social status in society, they exchange knowledge, skills, and experience with each other, which they use, apply, and practice after the formal completion of the program. Consequently, the program brings positive changes in the lives of all stakeholders including the program participants and learners. When all stakeholder groups feel heard and respected, they feel the program useful, relevant, and beneficial for them and their local families and communities. When all stakeholder groups actively engage, participate, and collaboratively learn from each other throughout the program lifecycle, they continue the program after its formal completion if they need to, Additionally, when all stakeholders gain expertise in one or more areas of the program, they also volunteer or participate in the same program implemented in different communities as experts. All these situations, efforts, and actions ensure the sustainability of the program. Hence, the first component (sustainable) of SAMREEN goal and objective guides and promotes program sustainability for learners.

(2) Attainable (Specific and achievable based on timing, scope, and allocated resources).
As mentioned earlier, that SAMREEN program goals are border and long-term, whereas objectives are brief and short-term, but it is also worth mentioning that both SAMREEN goals and objectives need to be attainable. Since each program goal and objective vary in terms of their length, it is important for learners and relevant stakeholders including program participants to determine the time, scope, and allocated resources of their program based on the previous steps of the program development process, their program goals and objectives need to be specific and achievable given the time, scope, and resources allocated for the program. Although stakeholders can continue the program, the program goals and/or objectives need to be designed based on the allocated funds and duration of a program. Hence, the second component (attainable) of SAMREEN goal and objective enables learners to determine a specific timeline to formally complete their program.

(3) Meaningful (Relevant and useful for all relevant stakeholders including program participants).
When program goals and objectives are meaningful and relevant for learners and relevant stakeholders including program participants, they are more likely be engaged in the program because they consider the program beneficial, useful, and important in addressing their needs and issues. The program needs to be developmentally and culturally responsive and appropriate for all stakeholder groups to increase their participation, engagement, retention, program outcomes, and sustainability. If participants and other stakeholder groups do not find the program relevant and meaningful, they lose their interest in the program. In order to make the program inclusive, engagement, and effective, an active participation of all program stakeholders is essential throughout the program

lifecycle. The program relevance motivates stakeholders to identify, share, and utilize resources for the success of their program. Therefore, it is important for learners to collaboratively work with all relevant stakeholders including program participants to make their program more relevant and meaningful to their needs, lives, and cultures. Hence, the third component (meaningful) of SAMREEN goal and objective enables learners to develop a relevant and meaningful objective, which is also beneficial for the program.

(4) Related (Consistency throughout the program, such as program description, SAMREEN goals and objectives, and program curriculum and delivery).
Since the MCEM programs are systematic and multilevel, it is important for learners to ensure consistency between all steps of the program. Hence, each chapter of this book focuses on one specific step that learners and other program stakeholders including program participants need to accomplish before moving to the next step and each step is connected and interrelated with the other. Therefore, learners need to review the previous steps before working and completing the current or next step of the program. Hence the fourth component (related) of SAMREEN goal and objective helps learner to ensure and account for a consistency between all program segments and steps.

(5) Engaged (Engagement of all relevant stakeholders including program participants throughout program lifecycle, engagement of program participants with curriculum, delivery, and assessment).
The MCEM programs foster engagement of learners and all relevant stakeholders including program participants throughout the program lifecycle. Additionally, program participants are engaged with each other, with the program curriculum, learners, and facilitators/instructors. Program stakeholders' engagement and collaboration are imperative and essential for the success of MCEM programs. Since the MCEM programs and multilevel, dynamic, and complex, learners need to make sure that they foster and promote stakeholders' engagement in all program areas and engagement levels. Such a collaborative and engaged program process provides stakeholders with many opportunities to share and utilize each other's resources and strengths and reduce vulnerabilities and risks for the success and sustainability of their program. Hence, the fifth component (engaged) of SAMREEN goal and objective fosters engagement of all stakeholders including program participants in all areas and engagement levels of the program.

(6) Evaluative (Clear, measurable, consistent, and straightforward, which can be assessed rigorously and in a meaningful manner).

Program evaluation is an integral part of any program. Different evaluation methods and techniques can be used to assess programs. The purpose of conducting an evaluation is to examine the progress of a program in relation to its goals and/or objectives. Hence, if the program goals and/or objectives are clear, consistent, measurable, and straightforward, the evaluator can smoothly and rigorously assess what the program has accomplished in relation to the program goals and objectives at any given time.

Sometimes, organizations or learners hire external evaluators to assess their program. These external evaluators usually do not know the background and history of the program for which they are hired. External evaluators are also not quite aware of the context and dynamics of the program. They briefly review the program, focus on the work related to the program which is accomplished, choose evaluation methodology, collect data, and share the results with the learners and sometimes stakeholders. When the program objectives are clear, consistent, and straightforward, it makes the assessment process much simpler and easier for an evaluator who is usually hired to conduct the assessment in a limited time. Moreover, if learners or any stakeholders have appropriate skills and expertise to assess the program, the evaluative quality of SAMREEN goals and objectives makes the assessment process less challenging and much smoother for them. Due to the clarity of a program, its goals, and objectives, the evaluation results are more accurate, meaningful, and useful for learners and program stakeholders. Hence, the sixth component (evaluative) of SAMREEN goal and objective increases clarity and ease in the assessment of a program.

(7) Neat (Organized, clean, well-written, placed in an orderly manner, and simple that can be understood by all relevant stakeholders including program participants regardless of their educational levels, skills, and background).

It is worth mentioning that some stakeholders in a program may not have high educational levels, technical skills, and/or expertise to actively participate in the assessment process and understand the evaluation results. Since their roles and active participation is important and useful for the program, their understanding of program goals, objectives, and evaluation results are also equally important to ensure their continuous participation and engagement in the program over the program lifecycle.

Hence, it is important for learners and other stakeholders to neatly develop and write their program goals and objectives, which can be understood by all stakeholders including program participants and external evaluators. A language used in writing the program goals and objectives needs to be simple, less technical, information is well-organized, placed in orderly manner, and clearly written. Hence, the seventh component (neat) guides learners to write SAMREEN goal and objective in an organized and orderly manner that can be simply understood by all program stakeholders.

It is worth mentioning that even though the MCEM programs may vary based on time, scope, focus, and funding, in order to develop and implement an effective program even though it has a limited time period, small scope, and fewer or no funding, learners need to develop at least one objective for each engagement level and developmental, sociocultural, and historical contexts. Learners can also develop one to two goals that cover the overall focus of the program and one objective each for the engagement levels and developmental, sociocultural, and historical contexts. Since the purpose of a MCEM program is to address program participants' needs or problems by decreasing the vulnerabilities or risks and improving resources or strengths, learners identify potential vulnerabilities and resources created by stakeholders for program participants from each of the engagement levels which change over time, and are influenced by developmental, sociocultural, and historical contexts. Learners can develop program objectives to improve participants' resources and decrease vulnerabilities for each engagement level, and developmental, sociocultural, and historical contexts. This procedure also indicates that the MCEM framework provides learners with a systematic process to develop, implement, and evaluate multilevel, complex, and comprehensive programs. Even though learners do not have advanced skills or background of program development, implementation, and evaluation, they can follow these steps to systematically develop, implement, and evaluate their MCEM programs. Thus, the MCEM framework provides a healthy balance between a scientific procedure (a systematic process) and relevance (acknowledging and using stakeholders knowledge and real-life experiences).

Moreover, learners can divide one SAMREEN goal or objective into many subgoals and/or subobjectives, which may further facilitate them in examining their program goals and objectives and conducting an effective and comprehensive evaluation during the program lifecycle. For instance, when learners develop an objective and assess it with the SAMREEN lens (Sustainable, Attainable, Meaningful, Related, Engaged, Evaluative, and Neat), they can develop one additional objective for each component of the SAMREEN objective that may help and facilitate learners to focus on each component of the overall objective and keep evaluating their program in relation to the subobjectives until they achieve it. For instance, the first component of SAMREEN objective is "Sustainable." So, after developing the main objective, learners can assess it with SAMREEN lens to make sure that it has all the SAMREEN objective components (seven components) and then further develop one subobjective for each of these components. The same rule applies when learners develop the SAMREEEN goals. One of the uniqueness of the MCEM programs is that they are quite flexible and adaptable. Consequently, they can range from quite simple to very complex programs as is also evident from the current discussion of SAMREEN goals and objectives. Learners need to examine the purpose of their program, time, scope, resources, and other contextual factors to determine the degree of complexity that they want in their MCEM program.

In sum, the SAMREEN program vision, goals, and objectives provide a foundation or a roadmap to learners and relevant stakeholders including program participants that they can focus on to develop next steps of their program. As the MCEM programs are flexible and adaptable, SAMREEN program vision, goals, and objectives can also be developed in various ways. However, it is essential for learners to maintain a consistency between all segments and components of their program including SAMREEN goals and objectives to maintain scientific rigor and transparency of their program. Since the MCEM programs are systematic and multilevel, every step of the program is connected and interrelated with one another. Therefore, learners need to review the previous steps that they accomplished before working on and developing the SAMREEN program vision, goals, and objectives.

CASE STUDY

This is the time when Karen is ready to develop her program vision, goals, and objectives. However, she has several questions wondering in her head regarding her program goals and objectives. For instance, what is the role of a vision statement for the program and how broader does it need to be? Whether she needs goals only, objectives only, or both for her program. How many goals and/or objective does she need? How would she know that her program goals and objectives are accurate and relevant to her program? How can she ensure consistency between her program goals and objectives? How can she assess the accuracy of her program goals and objectives? How does she know that her program goals and objectives will foster and promote engagement and inclusion? All these questions create concerns about the accuracy and successful accomplishment of this task. Since the program goals and objectives are developed based on the prior work she accomplished (as mentioned above in the previous chapters), and the program implementation and evaluation will be based and focused on these program goals and objectives, Karen wants to make sure that she has appropriate knowledge and skills along with specific guidelines so that she can accurately develop her program goals and objectives.

DISCUSSION QUESTIONS

(1) What is a SAMREEN program vision? Describe its different elements and their significance.

(2) What are the SAMREEN goals and subgoals?

(3) Discuss the difference between SAMREEN goals and subgoals.

(4) What are the SAMREEN objectives and subobjectives?

(5) Discuss the difference between SAMREEN objectives and subobjectives?

(6) Discuss the difference between SAMREEN goals and objectives?

(7) Discuss the relationship between SAMREEN goals and objectives.

(8) How can they be aligned and consistent with each other?

(9) How can learners make them aligned and consistent with the SAMREEN vision?

(10) What is the role of SAMREEN goals and objectives in a MCEM program?

(11) Why SAMREEN goals and objectives are important for the success of MCEM programs.

(12) How do SAMREEN goals and objectives improve a MCEM program?

(13) How do SAMREEN vision, goals, and objectives foster stakeholders engagement and participation in the program?

(14) What did you learn from this assignment?

ASSIGNMENT QUESTIONS

(1) What is your SAMREEN program vision?

(2) What is your SAMREEN program goal (s)?

(3) How does it include the components/qualities of a SAMREEN goal? Assess and describe your program goal by using the lens of SAMREEN goal (Sustainable, Attainable, Meaningful, Related, Engaged, Evaluative, and Neat).

(4) What is your program SAMREEN objective (s)?

(5) How does it include the components/qualities of a SAMREEN objective? Assess and describe your program objective by using the lens of SAMREEN objective (Sustainable, Attainable, Meaningful, Related, Engaged, Evaluative, and Neat).

(6) How are your program SAMREEN goals and objectives aligned with each other?

(7) How are your program SAMREEN goals and objectives aligned with the other parts of your program?

(8) How do program SAMREEN goals and objectives address the needs and issues of your program participants?

(9) How do your program SAMREEN goals and objectives indicate the program focus and success?

(10) What did you learn from this assignment?

Table 5. Examples of SAMREEN Goal and Objectives.

SAMREEN Goal	Components of SAMREEN Goal	SAMREEN Objective	Components of SAMREEN Objective
Parents of young children 0–8 years will work together to learn and practice useful parenting practice for effectively raising their children in a local community over the next 3–5 years.	(1) Sustainable: Parents will learn the knowledge and skills of raising young children. Children will grow and develop well over time. (2) Attainable: Parents have sufficient capacities/ abilities to learn parenting knowledge and skills. (3) Meaningful: It is important and relevant for parents to learn important knowledge and skills for raising their children. (4) Related: Program focuses on parents of young children aims at supporting parents and providing them with appropriate skills to raise their children for which parents' learning are facilitated	(1) Parents of young children 0–8 years will learn important and relevant parenting knowledge and skills that they can use and practice in effectively raising their children. (2) Young parents who need additional support (e.g., counseling, therapy, and financial assistance) will receive it from program stakeholders who are partnered in the program.	(1) Sustainable: Parents will learn, practice, and transform their parenting knowledge and skills into their children. (2) Attainable: Parents can learn, use, and practice parenting knowledge and skills and children can also learn from their parents over the program life cycle. (3) Meaningful: The program is relevant for parents, their children, friends, and extended family members. (4) Related: All components of the program as well as SAMREEN goal and objectives are aligned and consistent with each other. (5) Engaged: The program

(Continued)

Table 5. *(Continued)*

SAMREEN Goal	Components of SAMREEN Goal	SAMREEN Objective	Components of SAMREEN Objective
	through various ways and modalities. All components of the program and goal are consistent and aligned with each other. (5) Engaged: Parents and their children including all relevant stakeholders will be engaged during the life cycle of the program. (6) Evaluative: Program goals can be assessed over time by evaluating parents' knowledge, engagement, and practice in the program over time. (7) Neat: The goal clearly states that it focuses on helping parents of young children about parenting knowledge and skills to support them in		objective will engage all relevant stakeholder groups from the engagement level including the program participants. (6) Evaluative: The extent of positive change among program participants and engagement among stakeholders can be easily assessed to examine the effectiveness of the program over time. (7) Neat: The objectives can be easily understood by all relevant stakeholders regardless of the educational levels and/or technical knowledge. They are clearly aligned with the SAMREEN goal and indicates that these objectives are

Table 5. *(Continued)*

SAMREEN Goal	Components of SAMREEN Goal	SAMREEN Objective	Components of SAMREEN Objective
	effectively raising their children.		supporting the program goal and helping learners to pursue and achieve their broader and long-term goal.

SAMREEN Goal	SAMREEN Objectives	SAMREEN Subobjectives
Parents of young children 0–8 years will work together to learn and practice useful parenting practice for effectively raising their children in a local community over the next 3–5 years.	*Proximal-level objective:* Parents will learn, share, and practice useful parenting knowledge and skills with each other in a collaborative manner. *Influential-level objective:* Parents will learn the negative and positive effects of electronic and social media on them and their children. *Holistic-level objective:* Parents will learn, share, and practice resources and vulnerabilities in their cultural context with each other. *Developmental time/context objective:* Parents will learn developmental changes and needs of their young children and useful strategies that they can use to address them.	*Proximal level subobjective:* (1) Learners will educate parents about useful parenting knowledge, skills, and best practices to grow their parenting skills. (2) Parents will share useful parenting strategies with each other. (3) Childcare and elementary staff will be invited to share their knowledge and information with program participants. (4) Community local organizations and support groups will be invited to introduce their support, connect with participants, and share their programs to engage participants in the future.

(Continued)

Table 5. *(Continued)*

SAMREEN Goal	SAMREEN Objectives	SAMREEN Subobjectives
	Sociocultural time/context objective: Parents will learn parenting in the current societal context, its strengths, and challenges. *Historical time/context objective:* Parents will learn how parenting perceptions, demands, and support systems changed over time.	Similarly, learners can develop subobjectives aligned with each engagement levels and developmental, sociocultural, and historical time/context.

10

THE MCEM PROGRAM CURRICULUM AND DELIVERY

The objective of this chapter for learners is to learn how to develop a program curriculum for a MCEM program. Additionally, this chapter also discusses useful teaching methods and techniques to deliver and implement a MCEM program curriculum. The author also shares how learners can operationalize different program components that they chose when they described their program based on its definition (please review Chapter 5). Further, the author also shares how learners can engage stakeholders including program participants with program curriculum, make the program delivery interesting, relevant, and meaningful for them, and foster their positive learning experiences.

One of the uniqueness of MCEM programs is that they are inclusive and comprehensive in all aspects including program curriculum and delivery. For instance, as discussed in the previous chapters, the recognition, engagement, and inputs of all relevant stakeholder groups including program participants throughout the program process makes the MCEM program more inclusive and representative of all stakeholders. Similarly, when learners develop the MCEM program curriculum, it also needs to be inclusive and comprehensive. The MCEM framework considers culture and diversity as the central aspects of the program process. Hence, the MCEM program curriculum and delivery also need to consider these aspects central and important, which makes the implementation process more inclusive, culturally appropriate, and effective. As the MCEM framework provides learners with step-by-step guidelines to systematically develop, implement, and evaluate their programs, all steps, and components of the MCEM program are related to and connected with each other. Likewise, the MCEM program curriculum and delivery also need to be consistent and aligned with all other components that learners accomplished before reaching at this stage of the program. Below is a definition of the program curriculum.

A program curriculum is an organized and structured set of contents aligned with specific program goals and/or objectives and all other components of the program, which offers learners with education, knowledge, and understanding on relevant topics and improve their proficiency and skills on the contents to provide learners with positive and rigorous learning experiences and achieve learners' success and successful learning outcomes.

The MCEM programs can focus on prevention, intervention, or both. In a MCEM program that focuses on prevention, its primary purpose is usually to educate program participants and other relevant stakeholders about the problems, needs, and/or strengths that the program focuses and raise their awareness to help them prevent from those issues or strengthen them to deal with it future if they face it. Hence the MCEM program curriculum plays an integral role in educating participants about the program and raising their awareness about it. The MCEM program curriculum is also grounded in the MCEM framework. For instance, if learners developed four SAMREEN objectives, one for each engagement level and one for developmental, sociocultural, and historical contexts, then the MCEM program curriculum can be organized and structured with respect to these objectives. It is worth mentioning that learners can develop as many goals and/or objectives as they like depending upon the scope, time, and allocated resources of the program. Learners can include specific contents aligned with each objective in the program curriculum to educate program participants about them, raise awareness, knowledge, and understanding about the issue focused through the program. Once learners choose a program topic, they need to decide which program component (s), such as instructions, resources, activities, and services, they want to include in their program. Then learners include specific contents in their curriculum to operationalize or implement those program components. Learners use the program components and operationalize them by including specific contents to achieve their SAMREEN program goals and/or objective. For instance, if learners developed one objective for the proximal level, which is to educate young parents about positive parenting practices and they use "Instructions" to operationalize it. For this purpose, they use various methods and techniques, such as different styles of presentation (Arvola et al., 2021; Cuesta-Hincapie et al., 2024; Leijen et al., 2024; Moen, 2021); posters, whiteboards, charts, and pictures (Forsyth, 2023; Godwin et al., 2022; Nguyen, 2023), roleplays (Bajaj et al., 2024; Buldu, 2022; Daif-Allah & Al-Sultan, 2023), audio and video aids (Azor et al., 2020; Khabir et al., 2022; Wójcik et al., 2021), etc. to implement and deliver the instructions to foster participants' understanding on positive parenting practices, which is an objective of the program.

It is worth mentioning that the selection of these components (i.e. instructions) should be aligned with how learners described the program. If learners described their program with all four components, then they can use any of the components in their program curriculum, but if they chose only two or three components based on the need, scope, and nature of their program, then they need to develop their program curriculum according to those program components. Therefore, the MCEM program process is a systematic process such that each step relates to one another, which increases the rigor and trustworthiness of the MCEM program. Moreover, as it is evident from the definition of a program (please refer to Chapter 5) that a program should be developmentally and culturally appropriate. Hence, it is essential that learners examine the age-specific learning needs of their participants. For instance, if participants are children, learners need to create a curriculum that resonates and aligns with the ages of children. If the program focuses on teenagers and youth, learners need to include those instructions and activities, which are interesting, relevant, and exciting for their program participants. Similarly, if program participants are elderly people, learners need to consider their learning needs and styles. They may need less content, more time, longer breaks, and frequent discussions. The purpose, use, and significance of a program curriculum may vary based on the ages, developmental, stages, and learning needs of participants including individuals, families, and groups. Sometimes, learners have different age groups in their program. As mentioned above, participants bring distinct age-specific and learning needs and prefer certain styles of learning. Therefore, learners need to be prepared for such situations and use a variety of modes, methods, and techniques to deliver and implement their program to foster and promote positive learning experiences among program participants. Hence, there are many factors that guide learners to make the program curriculum developmentally appropriate, which results in positive outcomes (Li et al., 2021; Newton et al., 2024).

Similarly, learners also need to make sure that their program curriculum respects and aligns with participants' cultures (Kabir et al., 2022; Offei-Dua et al., 2022). Culture plays an extremely important role in participants' learning, engagement, and participation in the program curriculum and delivery (Herr & Anderson, 2015; Raza, 2022). If participants find the program contents more relevant and aligned with their cultural believes, values, and practices, they are more likely to learn and engage in the program curriculum, share their experiences, and practice it after the formal completion of the program (Herr, 2017;

Mathur & Rodriguez, 2022). Participants' cultures determine how they think, behave, and interact with each other and make sense of the program contents. Hence, learners need to make sure that the program curriculum culturally makes sense to participants. Since participants are a part of stakeholders' groups who also engage throughout the program process including program curriculum and delivery, leaners can also pilot test their program curriculum with a group of program participants before they deliver the program. This may help learners to receive any additional feedback, make revisions, and improve their program before its implementation. There are some other factors, such as religion, history, patriarchy, etc., which are also important for learners to consider for developing an appropriate and effective program curriculum. Due to an engaged, continuous, multilevel, and inclusive MCEM program process, learners create more opportunities and fewer challenges for their program curriculum and delivery. Finally, learners decide how they deliver the program curriculum to their program participants, which is a part of program delivery. Below is a definition of program delivery:

A program delivery is composed of various effective teaching approaches, methods, and techniques, which are carried out in a collaborative, engaged, and inclusive manner to deliver or implement a program curriculum with program participants according to their learning styles, abilities, and needs for educating them about the program curriculum and improving their understanding, knowledge, and skills of the contents.

Learners may vary in terms of their philosophy or views about teaching. Consequently, one learner may believe in the effectiveness of a collaborative, nontraditional, or modern teaching approach (Behmanesh et al., 2022; Gao et al., 2020; Keesey-Phelan et al., 2022; Rönnlund et al., 2021), and the other learner may consider a directive, top-down, or traditional teaching approach more beneficial for participants (Humphries & Clark, 2021; Osmani et al., 2021; Wang et al., 2021) whereas a third learner may thing to combine these two approaches (traditional and modern) to teach and educate participants about the program curriculum (Shurygin et al., 2023; Villar, 2022; Wang, 2022). Learners' pedagogical philosophies and views inform their teaching methods and techniques that they use to educate their participants about the program curriculum, and deliver these contents to program participants during the program implementation and delivery (Lam, 2021; Rasegh et al., 2022; Zhu et al., 2020)

Since the MCEM programs promote an engaged, inclusive, and collaborative learning process and create an environment that recognizes and respect the voices of all stakeholders from the very beginning of the program, the MCEM program curriculum and delivery is also grounded in collaborative teaching approaches, which are inclusive, culturally relevant, developmentally appropriate, and foster engagement and collaboration among participants. Hence, learners need to learn, identify, and utilize such approaches, which are aligned with the MCEM framework and that continuously promote stakeholders' engagement and collaboration in program curriculum and delivery. Participants may have unique learning styles, needs, and abilities; hence, learners need to understand and address the learning needs of each participant and simultaneously carry out a collaborative and cooperative learning process that encourages participants to share their real-life experiences and local/personal expertise and foster possibilities of engagement, collaboration, and connections among them. Such an inclusive, engaged, and collaborative learning process not only helps participants to understand the knowledge and skills delivered to them in the program, it also increases the interest, relevance, and involvement of program participants in the program during that phase and later in the program process, which contributes to program success and sustainability.

In order to develop a rigorous, trustworthy, and culturally appropriate program curriculum, learners need to conduct a literature review and explore all possible and reliable sources (please read Chapter 8 for detailed information on how to conduct literature reviews for a MCEM program) to explore and find information on the program that they think important and relevant and want to share with program participants during the program delivery and implementation phase to achieve the program goals and/or objectives. For instance, if the program objective is to improve positive parenting practices among young parents, learners need to find information, which helps them to implement all program components (i.e. resources, instructions, activities, and services) and related to all engagement levels, and developmental, sociocultural, and historical contexts. When all stakeholders including program participants are engaged in the development of the MCEM program curriculum, the program curriculum becomes more relevant, meaningful, and representative of all groups who are engaged in the program.

At the proximal level, program participants, their friends, and families belong to stakeholder group of "Families," and employers, support groups, local community organizations, and schools belong to the stakeholder group of "Community." Learners need to find topics and information related to these groups to improve participants' parenting practices (increasing participants' resources and strengths) and reduce their challenges and demands associated with their parenting practices (decreasing participants' vulnerabilities and risks). Similarly, topics related to the influential level include the role of print, electronic, social media, public policies, and programs in supporting parents and promoting healthy and positive parenting practices. For instance, the role of technology in today's parenting and the effects of screentime on children's behaviors and their interactions with parents. Likewise, from the holistic level, topics related to parenting are parenting in a cultural context, parenting practices among diverse parents, etc., can be included in the curriculum. Likewise, topics related to the developmental context, age-specific changes in young children and how parents can foster their young children's development by providing them with age-appropriate activities and environment. Related to the sociocultural context, topics include parenting in contemporary society, challenges and demands for parents in today's society, etc. Finally, related to historical context, topics include changes in parents' beliefs, practices and development of government policies and programs to support young parent families since 1960s. Hence, to make the MCEM program multilevel, culturally appropriate, and inclusive, learners consider and utilize all engagement levels, operationalize them by including all four program components (i.e. instructions, resources, activities, and services) into the program curriculum, and use effective and collaborative teaching methods and techniques to delivery and implement the program curriculum.

It is worth mentioning that since the engagement levels are reciprocally related, developmental, sociocultural, and historical contexts are also reciprocally related. Additionally, the dynamics of stakeholder groups change over time, and their reciprocal relationships with each other within and between the engagement levels are influenced by developmental, sociocultural, and historical contexts. Hence, learners can include and discuss these linkages and complexities in their program curriculum and delivery if they want to. It is important for learners to share and discuss any modifications or changes to the program curriculum with all relevant stakeholders before taking any actions. However, based on the nature, scope, and participants' backgrounds, learners should decide the extent, depth, and complexity of topics in their program curriculum. In-depth discussions among participants and their personal reflections are essential to engage participants in program curriculum, create relevance, and assess their understanding of topics/contents.

The components of a MCEM program (i.e. instructions, resources, activities, and services) provide learners with an opportunity to utilize various useful information and educational pieces to foster learners' knowledge, skills, and understanding of the topics focused through the program. For instance, to implement the instruction component, learners can create PowerPoint presentations and posters to provide participants with specific instructions and education. Learners can also use whiteboards, charts, cards, etc., to facilitate the learning of participants. For activities, learners can conduct small-group discussions, large-group discussion, roleplays, games, online surveys, debates, storytelling, journalling, etc. For resources, learners can create and share videos, assessments, websites, brochures, and any other informational resources to expand participants' understanding on the topic. Regarding services, based on the scope, learners' expertise, and funds, services can also be offered through professionals who are engaged as stakeholders in the program. For instance, certified counselors, parenting experts, mental health professionals, and/or relationship therapists can be engaged (or requested to be volunteered) or hired (if funds are available), and their services are offered to program participants. If learners don't have funds or suitable conditions to hire or engage any specialists for their program, they can also provide flyers, brochures, and pamphlets containing contact information of these specialists and specialized services to program participants. Learners can also collaborate with any relevant government and/or nongovernment organization that works with these specialists and utilize the services of these experts through that organization which they can offer to program participants. Hence, there are many ways through which learners can provide participants with specific and specialized services to meet their needs.

Moreover, the MCEM programs are quite flexible, adaptable, and learners' friendly due to the rigor and relevance of the MCEM framework. The MCEM programs can be offered and delivered through many different modes, which have been used in education and teaching such as in-person/face-to-face teaching (Holloway et al., 2023; Kobayashi, 2021; Song, 2021), online teaching including synchronous and asynchronous (An et al., 2024; Bong et al., 2024; Poon & Tang, 2024), and hybrid teaching (Dashtestani & Mohamadi, 2023; Feubli et al., 2024; Gamage et al., 2022). Participants usually belong to different cultures and backgrounds (Ólafsdóttir & Einarsdóttir, 2021). They have distinctive learning styles and needs (Brown et al., 2022). For instance, if program participants are nontraditional students, some of them may experience difficulties in attending educational sessions and need additional learning assistance and counselling services to successfully attend educational sessions or participate in the program delivery (Ivers et al., 2022; LeNoble & Roberts, 2020; Moore et al., 2020). Elderly program participants may need special accommodation, such as special seats, wheelchairs, transportation, etc. Sometimes, participants have any learning or developmental disabilities, which create additional needs and demands for learners (Brown et al., 2020; Harrison & Armstrong, 2022; Nannemann, 2021; Sellmaier & Kim, 2021). In order to provide participants with positive and useful learning experiences of the program, learners need to be prepared for these situations, scenarios, and challenges. Therefore, it is essential for learners to learn about their participants' needs and learning styles before delivering their program and working with participants. There are many sources and strategies that learners can use. Literature reviews and other reliable sources are useful tools and resources for learners to gain a better understanding of their program participants. Learners also interact and meet with participants prior to conducting their educational sessions or program delivery to gain insights about them. Since participants are a group of stakeholders who engage throughout the program process from the very beginning of the program, it also provides learners with substantial opportunities to learn about their participants. Stakeholders also usually know about program participants who can also provide insightful information to learners about program participants' backgrounds, learning styles, and needs. Learners can also attend community events, visit libraries, read local magazines, and newspapers to learn about the problem, its severity, and program participants. These are a few sources discussed, the MCEM program process fundamentally encourages learners and stakeholders including program participants to work together, collaborate, engage, and share, consequently, all partners have substantial opportunities to learn about each other. Since learners lead the program, they are more active and engaged due to their program success and sustainability, hence, they need to spend sufficient time with program participants to well-prepare themselves for the program delivery.

Additionally, the MCEM programs can be of several kinds, and consequently, the program curriculum may vary based on the form and nature of the program. Sometimes, due to limited time, scope, or instructors' expertise or comfort level, students do not directly work with program participants in the community, school, or workplace, but they choose resources and services for their program components when they describe the program. Consequently, students create an informational resource for their participants, which includes contents and information on a fundamental understanding of the program and contact information about relevant services and organizations. Students disseminate these resources among program participants and relevant stakeholders. Sometimes, students choose instructions and activities for their program. Hence, they record a presentation in which students discuss the program topic and provide specific information and details to educate program participants. Additionally, students also perform and record roleplays and small-group discussions to demonstrate a real-life application and share personal reflections on the topic for program participants and disseminate these contents among their program participants and other relevant stakeholders. Hence, a MCEM program can be developed and offered in many forms and modes. It is worth mentioning that although the forms and modes of a MCEM program may vary, stakeholders' engagement from the engagement levels and a systematic process is crucial that learners, instructors, and students need to carry out to develop, implement, and evaluate a successful and sustainable MCEM program. Again, the degree of complexity, engagement, and comprehensiveness of program curriculum and delivery may change but it is important for leaners to follow all steps or at least those which they consider important and crucial for the program based on the time, scope and nature of the program, SL requirements, and expertise.

Sometimes, a SL project is divided into a few courses and students complete their SL projects over a course of many semesters. This strategy provides students with additional opportunities and time to think and review different aspects of their MCEM program and a longer period to implement their program. Similarly, when students use the MCEM framework to develop, implement, and evaluate their MCEM program for practicums and internships, they have additional time to complete their program/project. If students work on their MCEM program in multiple courses (3–4 courses) or the form and nature of the MCEM program vary in each course, they can also receive a certificate (The MCEM Program Certificate) from their school/university, which also increases students' marketability in their professional field. It is worth mentioning that the MCEM programs provide students with rigorous, impactful, and applied SL experiences. Hence, the MCEM program process is quite extensive and different than just performing volunteer work with an organization/community partner. Volunteerism is also important to serve communities and develop positive citizenship behaviors among students. The MCEM program also includes students' direct volunteer work with their community partner when they implement their program, but it is much more advanced than that. Hence, instructors and schools need to be prepared and if they think that the MCEM programs provide their students with advanced applied, SL, and professional learning and experience, which results in positive personal, academic, and professional outcomes, then they can create a caring environment and additional support for instructors and students to use and practice the MCEM programs.

Further, as discussed earlier, there are many factors that guide learners to determine the degree of rigor, complexity, and engagement they want to use and apply for their program curriculum and the nature and scope of a program is one of them. For instance, if the problem that a MCEM program focuses is quite intense and its prevalence is also quite high, such as intimate partner violence, poverty, substance abuse, and child abuse and neglect, then leaners may need to make their curriculum quite extensively and the delivery period also may be different and longer for such programs to address severe and intense problems of program participants compared to those programs through which learners educate program participants about intimacy and building healthy intimate relationships. Hence, it is important for learners to critically think about the program, extensively read and review existing literature and other reliable sources about the problem, engage all relevant stakeholders in discussions, meet with program participants to learn about the intensively of the problem and their experiences, and observe program participants and their interactions with stakeholders who are situated at different engagement levels of society in real-world settings. The process and practice of recording, documenting, organizing, reflecting, and disseminating the information effectively and inclusively throughout the program lifecycle including program curriculum and delivery are essential qualities for a successful and sustainable MCEM program.

In addition, the MCEM programs are quite relevant, sustainable, and effective because they consider culture and diversity as the central aspects of the program process, foster stakeholders' engagement throughout the program lifecycle, and offer a multilevel understanding of the program along with developmental, sociocultural, and historical contexts. The MCEM program curriculum plays an integral role in ensuring the sustainability of a MCEM program. For instance, if an overall purpose of a MCEM program is to educate college students on how to manage and cope with their daily stressors. For this purpose, learners include quite effective, relevant, and participants' friendly teaching methods, techniques, and contents. Participants substantially improve their understanding on the topic, engage in discussions, make social connections, reflect on their personal experience, share important strategies based on their personal experiences, and learn from each other. Consequently, participants are more likely to use the information, knowledge, and skills that they learned after the formal completion of the program. When participants use and practice these skills after the formal completion of the program, maintain their connections, sharing, and engagement with each other, share their knowledge and skills with others who did not attend the program, and/or partner with other groups/organizations as a volunteer, it not only ensures the program sustainability but also contributes to sustainable community, school, and workplace's efforts and actions.

In conclusion, the MCEM program curriculum and delivery are integral to the success of a program and its implementation because learners implement the program by educating participants on different topics included in the program curriculum. The success of a MCEM program is partially linked with participants' learning and understanding of the program curriculum. If participants gain knowledge and skills through the program that they can use and share after the formal completion of the program, learners are more likely to achieve the program objectives which indicates the success and positive outcomes of their MCEM program. Additionally, the various components of SAMREEN objectives also help learners to focus and achieve other positive aspects of the program, such as increasing participants' relevance in the program curriculum and devising effective teaching methods and techniques to foster participants' engagement during program delivery and implementation.

CASE STUDY

Karen is developing her program curriculum. However, she is not quite sure which topics she needs to include in the program, the number of topics, and the type/nature of it. Based on her extensive reading of existing literature and exploration of other sources, she knows that the overall topic that she needs to focus on is parent-child attachment, challenges, and outcomes. She is also concerned about how her program curriculum will align with her program goals and/or objectives and other program components. She knows some relevant topics, such as parent-child attachment in diverse families, parenting and technology, and parent-child attachment in a cultural context. However, she is not quite sure how to organize and structure these topics in an effective way in her program curriculum that makes sense to her, prevents her from being overwhelmed, and also facilitates fruitful program delivery. She also wants to know the teaching methods and techniques which can be useful to educate their participants about the topics. Since she doesn't have extensive teaching experience and background, she is interested in exploring and reflecting on her pedagogical philosophy and views and how it can affect her choices of teaching methods and teaching that she would use to deliver her program. She chose all four components of the program at the beginning when she described her program, but she is not quite sure what sources, educational pieces, and information she needs to include to operationalize each component.

DISCUSSION QUESTIONS

(1) Why is a program curriculum important for a MCEM program?

(2) How can learners maintain consistency between program components and curriculum?

(3) How does the program curriculum help learners to operationalize program components?

(4) Which teaching methods and techniques are important for an effective curriculum delivery?

(5) What is the role of a program curriculum in improving participants' understanding of the program?

(6) How does learners' pedagogical philosophy and views affect their teaching approaches?

(7) Discuss the strengths and challenges of using the MCEM program curriculum.

(8) How can learners maintain a consistency between program curriculum and delivery?

(9) Which teaching methods and techniques are useful to foster participants' engagement and collaboration during curriculum delivery?

(10) Discuss the role of MCEM program curriculum in the program success and sustainability.

ASSIGNMENT QUESTIONS

(1) What is your pedagogical philosophy for the program?

(2) How does your pedagogical philosophy affect your teaching methods and techniques for the program?

(3) Which program components did you choose for your program and why?

(4) Which program contents did you use to operationalize each component?

(5) How are your program contents aligned with your program goals and/or objectives?

The MCEM Program Curriculum and Delivery

(6) Which teaching methods and techniques do you use for your program delivery and why?

(7) What challenges and opportunities do you expect to experience during your program delivery?

(8) What strategies do you use to overcome challenges and utilize opportunities?

(9) How do you foster participants' engagement and collaboration during program delivery?

(10) How does your program curriculum improve participants' learning of the program?

(11) How does your program curriculum make your program successful and sustainable?

(12) What did you learn from this assignment?

Table 6. Program Topic: Contemporary College Students and Daily Stressors.

Program Vision: Making college students free from daily stressors.

SAMREEN Program Goals	SAMREEN Program Objectives	The MCEM Educational Pieces	Program Components (Resources, Instructions, Activities, and/or Services)	Operationalization of Each Program Component	Teaching Approaches, Methods, Techniques, and Learning Styles	Cultural and Ethical Challenges	Pre-Program Assessment	Workshop/ Educational Session 1	Workshop/ Educational Session 2	Post-Program Assessment	Time Allocated for Each Activity
	Proximal level	Topics that you want to educate your participants about to achieve the program proximal level objective.	Which of the program components will you use to implement your topics/ educational pieces?	What material, sources, and information do you want to include for each component? For instance, if you chose resource, what resources, such as websites, online assessment, brochures, etc. do you want include to operationalize/ implement this component and include it in your program curriculum.	What are your teaching philosophies and views? What teaching methods and techniques do you want to use to deliver the program curriculum? How would you facilitate different learning styles, abilities, and needs of your program participants?	What are your plans to deal with any cultural and ethical challenges that you may face during your program implementation and evaluation?	Evaluate your program in the following manner: Ask the participants the following questions before conducting your first workshop: How would you rate your knowledge and understanding about the topic that we are going to cover/ covered in our program?	Include the demographics of your participants who participated in session 1, such as age, gender, ethnicity, etc.	Include the demographics of your participants who participated in session 2, such as age, gender, ethnicity, etc.	Evaluate your program in the following manner: Ask the participants the following questions after conducting your second workshop: How would you rate your knowledge and understanding about the topic that we are going to cover/ covered in our program?	

	Topics that you want to educate your participants about to achieve the program [level] objective.	Which of the program components will you use to implement your topics/educational pieces?	What are your teaching approaches? How would you facilitate different learning styles and needs of your program participants?	What are your plans to deal with any cultural and ethical challenges that you may face during your program implementation and evaluation?	1 = very low, 2 = low, 3 = moderate, 4 = high, 5 = very high Could you please describe and share your knowledge and understanding about the topic in your own words?
Influential level	Topics that you want to educate your participants about to achieve the program influential level objective.	Which of the program components will you use to implement your topics/educational pieces?	What are your teaching approaches? How would you facilitate different learning styles and needs of your program participants?	What are your plans to deal with any cultural and ethical challenges that you may face during your program implementation and evaluation?	1 = very low, 2 = low, 3 = moderate, 4 = high, 5 = very high Could you please describe and share your knowledge and understanding about the topic in your own words?
Holistic level	Topics that you want to educate your participants about to achieve the program holistic level objective.	Which of the program components will you use to implement your topics/educational pieces?	What are your teaching approaches? How would you facilitate different learning styles and needs of your program participants?	What are your plans to deal with any cultural and ethical challenges that you may face during your program	

(Continued)

Table 6. *(Continued)*

Program Vision: Making college students free from daily stressors.

SAMREEN Program Goals	SAMREEN Program Objectives	The MCEM Educational Pieces	Program Components (Resources, Activities, and/or Services)	Operationalization of Each Program Component	Teaching Approaches, Methods, Techniques, and Learning Styles	Cultural and Ethical Challenges	Pre-Program Assessment	Workshop/ Educational Session 1	Workshop/ Educational Session 2	Post-Program Assessment	Time Allocated for Each Activity
	Sociocultural and historical level	Topics that you want to educate your participants about to achieve the program sociocultural and historical level objective.	Which of the program components will you use to implement your topics/ educational pieces?		your program participants? What are your teaching approaches? How would you facilitate different learning styles and needs of your program participants?	implementation and evaluation? What are your plans to deal with any cultural and ethical challenges that you may face during your program implementation and evaluation?					

The MCEM Program Curriculum and Delivery   145

Table 7. Program Topic: Strengthening Employees' Listening Skills in the Workplace.

Program Vision: Improving workplace communication to the highest standards.

SAMREEN Program Objective	The MCEM Engagement Levels	The MCEM Educational Pieces	Program Components (Resources, Instructions, Activities, and/or Services)	Teaching Approaches and Learning Styles	Cultural and Ethical Challenges	Pre-Program Assessment	Workshop/ Educational Session 1	Workshop/ Educational Session 2	Post-Program Assessment	Time Allocated for Each Activity
Employees in the workplace will learn and practice different types and modes of positive listening and its benefits for them and the employer.	Proximal level	Topics related to the proximal level that you want to educate your participants about to achieve your program objective.	Which of the program components will you use to implement your topics/ educational pieces?	What are your teaching approaches? How would you facilitate different learning styles and needs of your program participants?	What are your plans to deal with any cultural and ethical challenges that you may face during your program implementation and evaluation?	Evaluate your program in the following manner: Ask the participants the following questions before conducting your first workshop: How would you rate your knowledge and understanding about the topic	Include the demographics of your participants and other stakeholders who will participate in session 1, such as age, gender, ethnicity, etc.	Include the demographics of your participants and other stakeholders who will participate in session 2, such as age, gender, ethnicity, etc.	Evaluate your program in the following manner: Ask the participants the following questions after conducting your second workshop: How would you rate your knowledge and understanding about the topic that we are	

(Continued)

Table 7. (Continued)

Program Vision: Improving workplace communication to the highest standards.

SAMREEN Program Objective	The MCEM Engagement Levels	The MCEM Educational Pieces	Program Components (Resources, Instructions, Activities, and/or Services)	Teaching Approaches and Learning Styles	Cultural and Ethical Challenges	Pre-Program Assessment	Workshop/ Educational Session 1	Workshop/ Educational Session 2	Post-Program Assessment	Time Allocated for Each Activity
	Influential level	Topics related to the influential level that you want to educate your participants	Which of the program components will you use to implement your topics/	What are your teaching approaches? How would you facilitate different	What are your plans to deal with any cultural and ethical challenges that you may face	that we are going to cover/ covered in our program? 1 = very low, 2 = low, 3 = moderate, 4 = high, 5 = very high Could you please describe and share your knowledge and understanding about the topic in your own words?			going to cover/ covered in our program? 1 = very low, 2 = low, 3 = moderate, 4 = high, 5 = very high Could you please describe and share your knowledge and understanding about the topic in your own words?	

The MCEM Program Curriculum and Delivery

	...about to achieve your program objective.	...educational pieces?	learning styles and needs of your program participants?	during your program implementation and evaluation?
Holistic level	Topics related to the holistic level that you want to educate your participants about to achieve your program objective.	Which of the program components will you use to implement your topics/ educational pieces?	What are your teaching approaches? How would you facilitate different learning styles and needs of your program participants?	What are your plans to deal with any cultural and ethical challenges that you may face during your program implementation and evaluation?
Sociocultural and historical level	Topics related to sociocultural and historical time/contexts that you want to educate your participants about to achieve your program objective.	Which of the program components will you use to implement your topics/ educational pieces?	What are your teaching approaches? How would you facilitate different learning styles and needs of your program participants?	What are your plans to deal with any cultural and ethical challenges that you may face during your program implementation and evaluation?

11

CULTURAL AND ETHICAL CHALLENGES

The objective of this chapter for learners is to learn about potential cultural, ethical, and developmental issues and challenges that they can face during a MCEM program process and important strategies to deal with them. This chapter also describes how the MCEM programs offer a culturally, ethically, and developmentally valued education to all relevant stakeholders including program participants to minimize many potential problems for learners, relevant stakeholders, and program participants throughout the program process including program curriculum and delivery.

The MCEM programs are dynamic, complex, and multilevel. Learners usually come across new and unique cultural, ethical, and developmental challenges throughout the program process. Hence, the fundamental principles of culturally, ethically, and developmentally valued educational processes discussed below are applicable to every stage of a MCEM program. Given the scope of this chapter, these principles are discussed and applied in the areas of program curriculum and delivery. Below is a definition of culturally valued education:

Culturally valued education honors, promote, and share participants' cultural values, beliefs, and practices and emphasizes the importance of understanding and integrating them into program curriculum and pedagogical approaches, which considers participants' background and real-life experiences as an essential part of the learning process to foster positive, collaborative, and meaningful learning experiences among participants and achieve successful outcomes.

Based on the definition above, it is important for learners to consider participant's culture as one of the central aspects in their program curriculum and delivery. One of the purposes of a MCEM program is to honor and promote culture, diversity, and inclusion throughout the program lifecycle including program curriculum and delivery. Due to the growing and emerging cultural diversity, individuals and families who attend a program come from diverse cultures and family backgrounds (Henert et al., 2021; Kara & Khawaja, 2024; Suarez et al., 2020). Participants' unique cultural values, beliefs, and practices are quite relevant and meaningful for them (Smith et al., 2022). Culture is people's relevant and meaningful ways of living life which includes people's beliefs, values, and practices, and determines people's behaviors and interactions with others and their perceptions and meanings that people associate with those behaviors and interactions. Hence, it is essential for learners to gain a comprehensive understanding of program participants' cultures particularly if they belong to various cultures (Raza, 2024a). Sometimes, participants apparently speak the same language, and their skin color or hair texture also looks the same, it is possible that their cultural values, beliefs, and practices might be different than learners and each other, due to many factors, such as childhood socialization, neighborhood environment, socioeconomic status, religion, and dating and mate selecting processes (Heidelburg & Collins, 2023; Raza, 2022). Hence, it is integral for learners to have a comprehensive knowledge and understanding about participants' cultures (Herr, 2017; Pinkerton & Martinek, 2023).

For this purpose, learners can read about their participants online, access books and scholarly articles, visit libraries, attend community events and conferences, and interact with these people (Domenech Rodríguez et al., 2022; Gradellini et al., 2021; Nozhovnik et al., 2022). It is worth mentioning that the process of MCEM programs helps learners to gain this information because learners identify, collaborate, and engage with program relevant stakeholders including program participants at the beginning of their program and throughout the program process as discussed in the chapters earlier. Hence, the MCEM program process creates a favorable environment for learners, program participants, and other stakeholders to share and learn each other's culture. Participants also have opportunities to discuss and reflect on each other's cultural values, beliefs, and practices and examine how their cultures affect their expectations, interactions, and perceptions toward each other and the learning program process (King et al., 2021; Lowe et al., 2021; Vaarzon-Morel et al., 2021). When learners, relevant stakeholders including program participants learn about new cultures and their unique qualities, they appreciate cultural differences and celebrate similarities, which further strengthens stakeholders' collaboration and engagement in the program process including program curriculum and delivery (Herr & Anderson, 2015; Raza, 2020a).

After learning about and gaining a comprehensive knowledge and understanding about participants' cultures, learners need to consider, acknowledge, and integrate diverse participants' cultures into their program curriculum (Coenraad et al., 2022; Gillispie, 2021; Le Pichon et al., 2024). For instance, if the program focuses on promoting positive parenting practices among parents of young children, then learners also need to integrate topics which discuss participants' parenting practice in their cultural context. In addition to integrating cultural aspects of participants into the program curriculum, learners also need to promote participants' culture during program delivery and provide participants with equal opportunities to share their cultural background and real-life experiences in relation to the topics discussed during program implementation/delivery (e.g. workshops, educational sessions, online material with participants' live reflections and interviews, etc.). When participants relate the program curriculum with their personal experiences and share their valuable real-life experiences, strategies, and practices with others, it not only empowers them, but they feel the program more useful and beneficial for their lives, which fosters their engagement and motivation in the program (Koseoglu et al., 2020; Papadopoulos et al., 2022; Pasternak et al., 2023). Additionally, it also provides other program stakeholders with opportunities to learn about diverse cultures, valuable strategies, and successful practices in relation to the program (Aldaheri et al., 2023; Karatasas et al., 2024; Mendenhall et al., 2024). This approach promotes a culturally valued educational process among participants to develop, grow, and sustain participant's positive learning experiences and show successful outcomes.

Since the purpose of MCEM programs is to promote and apply culture, diversity, and inclusion, learners can integrate participants' cultures at all engagement levels, and discuss developmental, social, and historical factors in their cultural contexts. For instance, if a program is on dating and mate selection. Families are situated at the proximal level. Learners can discuss dating and mate selection in a cultural context. For example, in many developing societies, such as Pakistan, India, Bangladesh, Afghanistan, etc., collectivistic culture is quite prevalent (Mendenhall et al., 2019; Saarikallio et al., 2021; Wang et al., 2023). In a collectivistic culture, parent-arranged marriages are still quite common and couples benefit from these arrangements because the entire cultural group (due to a collectivistic culture) supports married couples to succeed in their couple and family relationships (Flicker et al., 2020; Kumar & Singh, 2024; Raza et al., 2023b). Individuals are also prepared for these marital arrangements due to their cultural belonging and socialization. It is worth mentioning that there are variations in dating and mate selection patterns in these societies due to many factors, such as place of residence, socioeconomic status, parents' education, etc. (Raza, 2020a). One the other hand, in most of the western societies including the United States, Canada, Australia, and Europe where families practice individualistic culture, love marriages are prevalent (Olson et al., 2021). Families and society support these marriages due to cultural acceptance and practices. It is worth mentioning that there are also within-group variations, such that families also practice an evolved culture in which they practice some aspects of individualistic as well as collectivistic cultures, such as multigenerational families (Raza, 2024a, 2024b).

Similarly, if participants from different religions are participating in a MCEM program delivery and implementation, then learners can talk about dating and mate selection in different religions. For instance, in religion Islam, the patterns and practices of dating and mate selection are quite different compared to other religions. The meaning of intimacy, intermate relationships, interactions, traditions, customs, and experiences vary across religions (Raza et al., 2023b). Hence, learners can utilize this opportunity to learn about it and then educate their participants about it during the program delivery. Additionally, learners can invite participants from different religions and cultures to share their traditions, rituals, and practices with others in welcoming manners. It is important for learners to create a safe, inclusive, and respectful learning environment for all participants. For this purpose, learners can work with program participants at the beginning of program delivery and develop specific rules to run the workshops/educational sessions. Such approaches to integrate participants' cultures and make the program curriculum more culturally valued and relevant not only engage and motivate participants in the program curriculum, delivery, and implementation, but also show positive learning outcomes (Marsh et al., 2023; So et al., 2020; Wassell et al., 2022).

Below is a definition of ethically valued education:

Ethically valued education respects and honors participants' dignity, culture, and background and provides them with fair and equitable opportunities regardless of their social status in society and adequately addresses participants' learning needs based on their unique learning abilities and styles in an inclusive and collaborative manner to grow and foster participants' positive learning experiences and achieve successful outcomes.

As the above definition elaborates that participants can come and join the program from various social statuses, backgrounds, and cultures. It is important for learners to carry out honest, fair, and equitable learning process, which respects and honors the dignity and self-respect of each participant to make the program delivery inclusive, collaborative, and representative of all participants (Abbak Kacar et al., 2024; Birrell et al., 2024; Fleet et al., 2023). Even though participants belong to the same culture, speak the same language, and have quite similar physical features, they might have distinctive learning abilities and styles (Boysen, 2024; Kaplan Sayı & Yurtseven, 2022). Consequently, their learning needs might be different from one another (Evans et al., 2021). Therefore, it is important for learners to understand their participants, their learning abilities, and styles and find out the best possible pedagogical methods and techniques to engage participants, increase their knowledge, learning, and understanding of the program, and promote positive learning experiences among them (Chow & Tiwari, 2020; Henry et al., 2021). Learners need to find a good balance between creating a collaborative, sharing, and engaged environment and focusing on individualized needs of participants to achieve successful learning outcomes. A greater and comprehensive understanding about participants and other contextual factors may help learners determine an appropriate degree of balance between rigor and relevance. For instance, if there are participants who have special learning needs due to their unique learning abilities, it is important for learners to provide them with appropriate learning materials, instructions, and tools according to their learning needs and abilities, make appropriate sitting arrangements to accommodate them, and make the environment welcoming and inclusive for them to provide them with equitable learning opportunities in their program (Heron & Bruk-Lee, 2023; McNally et al., 2022; Sellmaier & Kim, 2021). When learners examine that participants have unique learning needs, styles, and abilities, they develop program curriculum and deliver it according to their participants' needs rather than making it overly rigorous, complex, and technical (Apanasionok et al., 2020; Coleman et al., 2023; Dymond et al., 2024). Consequently, learners foster, promote, and sustain ethically valued educational processes for their program, which also ensures the inclusion of all stakeholders including program participants throughout the program lifecycle including the program curriculum and delivery (Isaacson et al., 2024; Tan & Adams, 2023). The following is a definition of inclusive education.

An inclusive educational process provides all learners with equal support and access to program learning opportunities regardless of their learning needs, styles, abilities, and social status in society for achieving positive and sustainable learning and teaching outcomes.

As the above definition demonstrates that an inclusive educational process ensures that all program participants regardless of their learning needs, styles, abilities, and social status in society receive equal support and access to all learning opportunities throughout the program including program curriculum and delivery. Since the MCEM programs are informed by the MCEM framework, which considers culture, diversity, and inclusion as the central aspects of the program process, consequently, the educational process offered by the MCEM program is also likely to be inclusive, supportive, and accessible for all stakeholders including program participants.

It is worth mentioning that the inclusive educational process not only benefits program participants in their learning process and experiences, it is also advantageous to learners/facilitators because when they address all unique and relevant needs of their program participants in program curriculum and delivery, their participants are engaged and motivated, which increases opportunities for them to share and learn because they understand that their voices are heard and inputs are valued (Chen et al., 2022; Orr et al., 2021; Pan et al., 2023). Consequently, the inclusive educational process helps and supports program participants to learn and comprehend the program curriculum, which they also practice during and after the program completion to address their problems and needs, educate others, and partner with schools, communities, and workplaces to offer their services as volunteer experts (Ajaps, 2023; Amjad et al., 2024; Fang et al., 2021). Learners/facilitators also achieve their specific objectives related to program curriculum and delivery when they attain positive learning outcomes of their program participants. Hence, an inclusive educational process benefits learners, program participants, and the program to achieve successful and sustainable outcomes.

Sometimes, learners find program participants of different ages, genders, etc. whose developmental needs are unique and different from one another (Garvey et al., 2020; O'Connor et al., 2020). Some participants may have any learning and developmental disabilities (Klodnick et al., 2021). Hence, learners need to make sure that their program curriculum and delivery is according to the developmental needs of their participants. Following is a definition of the developmentally valued education:

Developmentally valued education creates and promotes a learning environment, which encourages learners to engage in a reciprocal, experiential, and need-specific learning process to experience growth, change, and stability in various domains, such as biological, social, emotional, cognitive, academic, etc. and during each stage, such as childhood, adolescence, youth, adulthood, middle and older age of their lives to grow and foster positive learning experiences and achieve successful and sustainable learning outcomes.

When program participants attend program delivery and implementation, they receive many benefits and experience growth in their social, emotional, cognitive, academic domains and these benefits and participants' experiences related to these and other relevant domains may vary within each developmental stage which they currently experience or go through when they participate in the program and its implementation, such as childhood, adolescence, youth, adulthood, middle and older age (Raza, 2022). Similarly, their learning needs related to these domains within each developmental stage also vary, which learners need to address in their program curriculum and delivery (Clarke, 2022). For instance, children's learning needs based on their social, emotional, and cognitive levels may be different compared to adults (Graham et al., 2020; Marcussen et al., 2020; Terrizzi et al., 2020). Additionally, there are variations within each developmental stage, such that those with any learning or intellectual disabilities (e.g. children with learning and intellectual disabilities) may have different and unique learning needs compared to other participants who belong to the same developmental stage (Bődi et al., 2023; Ortega et al., 2023). Hence, learners need to collaboratively work with other program stakeholders to effectively prepare and implement their program curriculum and delivery. If learners feel that they don't have sufficient skills and stakeholders also don't have expertise of that degree to develop and implement an effective program curriculum and delivery, then they need to reach out to other experts, organizations, and professionals, to either hire them or ask them to volunteer and offer their services for the program (de Heer et al., 2020; Kim, 2024; Raviv et al., 2022).

It is worth mentioning that though these terms and concepts discussed in this chapter, such as culturally, ethically, inclusive, and developmentally valued education relate to each other and also share some aspects with each other, the author conceptualized and defined them differently. Hence, if learners cannot use and apply all terms and concepts for their program including program curriculum and delivery, they can choose one or a few of them and devise specific teaching methods and techniques aligned with these terms and concepts to effectively apply and operationalize them for fostering positive learning experiences of program participants.

In conclusion, learners face cultural, ethical, and developmental problems and challenges throughout their program including program curriculum and delivery, which they need to effectively deal with and resolve them to successfully carry out a MCEM program. It is important for learners to gain a comprehensive understanding of participants' cultural and developmental needs and examine the issues of ethics and inclusion in the program process including program curriculum and delivery. Consequently, learners use and apply specific teaching methods and techniques in their program curriculum and delivery to respect and honor all participants regardless of their background and social status in society and promote fair and equitable learning opportunities among participants according to their specific learning needs, abilities, and styles to address their individualized needs and simultaneously engage them in a collaborative and inclusive learning process to foster participants' positive learning experiences and achieve successful learning outcomes for their participants and the MCEM program.

CASE STUDY

After reading and reviewing extensive relevant research and other reliable sources about her program, Karen realized the importance of culturally, ethically, and developmentally valued education for her program. Karen program participants are from different cultures and backgrounds. She values her participants' unique real-life experiences and believes that it is a crucial part of their learning process. Karen wants to encourage participants to share their real-life experiences so that participants can increase their cultural knowledge and learn from each other. However, Karen does not have sufficient information about her participants' cultural values, beliefs, and practices. She aims at learning additional research about her participants' learning needs, cultures, and developmental context. She also plans on watching movies, attending events, visiting websites, and local organizations, and interacting with her program participants of different cultures so that she can accurately and effectively integrate their culture, its important aspects, and strengths into her program curriculum and pedagogical approaches to foster positive and collaborative learning experiences among participants. Karen also expects that her participants may have unique learning abilities and styles, which she needs to consider and examine. Consequently, she may need to explore and devise effective teaching methods and techniques, which can adequately address participants' learning needs based on their learning abilities and styles in a collaborative and inclusive manner. She is also integrating various sources, information, and modalities through which she can appreciate, honor, and promote participants' unique culture and background. She also wants to create a learning environment, which promotes and offers fair and equitable learning opportunities among all participants in a collaborative and inclusive manner. She believes that her approaches, strategies, and actions will prove to be a key in fostering participants' positive learning experiences and achieving successful outcomes.

DISCUSSION QUESTIONS

(1) Why is culture an important aspect to consider in program curriculum and delivery?

(2) Discuss the benefits of culturally valued educational processes?

(3) How does a culturally valued educational process honor and respect participants' cultural values, beliefs, and practices?

(4) How does a culturally valued educational process make the program curriculum and delivery more relevant and meaningful for program participants?

(5) What is an ethically valued educational process?

(6) Discuss the benefits of ethically valued educational processes?

(7) How does an ethically valued educational process make the program curriculum and delivery more engaged and inclusive for program participants?

(8) What is a developmentally valued educational process?

(9) Discuss the benefits of developmentally valued educational processes?

(10) How does a developmentally valued educational make the program curriculum and delivery more engaged and inclusive for program participants?

(11) Discuss the linkages between culturally, ethically, and developmentally valued educational processes.

(12) How do culturally, ethically, and developmentally valued educational processes help learners to foster participants' positive learning experiences?

(13) How do culturally, ethically, and developmentally valued educational processes help and guide learners to achieve successful learning outcomes?

ASSIGNMENT QUESTIONS

(1) What cultural challenges do you expect in your program curriculum and delivery process?

(2) How does a culturally valued educational process help and guide you to address and/or minimize these challenges?

(3) What actions would you carry out to use and apply the principles of a culturally valued educational process?

(4) What ethical challenges do you expect in your program curriculum and delivery process?

(5) How does an ethically valued educational process help and guide you to address and/or minimize these challenges?

(6) What actions would you carry out to use and apply the principles of an ethically valued educational process?

(7) How do a culturally valued educational process and an ethically valued educational process support and substantiate each other?

(8) How do a culturally valued educational process and an ethically valued educational process foster positive learning experience of your participants?

(9) How do a culturally valued educational process and an ethically valued educational process help and guide you to achieve successful learning outcomes?

(10) What did you learn from this assignment?

12

THE SAMREEN EVALUATION

The objective of this chapter for learners is to learn the SAMREEN evaluation design for assessing the MCEM programs in various areas and at different engagement levels over the course of a program lifecycle. The author developed the SAMREEN evaluation design and operationalized it, which is grounded in the MCEM framework. The SAMREEN evaluation design can be used to evaluate the MCEM programs as well as non-MCEM programs. The author also presents a critical comparison between the SAMREEN evaluation design and other contemporary evaluations and designs to offer an understanding on how the SAMREEN evaluation design is engaged, multilevel, and culturally relevant compared to other evaluations methods and designs which have been used in the field of program development and evaluation to evaluate programs in various settings.

Following is a definition of the SAMREEN evaluation:

The SAMREEN evaluation is a continuous, engaged, systematic, and multilevel process during which all relevant stakeholders including program participants discuss, choose, and carry out accurate and meaningful methods and techniques to assess the progress, success, and effectiveness of a program in various areas and at multiple engagement levels over the course of a program lifecycle.

As mentioned above the SAMREEN evaluation is quite different from existing and traditional assessments, such as formative assessment and summative assessment (Orozco, 2024; Theall & Franklin, 2010; Trumbull & Lash, 2013; Wang, 2024). Formative evaluation can be conducted regularly, such as on a monthly, weekly, or daily basis (He et al., 2024; Nicol & Macfarlane-Dick, 2006; Ochsen et al., 2023). It is usually less formal and simple compared to a summative evaluation. Although it provides important information about the ongoing progress and implementation of a program, it can be time and resource consuming because organizations need to collect, analyze, and report data with a frequency they determine to conduct a formative assessment for their program (Huang et al., 2021; Liu et al., 2021). On the other hand, a summative assessment is usually conducted at the completion of a program to assess its impacts and effectiveness on target population, and it is usually a one-time evaluation (Looi et al., 2021; Reed & Mercer, 2023; Trumbull & Lash, 2013). It is a more formal, complex, and rigorous evaluation compared to a formative assessment, which helps organizations to collect data on specific areas that they want to assess to examine the impacts and effectiveness of their program on target population in those areas (Broadbent et al., 2021; Vicente et al., 2021; Postmes et al., 2023). It also requires specialized knowledge and expertise, and organizations usually hire external evaluators or experts to conduct a summative evaluation for their program (Lefebvre et al., 2020; Lyness et al., 2021; Reed & Mercer, 2023).

The SAMREEN evaluation takes the evaluation to a next level of assessment. For instance, the SAMREEN evaluation is multilevel, engaged, and meaningful in many ways compared to formative and summative assessments. For instance, it encourages and promotes the engagement of all stakeholders inclusively in the evaluation process regardless of their education, skills, and social status in society who already have been participating and working in the program from its very beginning. It is aligned with SAMREEN goals and objectives that learners develop for their program, which informs the next steps of the program such that how, what, when, where, and with whom the program will be carried out. It helps learners to assess each element of their SAMREEN goals and objectives throughout the program lifecycle. It is neither quite expensive nor external to the program because stakeholders who learn and practice the SAMREEN evaluation can conduct it and assess a MCEM program at any given time or overtime. It can be carried out at one or multiple program engagement levels which ranges from very simple to quite complex evaluation. When stakeholders participate and conduct a SAMREEN evaluation to assess the program overtime, which they collaboratively developed, and have been implementing together, they understand the evaluation process, feel the evaluation process more relevant, and are more likely to utilize the evaluation results to improve their program. It removes the difference between the types, hierarchies, and timing of evaluations (e.g., formative and summative evaluation) and when they are supposed to be conducted during or at the completion of a program because learners can use the SAMREEN evaluation at any time throughout the program lifecycle including the completion of a program. Additionally, since the MCEM programs consider and promote diversity, culture, and inclusion as the central aspects of a program, the SAMREEN evaluation design also follows the same fundamental principles, consequently, the evaluations become more relevant, meaningful, and inclusive for all stakeholders including program participants. Hence, the SAMREEN evaluation is more advanced, engaged, and multilevel, and simultaneously, it is less time and resource consuming because stakeholders who are already engaged in the program conduct that evaluation or even if they need any additional assistance, they can engage or collaborate with other organizations or experts to volunteer their services or hire them for a short-period of time because stakeholders have substantial knowledge of the SAMREEN goals and objectives, SAMREEN evaluation procedure, and their program who can handle it after receiving a brief external assistance. For instance, stakeholders can use the assessment tolls provided for conducting a SAMREEN evaluation (please review the table at the end of this chapter) and collect data in one or more program areas and at any engagement levels that they want to assess and hire or volunteer someone who can analyze their data and create reports based on the evaluation findings. Once they learn this procedure, they can also collaboratively use it themselves in the future. The SAMREEN evaluation also provides consistency between the program components, such as program goals, objectives, implementation, and evaluation tools, which improves the efficiency, rigor, and effectiveness of the program. Further, when organizations conduct formative or summative evaluation, they need to determine and identify the area(s) they want to assess, sometimes, it happens at a given time due to the pressures, funds, and demands from a donor agency or government authority, and/or new hiring of an external evaluator at that time, but the SAMREEN evaluation assesses the progress and effectiveness of a MCEM program in those areas and at the engagement levels, which are informed by its program goals and objectives, already embedded into the program, and in a flow from the beginning of the program. Hence, the SAMREEN evaluation advances the evaluation procedure in terms of its rigor, relevance, and usefulness.

Additionally, stakeholders bring their resources, strengths, and expertise in the program, which they share with each other, and offer for the success of the program, consequently, stakeholders transfer their knowledge and skills to one another, which can also be the skills of accurately conducting a SAMREEN evaluation. Sometimes, when stakeholders develop, share and discuss their plans for a MCEM program including the evaluations, determine how they would like to assess their program by using a SAMREEN evaluation, and reflect on their strengths and weakness, consequently, they acquire appropriate knowledge and skills if they need to for conducting accurate evaluations of their program before they reach out to a point of assessing their program.

As we learned that there are seven components of SAMREEN goals and objectives (please review Chapter 9 of this book), such as Sustainable, Attainable, Meaningful, Related, Engaged, Evaluative, and Neat, the SAMREEN evaluation emphasizes the assessment of all these components and provides assessment tools (which are included at the end of this chapter) to evaluate each of these components. As it was discussed in the earlier chapters that once learners develop SAMREEN goals and/or objectives based on the work learners accomplished since the initiation of a MCEM program, the SAMREEN goals and/or objectives become a foundation for the rest of the program, such as program curriculum, delivery, and assessment. Since each component of SAMREEN goals and objectives represents a specific and valuable aspect of the MCEM program, the assessment of it increases the rigor and trustworthiness of the entire program. Moreover, the assessment of some components may be shorter or more important and relevant for one phase compared to the other. Learners conduct these assessments in various program areas and at multiple engagement levels. Hence, the SAMREEN evaluation guides learners to carry out a continuous, complex, sensitive, and multilevel assessments of the MCEM programs throughout the program lifecycle, which are quite relevant and meaningful for all stakeholders including program participants. It is evident that formative evaluation is also ongoing, but it focuses on traditional learning objectives, which are usually quite general and do not contain any specific element like SAMREEN, and the evaluation is also not multilevel (Nicol & Macfarlane-Dick, 2006; Trumbull & Lash, 2013). For instance, if there are a few specific learning objectives of a course, instructors conduct formative evaluation through discussion, reflections, weekly assignments, and quizzes, whereas a summative evaluation is conducted by giving students a comprehensive final exam or a paper at the end of a semester (Theal & Franklin, 2010; Trumbull & Lash, 2013). Similarly, the formative evaluation is conducted to assess participants' engagement, participation, retention, etc. in a program, but since program objectives do not inform or guide any specific areas or aspects of the program like SAMREEN objectives do such as Sustainable, Attainable, Meaningful, Related, Engaged, Evaluative, and Neat, there is no specific direction on the extent, continuity, significance, and engagement levels for carrying out the assessment. When learners use a SAMREEN evaluation design in assessing their MCEM programs, these assessments naturally happen in the program. For instance, the MCEM programs promote, maintain, and sustain stakeholders' engagement throughout the program, and when learners record it regularly, it shows a success for the component "Engaged" of the SAMREEN goals and/or objectives.

Moreover, the existing literature shows that SMART objectives have been used and prevalent in curriculum and program development (Doran, 1981). SMART stands for specific, measurable, achievable, realistic, and time-bound (Bjerke & Renger, 2017; CDC, 2018; Hessel et al., 2011). Thus, when we compare these components of SMART objectives/goals with SAMREEN objectives/goals components, some of them provide quite similar directions and guidance to learners on what to focus on in their program. For instance, specific and attainable, measurable and evaluative, achievable and attainable, realistic and attainable, and time-bound and attainable. There are additional components in SAMREEN goals and objectives, such as Related, Engaged, Neat, and Sustainable, which also makes SAMREEN an advanced and next level goals and objectives for a program. Additionally, SMART goals or objectives are usually assessed through traditional assessments, such as formative and summative assessments. Programs can also be assessed by using other designs, such experimental design, quasi-experimental design, case-control design, etc. (Creswell & Creswell, 2018; Remler & Van Ryzin, 2022), but these designs and methods assess an overall program, whereas SAMREEN evaluation design specifically focuses on the assessment of each component of the SAMREEN goals and/or objectives and also conducts it at multiple engagement levels of a program. For instance, in these traditional designs (although they are quite rigorous), one group of participants receive a program/treatment, whereas the other group does not receive that program, the purpose of conducting an evaluation is to find the overall impact of a program on the outcome/dependent variable (Remler & Van Ryzin, 2022). As mentioned earlier, the SAMREEN evaluation can be used in both MCEM and non-MCEM programs. Hence, the SAMREEN evaluation design is a new, unique, and advanced evaluation design, which is an important addition to the field of program development, evaluation, and research. The above evidence and discussion indicate that the SAMREEN evaluation design also provides a paradigm shift in evaluation research. Additional details on the use, application, and operationalization of the SAMREEN evaluation design will be shared in a different edition.

This section provides learners with information on each element of the SAMREEN evaluation design. The first component of the SAMREEN goal and objective is "Sustainable." The MCEM programs promotes a reciprocal exchange of knowledge, skills, and experiences among all relevant stakeholders including program participants, which brings positive changes in the perception and attitudes of participants, provide them with appropriate knowledge and skills to resolve their important problems, address immediate needs, and/or strengthen their capacities to deal with future problems. As discussed in the previous chapters, due to an effective operationalization of the MCEM framework, the MCEM programs are quite flexible (learners can develop various kinds of MCEM programs), adaptability (the MCEM programs can be implemented in various settings and environments around the world), and sustainable (due to a transformational and engaged process among all relevant stakeholder groups including program participants). Hence, learners need to assess the degree and nature of these aspects of their program. Sustainability also means that a MCEM program likely continues after its formal completion and the process of developing, implementing, and evaluating a MCEM program lays a foundation for it.

When stakeholders including program participants learn, understand, and apply appropriate knowledge and skills offered in the MCEM program, they are satisfied and feel confident about it, which increases learners' motivation and courage to continue program efforts after its completion. This is another aspect that learners need to assess, which may also help them identify any gaps in learners' knowledge, understanding, and skills during the program that they can address with additional planning and actions.

Additionally, sustainability also means that a MCEM program or its knowledge and skills should be disseminated, spread, and shared among other groups within and/or outside of the target population. Program stakeholders are the ones who can play a crucial role in that regard. When stakeholders are happy about the program, they learn something relevant and important from the program, and they believe that it can be useful for other groups and communities, they are likely to spread the news and refer the MCEM program to other groups and communities. Hence, learners also need to consider and assess this aspect of the program. After extensively and continuously participating in the program process throughout its lifecycle, program stakeholders usually become experts on the program and its process, they can engage and participate in the same program offered to other groups and communities as a volunteer expert which also indicates the sustainability of a MCEM program. Therefore, learners need to evaluate this area of a MCEM program as well. When learners observe and believe that their MCEM program is valuable and sustainable, they make their best efforts to continue their program and spread it among other groups and communities. Learners are the leaders of their program who are responsible for motivating, encouraging, facilitating, and guiding their stakeholders including program participants through effective communication, demonstration, and practice throughout the program lifecycle. Thus, when the program formally completes, learners have a firm belief based on their experience and observation that the MCEM program ensures and achieves sustainability. Hence, this aspect of a MCEM program also needs to be assessed. Finally, when program stakeholders find the program beneficial and effective for themselves, observe its positive outcomes and changes in their lives and the others, feel encouraged, realize the importance of it, consequently, they will also consider it beneficial for other community families and groups who did not participate in the program and recommend the program to them. Hence, it is essential for learners to record and share the success stories with program stakeholders including program participants throughout the program lifecycle. It is also essential for learners to assess this aspect of their program.

The description above regarding the SAMREEN evaluation design provides learners with a detailed procedure and accurate tolls to assess many areas and aspects of the MCEM program at multiple engagement levels over time based on only one component "Sustainable" of the SAMREEN goals and objectives. The tools to assess all components of SAMREEN goals and objectives are included at the end of this chapter.

In conclusion, the SAMREEN evaluation is an integral part and process of the MCEM programs, which helps learners and program stakeholders including program participants to assess the progress and effectiveness of a MCEM program in all areas and at multiple engagement levels of the program over time. Therefore, it is important for learners to ensure an active engagement, collaboration, and continuous participation of all relevant stakeholders including program participants and find a balance between scientific procedure and stakeholders' real-life experiences and expertise to maintain inclusiveness, transparency, and representativeness in the SAMREEN evaluation over the program lifecycle.

CASE STUDY

Karent successfully developed her program curriculum and chose teaching methods and techniques that she wants to use for effectively deliver/implement her program. She is now thinking about her program evaluation. She heard about program evaluation that it is quite a technical work which requires advanced and specialized knowledge on the subject to accurate perform it. She wants to know which aspect(s) of the program she needs to evaluate and how she should evaluate it. She is also not quite sure about the accuracy of her assessment, its consistency with the other program components, and relevance to stakeholders including program participants. She read a few program evaluations of relevant programs which focused on parenting but feel overwhelmed due to the use of advanced procedures, designs, and language. She also has been thinking about the timing of her program evaluation, whether it is a one-time activity, or it needs to continue throughout the program lifecycle.

DISCUSSION QUESTIONS

(1) What is a SAMREEN evaluation design?

(2) How is it different from the other traditional evaluations?

(3) How does it create engagement of and relevance for program stakeholders?

(4) Discuss different elements of SAMREEN evaluation?

(5) Share the strengths and relevance of SAMREEN evaluation in the MCEM programs?

(6) Why is a SAMREEN evaluation important for the MCEM programs?

(7) How is a SAMREEN evaluation relevant to and representative of program stakeholders?

(8) How is a SAMREEN evaluation effectively used to assess and improve the program?

(9) Discuss the challenges that learners and stakeholders can experience regarding a SAMREEN evaluation.

(10) What are the useful strategies to overcome or manage these challenges?

ASSIGNMENT QUESTIONS

(1) How do you want to use a SAMREEN evaluation design to assess your program? Why?

(2) How is your evaluation an effective procedure to assess your MCEM program compared to other potential evaluation procedures?

(3) What do you want to assess in your program? How will you assess it?

(4) How is your evaluation procedure consistent and aligned with your other MCEM program components?

(5) How will you make your evaluation procedure more relevant to and representative of all program stakeholders?

(6) How will you ensure an active participation and collaboration of all stakeholders in your evaluation process?

(7) How will you use the evaluation results to improve your program?

(8) How will you use and disseminate your evaluation results in your program?

(9) What did you learn from this assignment?

Table 8. Selected Questions to Evaluate the MCEM Programs.

SAMREEN (Sustainable, Attainable, Meaningful, Related, Engaged, Evaluative, and Neat).

Sustainable	(1) The MCEM program is/was transformational.		1: I strongly disagree
	(2) The MCEM program will likely continue after its formal completion.		2: I disagree 3: I agree 4: I strongly agree 0: I don't know/not sure
	(3) I feel satisfied and confident about the topic after attending the MCEM program.	(1)	How do you feel about the changes that the MCEM program brought in your life?
	(4) I will continue to use and apply the knowledge and skills that I learned from the MCEM program.	(2)	How do you think about the continuity of the MCEM program after its formal completion?
	(5) I recommend the MCEM program for other groups of the population.	(3)	How do you feel about your knowledge and skills on the topic/issue focused in the MCEM program?
	(6) I am willing to participate and work with any MCEM program in future.	(4)	How will you use and apply the knowledge and skills that you learned from the MCEM program?
	(7) The MCEM program achieves success and sustainability.	(5)	How do you feel about recommending the MCEM program to other groups within and outside of your community?
	(8) The MCEM program is effective and beneficial for all groups of the population.	(6)	How do you feel about your willingness to participate in the MCEM programs in future on similar or different topics?
		(7)	What are your views on the success and sustainability of the MCEM program you attended?
		(8)	How do you see the benefits of MCEM programs for other groups of the population within and outside of your community?
Attainable	(1) The MCEM program goals and objectives are/were successfully achieved.		1: I strongly disagree 2: I disagree 3: I agree
	(2) The MCEM program goals and/ or objectives are/were measurable and assessable.		4: I strongly agree 0: I don't know/not sure

(Continued)

Table 8. *(Continued)*

	(3) The MCEM program is/was well structured and organized. (4) The MCEM program shows flexibility in scope and purpose. (5) The MCEM program is adaptable in various settings and with different groups of the population. (6) The MCEM program goals and objectives can be achieved in various areas over time. (7) The MCEM program achieve/achieved positive and successful outcomes.	(1) How were the program goals and/or objectives achieved? (2) What are your views on the accuracy and assessment of program goals and/or objectives? (3) What are your views on the organization and structuring of the MCEM program? (4) How flexible is the MCEM program in terms of its purpose and scope? (5) How adaptable is the MCEM program when they are offered to various groups and implemented in different settings? (6) How do the MCEM goals and/or objective focus on different areas/aspects which can be achieved over the course of a program life cycle? (7) What are your views on the success and positive outcomes of the MCEM program you attended?
Meaningful	(1) The MCEM program was quite relevant to our issues and needs. (2) I find/found the MCEM program meaningful to my real-life situations and experiences. (3) The MCEM program addresses/addressed our immediate issues and needs. (4) The MCEM program is/was developmentally appropriate. (5) The MCEM program is/was culturally responsive, relevant, and appropriate. (6) The MCEM program considers/considered and addresses/addressed cultural and ethical issues for all stakeholders including program participants.	1: I strongly disagree 2: I disagree 3: I agree 4: I strongly agree 0: I don't know/not sure (1) How relevant was the MCEM program to your personal needs and issues? (2) How meaningful was the MCEM program to your real-life situations and experiences? (3) How effective was the MCEM program in addressing your immediate issues and needs? (4) How do you see the developmental appropriateness of the MCEM program you attended?

Table 8. *(Continued)*

	(7) The MCEM program is/was inclusive and representative of all program stakeholders. (8) The MCEM program considers culture and diversity important in understanding and addressing community needs and issues. (9) The MCEM program addresses the issues of social justice, inclusion, and equity throughout the program's lifecycle.	(5) How was the MCEM program culturally responsive, relevant, and appropriate? (6) How effective was the MCEM program in addressing cultural and ethical issues of all stakeholders including program participants? (7) How inclusive and representative was the MCEM program for all program stakeholders? (8) How important were culture and diversity in the MCEM program to understand and address community needs and issues? (9) How effectively did the MCEM program address the issues of social justice, inclusion, and equity throughout the program's lifecycle?
Related	(1) I find consistency among all components of the MCEM program. (2) The MCEM programs were quite easy to follow and attend. (3) The MCEM program curriculum is/was aligned with the other program components. (4) The MCEM program curriculum and delivery has/had various modalities for learning. (5) The MCEM program curriculum and delivery is/was quite engaged, relevant, and meaningful to our issues and needs. (6) The MCEM program curriculum and delivery is/was inclusive and represented of us and our needs and issues. (7) The MCEM program curriculum and delivery facilitates/facilitated an active participation and engagement of all participants.	1: I strongly disagree 2: I disagree 3: I agree 4: I strongly agree 0: I don't know/not sure (1) How did you find consistency among all components of the MCEM program? (2) How do you feel the degree of complexity in following and attending the MCEM program? (3) How was the alignment of the MCEM program curriculum with the other program components? (4) What are your views on the modalities used for the MCEM program curriculum and delivery? (5) How did you find the MCEM program curriculum and delivery in terms of its engagement, relevance, and meaningfulness to your issues and needs?

(Continued)

Table 8. *(Continued)*

	(8) The MCEM program delivery and implementation was consistent with the program curriculum. (9) The MCEM program implementation/delivery is/was aligned with the other program components.	(6) How inclusive and representative was the MCEM program curriculum and delivery to your needs and issues? (7) How did the MCEM program curriculum and delivery facilitate active participation and engagement of all participants? (8) What do you feel about the consistency between the MCEM program curriculum and delivery? (9) What do you feel about the consistency between the MCEM program curriculum and delivery and the other program components?
Engaged	(1) The MCEM program fosters/fostered engagement and participation among stakeholders including program participants. (2) The MCEM program is/was quite relevant, engaged, and effective in all areas of the program. (3) The MCEM program is multilevel, comprehensive, and multicoated. (4) The MCEM program promotes and guides engagement among all relevant stakeholders including program participants through the program lifecycle. (5) The MCEM program facilitates a continuous engagement in curriculum and delivery and among stakeholders including program participants through the program lifecycle. (6) The MCEM program promotes engagement, participation, and increase motivation among all program stakeholders in various areas of the program over time.	1: I strongly disagree 2: I disagree 3: I agree 4: I strongly agree 0: I don't know/not sure (1) How does the MCEM program foster engagement and participation among stakeholders including program participants? (2) How do you feel about the MCEM program in ensuring and fostering, relevance, engagement, and effectiveness in all areas of the program? (3) How was the MCEM program multilevel, comprehensive, and multicoated? (4) How did the MCEM program promote and guide engagement among all relevant stakeholders including program participants through the program lifecycle? (5) How did the MCEM program facilitate a continuous engagement in curriculum and delivery and among stakeholders including program participants through the program lifecycle?

Table 8. *(Continued)*

Evaluative	(1) The MCEM program is/was successfully assessed in different areas. (2) The MCEM program is/was flexible in using various accurate methods and techniques for its assessment. (3) The MCEM program facilitates an ongoing program assessment in different areas of the program. (4) The MCEM program evaluation is quite simple, clear, and straightforward. (5) The MCEM program can be implemented and evaluated in diverse cultures and societies around the world. (6) The MCEM program evaluation methods and techniques can be understood by all stakeholders regardless of their educational background and technical knowledge. (7) The MCEM program is useful and successful in fostering engagement among all relevant stakeholders including program participants in program evaluation.	(6) How do the MCEM program promote engagement, participation, and increase motivation among all program stakeholders in various areas of the program over time? 1: I strongly disagree 2: I disagree 3: I agree 4: I strongly agree 0: I don't know/not sure (1) How do you feel about the assessment of the MCEM program in different areas? (2) How flexible is the MCEM program in using various accurate methods and techniques for its assessment? (3) How does the MCEM program facilitate an ongoing program assessment in different areas of the program? (4) How do you feel about the MCEM program evaluation in terms of its simplicity, clarity, and straightforwardness? (5) How can the MCEM program be implemented and evaluated in diverse cultures and societies around the world? (6) How can the MCEM program evaluation methods and techniques be understood by all stakeholders regardless of their educational background and technical knowledge? (7) How is the MCEM program useful and successful in fostering engagement among all relevant stakeholders including program participants in program evaluation?

(Continued)

Table 8. *(Continued)*

Neat	(1) The MCEM program goals and/or objectives are/were simple, clear, and straightforward. (2) All steps and phases of the MCEM program are/were well-written and easily understood. (3) The MCEM program curriculum was well-designed, organized, and structured. (4) The instructions during program implementation and delivery is/was quite simple, clear, and straightforward. (5) The MCEM program development, implementation, and evaluation guidelines and instructions are quite easy to follow, apply, and implement. (6) All stakeholders including the program participants can understand the MCEM program guidelines.	1: I strongly disagree 2: I disagree 3: I agree 4: I strongly agree 0: I don't know/not sure (1) How do you feel about the MCEM program goals and/or objectives in terms of its simplicity, clarity, and straightforwardness? (2) How were all steps and phases of the MCEM program well-written, properly laid, and easily understood? (3) What are your views on the design, organization, and structuring of the MCEM program curriculum? (4) How were the instructions during program implementation and delivery in terms of its simplicity, clarity, and straightforwardness? (5) How did you find the instructions and guidelines regarding program development, implementation, and evaluation when you followed, applied, implemented them? (6) What are your views on the degree of stakeholders' understanding of the MCEM program instructions and guidelines?

13

THE MCEM PROGRAM REVIEW AND SHARE

The objective of this chapter for learners is to learn important approaches, strategies, and processes of reviewing, sharing, and disseminating the findings and outcomes of a MCEM program after its formal completion among program stakeholders and outside of the program. Program review and share is an important step that learners carry out at the end of a MCEM program to engage existing and new stakeholders in their program, market their program, and increase the sustainability of their program.

Following is a definition of the MCEM program review and share: The MCEM program review and share is a formal and detailed review process of a program which is held between learners, stakeholders (existing and new stakeholders), and program participants during which they review, share, discuss, and reflect on the program, its process, and outcomes along with important lessons learned and strategies, which guide existing stakeholders and engage new stakeholders to make appropriate and accurate plans and arrangements for future to ensure the growth, success, and sustainability of the program.

The MCEM program review and share is an important step of a MCEM program that is conducted at the formal completion of the program. The MCEM programs may vary based on the scope, funding, importance, and timeline (Raza, 2022). It is important for learners to determine and share a program period/timeline from the beginning to a completion date with all relevant stakeholders including program participants so that everyone is on track and aware of the formal completion of the program (Raza, 2021). When the program is completed and ended, learners need to gather all program stakeholders including the program participants and also invite new stakeholders who are interested in the program for a program review and share

(Raza, 2020a). It is quite useful for learners to invite all people, families, groups, and organizations who may be interested in learning about the program outcomes and using it in the future (Herr, 2017; Herr & Anderson, 2015; Bell et al., 2021; Vamos et al., 2021).

During the program review and share meeting (s), learners present a review of the program including its process and outcomes (Raza, 2020b; Yan et al., 2022). Learners need to share how the program achieved its goals and/or objectives (Lewis-Thames et al., 2023; Raza, 2021). It is also important to share the gaps between the designed and achieved goals and/or objectives with stakeholders so that if any group or organization wants to use this program learn about program challenges and gaps and make appropriate plans and strategies to address or overcome them throughout the program lifecycle (Hollman et al., 2022; Pugh et al.,2021; Vo et al., 2024) This may also help to achieve the program goals and objectives in the future which are either partially achieved or left unaddressed due to any reasons, such as a lack of time, expertise, funds, etc. (Brown et al., 2023; Herr, 2017; Raza, 2020a). This may foster collaboration among existing and new stakeholders and increase program sustainability (Liu, 2021; Preuss et al., 2024; Vartiainen et al., 2022).

Learners also need to share and discuss the challenges they faced during the program, important strategies, and lessons learned with attendees, which may be useful for stakeholder groups who may want to continue the program after its formal completion (Bagnall et al., 2021; Kern et al., 2024; Lawlis et al., 2024). It is worth mentioning that the aim of MCEM programs is to increase sustainability, consequently, stakeholders are engaged and encouraged to transform the knowledge and skills to each other and continue the program after its formal completion (Raza, 2020a, 2021). When learners share important and useful strategies with those stakeholders who are responsible to continue the program, it saves stakeholders' time, efforts, and resources, and increases their efficiency and productivity (Arnell et al., 2022; Holcomb et al., 2022; McCurtin & O'Connor, 2020). Program review and share meeting(s) may also facilitate learners to make effective plans and explore new strategies with existing and new stakeholder groups if they want to implement this program in a different community or through a different mode (Hearne et al., 2024; Mörk, 2022; Raza, 2022).

It is also important for learners to provide program stakeholders with sufficient time and opportunities to share their experiences and reflect on the program (Bruck et al., 2022; Ripoll Gonzalez & Gale, 2020). Hence, learners can conduct multiple meetings if they need to. Each stakeholder, group, and organization who was involved in the program process is important regardless of their social status, education, and skills (Bacci et al., 2021;

Molloy et al., 2024). They played an important role in a certain capacity during the program process. Therefore, their reflection of the program can be quite beneficial for program growth and sustainability (Cho & Egan, 2023; Herr, 2017; Raza, 2020a). It is also possible that those stakeholders who did not participate in the program due to any reasons or left the program utilize this opportunity and participate to continue program efforts in the future (Herr, 2017; Herr & Anderson, 2015; Meinhardt et al., 2022; Vanner, 2024). Hence, the MCEM program review and share is extremely important for all relevant stakeholders including learners and program participants (Raza, 2021). Learners need to be prepared for it and conduct the MCEM program review and share in an effective manner that is beneficial for all stakeholders including program participants.

Moreover, learners also need to document the program review and share meetings, which can be a guide to continue the program for stakeholders in the future (Heesch et al., 2020; Yılmaz et al., 2021). For instance, if any program goals and/or objective was not addressed due to a lack of funding or time, then stakeholders who are responsible to continue the program in the future after its formal completion would also know the strategies, lessons learned, and make useful plans during the program review and share to address the unaddressed goals and/or objectives (Raza & Richey, 2021; Zheng et al., 2020). For instance, stakeholders may explore and discuss new donor agencies or funding sources, overspending, money management systems, external technical assistance, internal donation from existing or new stakeholders, etc. This may help stakeholders who are responsible to continue the program to effectively deal with the challenges in the future, make/pursue specific plans, and achieve program goals and/or objective (s) which were initially not achieved.

It is also worth mentioning that priorities or focuses of learners or organizations may change over time. For instance, if one learner or organization has been carrying out a program for 3–5 years. It is possible that they run out of funds, find a more immediate or serious issue/need in their community, their priorities are changed, they do not want to deal with challenges associated the program anymore due to changes in social and political environment, or it is not feasible for them to continue the program (Hallé et al., 2024; Metcalf et al., 2024; Soneson et al., 2022). If the program needs additional work and continuity through an organized platform (a trained learner or a local organization), then the current learners can hand over the program to new learners or community organization/partner who can continue working with existing and new program stakeholders including program participants (Davis et al., 2022; DiSantostefano et al., 2024). Based on the nature and aim of a program, the program can also expand after its first formal completion. A program can enter from one phase (one formal completion) into another phase (another formal beginning with new or additional fundings; Snell-Rood et al., 2021; Westerman et al., 2020). For instance, if learners and program stakeholders find out that there are some domains, which were not addressed during the first program lifecycle and they are able to secure additional or new fundings to start a new phase, they can do that particularly if it is beneficial for program participant/target beneficiaries and local communities (Kouamé et al., 2022; Marshall et al., 2024). It may be helpful to comprehensively address the problem/issue and better prepare program participants and relevant stakeholders to either alleviate the problem entirely or keep it to a minimum degree through their sustainable efforts after the completion of a second or following phases (Raza, 2022). The contemporary problems are dynamic and multifaceted and one of the advantages of the MCEM programs is that they are flexible and adaptable, which can be implemented in various settings with diverse groups of the population and for one or more phases (Kearney, 2021; Raza, 2021).

Sometimes, given the prevalence and importance of a problem that the MCEM program is addressing, learners can also carry out advocacy campaigns and coordinate with government personnel and political leaders to integrate their program into the mainstream policy or a government program particularly when it is about to complete and stakeholders think that sustainable efforts are needed in the future to either alleviate this problem, keep it to the minimum degree, or address the needs of program participants (Erchick et al., 2022; Esper et al., 2024). These discussions and plans are usually discussed and initiated during the program. The MCEM program review and share process facilitates program stakeholders in determining a specific direction to sustain the program after its formal completion (Raza, 2021, 2022).

It is worth mentioning that the program review and share which is conducted at the formal completion of a MCEM program is different than the other reviews and shares that stakeholders conduct throughout the program lifecycle. The MCEM programs facilitate, promote, and guide learners and all relevant stakeholders including program participants to actively engage in the program from multiple engagement levels. These stakeholders keep interacting with each other, share their experiences and expertise, and utilize resources and strengths for the success of their program. Hence, continuous engagement and collaboration among all relevant program stakeholders is imperative throughout the program lifecycle for the success and sustainability of a MCEM program and the MCEM programs create a sustainable environment for it.

In conclusion, the MCEM program review and share is a crucial step of a MCEM program, which provides learners and relevant stakeholders including program participants with an opportunity to share, review, discuss, and reflect on the program, its process, and outcomes. It also provides them with an opportunity to share their experiences, challenges, and important lessons learned with each other and engage new stakeholders for contributing to sustainable program efforts in the future. Consequently, learners and program stakeholders make appropriate plans to successfully continue the program in the future after its formal completion, which ensures the growth, success, and sustainability of the program.

CASE STUDY

Karen successfully completed all three phases of her MCEM program, including program development, implementation, and evaluation. She is now formally closing her program and wants to ensure the sustainability of her program. She is also interested in sharing important lessons learned and would like to hear from other program stakeholders. She also wants to reach out and invite new stakeholders to market and expand her program. She is not sure how to disseminate and share her program outcomes among program stakeholders and those who were not a part of the program but would be relevant and may be interested in participating in or adopting the program in the future. She has been thinking about who she needs to invite in addition to her program stakeholders in her program review and share meetings. She doesn't have any prior knowledge about the nature, scope, and degree of a program review and share, which is conducted after the formal completion of a program. She is not sure about the extensiveness of a program review and share, who she needs to provide opportunities to talk and share during this process, and how and what she needs to record and document regarding program review and share. She also wants to learn how to structure the program review and share meetings to effectively conduct it. Hence, she decides to read existing research on program review and share. She also plans to read and review different programs and websites to learn about this process. She also scheduled a few meetings with other organizations and experts to consult about it. Additionally, she also has plans to meet with her program's relevant stakeholders including program participants to discuss it.

DISCUSSION QUESTIONS

(1) What is a program review and share?

(2) Why is it important for a MCEM program?

(3) How does it engage existing and new stakeholder groups in future program efforts?

(4) How does it ensure the sustainability of a MCEM program after its formal completion?

(5) How can learners make a program review and share more engaged and representative of all stakeholders?

(6) How long (e.g. number and duration of stakeholders' meetings) should learners plan to carry out a program review and share?

ASSIGNMENT QUESTIONS

Students will give a brief presentation (7–10 minutes) in which they will share their experiences and reflections on the service-learning project. Below are step-by-step guidelines for the service-learning project presentation.

(1) What is the topic/title of your SL program?

(2) Briefly describe your program. For instance, what is your program about? What is the focus and the purpose of your program? Why is your program important in addressing important areas/issues of diversity in early childhood education?

(3) Share your community partner, their overall focus of work, and how your program fits in their existing community efforts.

(4) How did you use the MCEM framework for your SL program?

(5) Describe the demographic characteristics of your program participants and relevant stakeholders, such as age, gender, race, income, family structure, etc.

(6) Share stakeholders' influences that they created for your program participants at the three engagement levels of the Multilevel Community

The MCEM Program Review and Share

Engagement model. How did stakeholders' influences change over time and were shaped by developmental, sociocultural, and historical contexts?

(7) Discuss the resources and vulnerabilities that you identified based on stakeholders' influences for your program participants in relation to your MCEM program at the three engagement levels of the MCEM. How did these resources and vulnerabilities change over time and were shaped by developmental, sociocultural, and historical contexts?

(8) Share your SAMREEN (Sustainable, Attainable, Meaningful, Related, Engaged, Evaluative, and Neat) program goals and/or objective.

(9) Describe your program curriculum, method of delivery, and teaching approaches.

(10) How did you use the information that you collected by conducting a literature review?

(11) How did you work with program stakeholders and participants to develop and implement your program curriculum?

(12) Discuss your MCEM program implementation/delivery (at least two workshops/educational sessions) with your program participants.

(13) How did you facilitate different learning styles and needs of your program participants?

(14) Discuss some ethical and cultural challenges that you faced during the program implementation/delivery. How did you overcome those challenges?

(15) Share your overall experience of the SL project and important lessons learned.

(16) Provide a conclusion and your overall reflection of the SL project.

(17) Provide references.

14

THE MCEM PROGRAM REFLECTION AND TRUSTWORTHINESS

The objective of this chapter for learners is to learn how to develop and maintain a reflective process and program trustworthiness in the MCEM programs throughout the program lifecycle. The author also shares specific steps and measures that learners can carry out to ensure that their MCEM programs are without any biases and prejudices, which helps learners to develop trust and good rapport among program stakeholders and beyond.

The following is a definition of the program trustworthiness:

Program trustworthiness demonstrates that the program is inclusive and transparent to all stakeholders who are actively engaged and participate in the decision-making process of all aspects of the program and simultaneously meets a certain degree of rigor (scientific standards) in pursuing its specific goals and objectives and achieving successful and sustainable outcomes.

One of the advantages of using the MCEM framework in developing MCEM programs is that a MCEM program is likely to be inclusive, transparent, and representative of all stakeholder groups due to its systematic process of stakeholders' engagement and collaboration. Usually, such comprehensive programs that foster and promote engagement among many stakeholder groups are quite expensive and require substantial fundings. However, the MCEM programs can be developed with small funds or even no external funds due to an active engagement of all stakeholder groups in the program process. It is worth mentioning that stakeholder groups bring unique knowledge and expertise into the program (Berger et al., 2024; Godier et al., 2022; McLennan et al., 2023). Some stakeholders may be better in their socioeconomic background than the others who can financially support the program (Raza, 2021; Reid et al., 2022; Song & Ferguson, 2023). Therefore, learners need to make sure that they spend substantial time and efforts to identify, engage, and utilize all program relevant stakeholders, their resources, and strengths for all aspects of the program.

When all relevant stakeholders including program participants actively participate in a MCEM program process, it makes the program inclusive and representative of all groups (Raza, 2022). When all stakeholder groups including the learners identify community needs and issues, consequently, stakeholders find the program more relevant and meaningful for them and their community because the needs and/or problems which are addressed through the program are identified by them through a collaborative process (Hayward et al., 2022; Lee & Raschke, 2020; Waisman-Nitzan et al., 2023). When stakeholders find the program useful for them and their community families, they become motivated and passionate about the program (Hughes et al., 2020; Levasseur et al., 2021). Their motivation and passion for the program encourages them to identify and access resources, find and allocate their time and efforts, and collaborate with each other to successfully develop the program, implement it, and evaluate that program to examine its impacts and effectiveness on target population (Song & Ferguson, 2023; Winberg et al., 2022).

It is worth mentioning that although learners need to make sure that the MCEM programs are inclusive and engaged, it is equally important for learners to keep the program rigor/scientific standards high because it usually happens that when such MCEM comprehensive programs are developed, rigor can be compromised. For instance, when learners collaborate and consult with program stakeholders in the program process, they need to develop and maintain certain rules and directions that govern and monitor participants' interactions, feedback, and inputs during the development of a program (Hilliger et al., 2024; Kröger et al., 2022). Learners need to document and record every event, meeting, and discussion that is held among stakeholders on the program development. Learners' purpose is to facilitate program stakeholders in the decision-making and simultaneously keep a program focus to save time, effort, and resources of program stakeholders (Cahill et al., 2023; Le Gouais et al., 2023; Raza, 2021). It also prevents learners and program stakeholders from any negative influences or opportunists whose intentions are to distract stakeholders or create hurdles in the program process. It is also important for learners to provide fair and equal opportunities to all stakeholders to share and express themselves during the program process and avoid any favoritism (Koly et al., 2024; Raza, 2022). Learners also need to develop, share, and stick to specific timelines with stakeholders to maintain a program focus, and efficiently use stakeholders' time and energy, and prevent stakeholders from feeling any pressure or burden from the program

(Batastini et al., 2020). Remember that stakeholders are volunteers in the program who are not receiving any financial benefits, hence, it is the responsibility of learners to respect and value stakeholder's time and energy to prevent stakeholders from feeling overwhelmed and discouraged to effectively engage and utilize them in the program process. Therefore, learners ensure that each step is systematically followed and completed in a collaborative manner. The MCEM program provides learners and program stakeholders with a systematic process to develop, implement, and evaluate their programs, which decreases learners' burden and take some pressure off from them because learners need to discuss and follow the steps and systematic process with program stakeholders to develop, implement, and evaluate the MCEM programs.

In addition, although the MCEM programs are multilevel, complex, and dynamic based on the scope, time, and prevalence of problems they address, the MCEM programs do not require complex or highly advanced scientific procedures for achieving a certain degree of rigor. Learners and program stakeholders can perform those procedures which are manageable and according to their expertise. For instance, if they are documenting how they are using and implementing each step of the MCEM program by maintaining weekly reports, minutes of meetings, videos, events records, etc. along with a reflective journaling, it provides evidence of their rigor and stakeholder engagement in the program process. Based on the funding, learners and stakeholders can also determine if they need any additional outside assistance. Since the MCEM programs bring stakeholder groups including individuals, families, groups, and/or organizations together, it is likely that learners may find an organization or a group of experts as part of their program stakeholder groups who have relevant expertise that they can offer for the MCEM program. Hence, it is important for learners and program stakeholders to spend extensive time and continue their efforts in identifying, accessing, and utilizing all relevant program stakeholders, their resources, and strengths for the success of their program (Raza, 2018).

Moreover, learners and stakeholders' personal and program reflections are extremely important to share, record, and document, which demonstrates the degree of program rigor and relevance within and outside of the program (Corneli et al., 2023; Meinhardt et al., 2022; Woods et al., 2021). For this purpose, learners can write their reflective journals during the program process in which they can write about the challenges, opportunities, biases, positionality, etc. and share strategies, actions, lessons learned that they used and carried out to address and overcome them (Berezan et al., 2023; Horton et al., 2021; Pieper et al., 2021). When learners examine and reflect on their biases, beliefs, and preconceived notions, it helps learners to determine their effects on learners' behaviors and interactions with program participants (O'Reilly & Milner, 2020; O'Loughlin & Griffith, 2020). Learners' biases, false beliefs, and inaccurate perceptions about program stakeholders can negatively affect stakeholders' collaboration, engagement, and retentions. When learners find out how their biases and beliefs can potentially affect or currently affecting program stakeholders, they are more likely to discover and use appropriated strategies to minimize or overcome them, which fosters a positive and collaborative process between learners and program stakeholders (Bonesso et al., 2024; Porter & Couper, 2023). Learners are the key to a program's success as they are the ones who lead and facilitate stakeholders' engagement in the program for its success. Hence, it is essential for them to overcome their biases and prejudices during the program process to ensure a transparent, neutral, and constructive program process (Lara, 2020; Najjarnejad & Bromfield, 2022). Additionally, it is also important for program stakeholders to record, share, and reflect on their believes and value systems, which provides them with opportunities to learn about each other's backgrounds, behaviors and interactions, and the meaning they associate with these behaviors and interactions, which reduces the conflicts, misunderstanding, and disagreements in the program process (Cahill et al., 2022; Olsson et al., 2024). For instance, if stakeholders are from different cultures, such as one stakeholder group is from South Asian, whereas the other stakeholder group is from United States, the use and meaning of making eye contacts are different between these countries due to practicing distinct cultures (individualistic vs collectivistic). In South Asia, such as Pakistan, it is not considered appropriate to make frequent eye contacts with older adults and parents, whereas in the United States, eye contacts are very important regardless of age, gender, and relationship type. Hence, learners need to learn about their stakeholders, examine their cultural context and practices, facilitate and create a safer environment for stakeholders' sharing and engagement, and be prepared for such situations (Herr, 2017; Morris et al., 2023; Raza, 2022).

It is worth mentioning that stakeholders may need to continue the program after its formal completion. Hence, in order to secure additional fundings or engage existing and new stakeholders, they may need to market their program and demonstrate its rigor, relevance, and success. Stakeholders would like to successfully continue their program after its formal completion when the program is useful, meaningful, and trustworthy (Madden et al., 2021; Martínez et al., 2021). Therefore, learners and stakeholders can choose and use various useful procedures and strategies to demonstrate the transparency and trustworthiness of their program, which increases the success and sustainability of the program (Cross et al., 2021; Yılmaz et al., 2021).

Moreover, a continuous recording, documentation, and reflections of learners and program stakeholders about the program and themselves may also save the time and efforts that learners and stakeholders usually invest in conducting multiple evaluations of their program (Subban et al., 2024; Vanner, 2024). If learners and stakeholders are confident that they are monitoring, assessing, and supervising the program rigorously and maintain a certain degree of scientific standard, which demonstrates program transparency and maintain its trustworthiness within and outside of the program, they may not need multiple formal evaluations or external experts to conduct these evaluations for their program (Alzahrani et al., 2023; Zheng & Toribio, 2021). Such approaches are more applicable and useful in those scenarios when there is no external fundings for the program and formal/external program evaluations are not required by a donor/funding agency. It is worth mentioning that the SAMREEN evaluation design also facilitates leaners and program stakeholders to carry out a straightforward evaluation process throughout the program lifecycle to assess different areas and multiple levels of the program, which is more useful and effective in those situations where they are fewer or no funds for program evaluations.

Further, it is worth mentioning that all three phases including program development, implementation, and evaluation are equally important and essential for the success and sustainability of a MCEM program (Raza, 2020b). Sometimes the evaluation phase/part is neglected due to a lack of expertise or no external requirements. The MCEM program evaluation is integral which not only helps learners and program stakeholders to demonstrate the transparency and trustworthiness of their program, but it also fosters stakeholders' engagement and participation in the program (Raza, 2020a). When learners or organizations leave the community after the formal completion of a program, program stakeholders can effectively utilize the assessments or records to replicate the same procedures which results in successful program implementation, outcomes, and sustainability to continue program efforts in the future (Raza, 2022). Hence, the program trustworthiness not only facilitates learners and program stakeholders to promote their program and engage existing and new stakeholders in the program before, during, and after the formal completion of the program, but it also helps learners and stakeholders to demonstrate that the MCEM program meets the rigor and scientific standards in all aspects and areas and at multiple program engagement levels (Raza, 2020a, 2020b, 2021; Raza et al., 2021).

In conclusion, the MCEM program's transparency and trustworthiness is an integral part of a MCEM program, which demonstrates that the program meets a certain degree of scientific standard, and it also shows the relevance and meaningfulness of the program for all program stakeholders. Learners and program stakeholders can use various methods and techniques which are discussed in this chapter to record and document their personal and program reflections throughout the program lifecycle, which helps to foster positive and constructive engagement during and after the formal completion of a MCEM program.

CASE STUDY

From the beginning of the program, Karen has been very proactive in maintaining the transparency and trustworthiness of her program. For this purpose, she has been continuously assessing different areas and aspects of her program at multiple engagement levels with program stakeholders to examine the program and make appropriate changes for its improvement and effectiveness. In addition to these assessments, she learned about record keeping, documentation, data management, and report writing. She also reviewed what other organizations have been doing in documenting their programs. Consequently, she and other relevant program stakeholders have been recording the program continuously and extensively. For instance, Karen records every meeting, event, and workshop. Additional evidence, such as participants' pictures, attendance sheet, minutes of meeting, etc. are also recorded and maintained. She collaboratively writes, maintains, and shares weekly reports. She also releases a monthly new letter and sends it to her program stakeholders. Moreover, she also understands that there are self-biases that she and her program stakeholders may feel and experience due to their values, beliefs, and worldviews, which could negatively affect the program and hinder its progress. Hence, she has been writing and maintaining her reflective journal and she also advised her program stakeholder groups to write and maintain their reflective journals in which they write about their biases, challenges, experiences, and lessons learned. She discusses her reflective journal during her monthly meetings regularly with program stakeholders and also invites other stakeholders to share their reflective journals in a safe, supportive, and respectful environment. She believes that a systematic recording of the program along with continuous and critical reflections helps her and other program stakeholders to maintain a good balance between rigor and relevance. Consequently, it improves the transparency and trustworthiness of the program.

DISCUSSION QUESTIONS

(1) What is the MCEM program trustworthiness?

(2) Discuss different aspects of the MCEM program trustworthiness?

(3) Why is MCEM program trustworthiness important?

(4) How does it foster stakeholders' engagement in the program?

(5) How does it facilitate the MCEM program evaluation?

(6) What is MCEM program reflections?

(7) Why is it important for learners and program stakeholders' to write reflections throughout the program lifecycle?

(8) How do program and learners' reflections increase MCEM program trustworthiness?

(9) How does program trustworthiness increase the rigor of MCEM programs?

(10) How does program trustworthiness increase success and sustainability of the MCEM programs?

ASSIGNMENT QUESTIONS

(1) Describe yourself as a learner/stakeholder in the MCEM program?

(2) What biases did you face in the program?

(3) How did it hinder the program process and success?

(4) How did you carry out a reflective process throughout the program?

(5) What were the advantages and disadvantages of recording your reflections?

(6) What strategies did you use to deal with these self-biases, prejudices, and challenges?

(7) What procedures did you use to ensure that your program meets scientific standards?

(8) What procedures were more effective and useful than the others? How? Why?

(9) How did these procedures help you record, assess, and supervise all aspects of the program?

(10) How did these procedures increase the program trustworthiness?

(11) How did trustworthiness ensure the success and sustainability of your program?

(12) What did you learn from this assignment?

15

THE MCEM PROGRAM SUSTAINABILITY, LESSONS LEARNED, AND FUTURE DIRECTIONS

The objective of this chapter is to discuss how the MCEM programs are successful and sustainable, which promote and foster school, community, and workplace engagement and SL. This chapter also shares important lessons learned for learners to carry out a successful MCEM program and ensure its sustainability over time. The author also discussed important suggestions for instructors to effectively guide and facilitate students in their SL projects.

The following is a definition of community engagement:

Community engagement is a process of collaboration, engagement, and active participation of all stakeholders including individuals, families, groups, and/or organizations in the decision-making to achieve certain goals and objectives which focus on addressing specific community needs and/or issues that directly or indirectly affect their lives, well-being, and development to ensure community success, sustainability, and positive outcomes.

One of the advantages of MCEM programs is that they not only show positive program outcomes and sustainability but also foster community engagement. As the above definition of community engagement demonstrates that it is a process of collaboration, engagement, and active participation of all stakeholders in the decision-making. As discussed in the previous chapters that learners need to spend substantial time and effort to identify, reach out, engage, and utilize all program relevant stakeholders in the program. These stakeholders include individuals, families, groups, and/or organizations who collaborate with each other, strengthen each other's resources, and minimize vulnerabilities to systematically develop, implement, and evaluate a MCEM program that focuses on addressing the needs and/or issues of program participants and all relevant stakeholders directly or indirectly. A MCEM program process promotes the engagement of all relevant stakeholders, recognizes their voices and inputs, and provides each stakeholder group with fair and equitable opportunities to actively participate in the decision-making process. Hence, those individuals, families, groups, and/or organizations who are engaged in other programs/projects become potential stakeholders in the MCEM program and bring their knowledge, skills, and expertise to the program. Consequently, different stakeholder groups who play various roles and tasks and are situated at different engagement levels of society learn from each other, make social connections, and share their concerns and ideas on the needs and issues of school, community, and workplace. This process of active collaboration, engagement, and participation among all relevant stakeholders including learners and program participants fosters community engagement. Since the program focuses on relevant needs and issues of program participants and stakeholders who collaboratively and systematically develop the program, these individuals, families, groups, and/or organizations find the program meaningful and useful for their lives, well-being, and development. This indicates that the MCEM programs foster community engagement, which provides all relevant stakeholder groups with opportunities to not only focus on the needs and/or issues that focus through the MCEM program but also critically think, share, reflect on other important community problems. Such an engaged and collaborative process results in school, community, and workplace collaboration and sustainability because stakeholder groups learn from each other and share/transform their unique and valuable knowledge and expertise with each other.

The following is a definition of program sustainability:

Program sustainability is a process of acquiring, using, preserving, and transforming community knowledge, skills, and/or any relevant social, economic, political resources for sustainable efforts toward addressing community needs and issues and achieving short-term and long-term goals and objectives to foster well-being and development of all stakeholders.

As the above definition of sustainability implies that when stakeholders share, receive, and utilize their knowledge, skills, and expertise to address immediate and important new and emerging needs and issues of community families and make collaborative efforts to achieve short-term and long-terms goals and objectives related to existing programs and/or new programs, it ensures community sustainability and show successful community outcomes in the form of improving the well-being and development of all stakeholders including program participants/target families.

When all relevant stakeholders including program participants and learners actively engage in the program process during which they learn, share, and transform their unique knowledge, skills, and expertise to each other, it fosters not only the MCEM program sustainability, but it also contributes to community sustainable efforts. As discussed above, when stakeholder groups work together and collaborate in the program process, they learn from each other and make connections. It is possible that one stakeholder group is more active and efficient in the economic domain of society, and the other stakeholder group is more influential in the social realm of society, whereas another stakeholder is more active and productive in the political sphere of society. When they engage in the MCEM program process, it also provides them opportunities to discuss and share their own areas and introduce other stakeholders with potential resources and opportunities which are available in their area. Consequently, it may also provide them with opportunities to collaborate on other programs/projects that focus on other community needs and issues. As a result, they may be able to share and effectively utilize each other's resources including economic, social, and political resources for improving the well-being and development of individuals, children, and families in schools, communities, and workplaces. Hence, the MCEM programs foster community sustainability, address broader community needs and issues, and make important contributions in existing or sustainable efforts and programs.

Since the MCEM programs are multilevel, engaged, and inclusive, which makes them successful and sustainable, they can be challenging and overwhelming for learners. Hence, it is important to carefully think about every step and decide the degree of complexity that learners want to apply in the program process. For instance, one of the advantages of MCEM programs is that they are quite flexible and adaptable, that is why they are developed and implemented in different societies and cultures around the world. If learners have limited time and they are developing, implementing, and evaluating the MCEM program in a period of 4–6 months, then they may need to choose and decide which steps and/or process they carry out during this timeframe to effectively complete their MCEM program. As discussed earlier, learners can develop a MCEM program which is simple and small in scope and expand this program later. Based on time, funds, scope, and other different factors, learners can use and apply a relatively small degree of complexity, rigor, and depth in their MCEM program. This book is a complete guide to successfully develop, implement, and evaluate the MCEM programs on different topics, with diverse groups of population, and in various settings in societies around the world. Hence, learners need to read this book and complete the assignments and discussions to gain a better understanding of the MCEM programs and then apply this knowledge to systematically develop, implement, and evaluate their programs. There is an extensive list of topics provided in the textbook that learners can use and choose their program topic from that list. The MCEM programs on these topics already have been developed and tested successfully. Learners can also choose different topics and follow the steps provided in this book to systematically develop, implement, and evaluate their MCEM programs.

In conclusion, the MCEM programs are flexible and adaptable and simultaneously they can range from low to high degree of rigor, engagement, and complexity. Hence, learners need to critically examine important factors, such as time, scope, context, funds, expertise, etc. and then determine the degree of depth and complexity they can go into in developing, implementing, and evaluating their MCEM programs. The MCEM programs not only show successful program outcomes and sustainability but also address broader community needs and issues and make important contributions in existing or sustainable efforts and programs for school, community, and workplace. The author provided useful suggestions for instructors to effectively facilitate and guide students in their SL programs, which are as follows.

(1) It is essential for instructors not to overwhelm students by sharing all or a lot of information about SL projects at the beginning of a semester because this is a time when students adjust and settle into a new semester. Some transfer students come and join a new institution, whereas other students have their first semester in that institution. There are possibilities that many students take the SL course first time who haven't worked with the instructor before. Hence, given all these factors, instructors need to be mindful and efficient when they share information with students on SL projects at the beginning of a semester.

(2) Instructors need to include the information on the SL projects on the syllabus, record a course review video for online classes, and/or discuss it with students in a seated class at the beginning of a semester.

(3) During the first few weeks, instructors can start sharing information about their SL projects every week, which include any specific guidelines, information on community partners, and introductory videos.

(4) Instructors need to provide students with information about their SL projects on a weekly or biweekly basis and include it in those modules which are relevant to that information. They can also create a separate

module/folder in which all relevant SL materials, assignments, and lecture videos are included if that is more convenient for them and their students. Hence, many useful strategies and modes can be used to facilitate students in their SL projects.

(5) It is important for instructors to create additional and specific documents, record videos, and develop informational resources to share with students so that they can learn the steps, assignments, and process of their SL projects.

(6) Instructors need to develop, finalize, and share a list of potential community partners with students from which students can choose their community partner for their SL projects in the early few weeks of a semester. It is also useful to provide students with a description and examples on how they can choose the best and most relevant community partners for their SL projects given the topic and focus of their program. For instance, if their project is about child development, then an organization which focuses on children and their developmental needs and outcomes would be a good fit for that project.

(7) If possible, instructors should share students' projects that were completed in prior semesters/courses as an example. Students can use these projects as examples in creating their own unique SL projects. This reduces substantial additional work, pressure, and burden for students and instructors.

(8) It is important for instructors to be adaptable and flexible if students find any community partners other than what they included in the list. Remember the community partner is only one stakeholder situated at the proximal, and there are many other stakeholders who are situated at the same or different engagement levels when students develop their MCEM programs. Students need to know and realize that all stakeholders are important who play equally important roles for the success and sustainability of a program.

(9) Instructors need to inform students in advance, when they are going to implement their program, how many educational sessions/workshops they will conduct, duration, and modes of delivery so that students already schedule their sessions prior to those modules to meet everyone's schedules and the assignments' due dates.

(10) If there are specific requirements from the institution, such as any agreement form, number of volunteer hours for SL projects, assessments,

etc. it is useful to develop a document, include that information in it, and share it with students.

(11) Sometimes, students just want to do the volunteer work due to the complexities involved in doing SL projects. It is the responsibility of instructors to explain and discuss with students that additional volunteer hours required for SL are already integrated into the SL assignments. As students successfully complete their SL assignments, they meet those requirements automatically. It is important to include this information in the course syllabus.

(12) Instructors need to learn and use such skills which help them to showcase and demonstrate the importance of SL projects before their students, how SL projects provide students with highly impactful learning experiences and have long-lasting and sustainable learning benefits for them because sometimes new students don't understand and/or realize the importance of these projects. Consequently, the efforts, time, and additional work that instructors put together to offer and integrate SL into their courses are taken for granted and become less effective.

(13) It is essential for instructors to be flexible and accommodate students if they miss any SL assignments due to any valid reason. However, it is important for students not to skip any SL assignment because every next assignment relates to the prior assignment. Hence, students need to regularly complete their SL assignments. Regular reminders and prompts can be useful to keep students on track in completing their SL assignments regularly.

(14) Instructors need to make sure that they are accessible and approachable to students to support and facilitate them in their SL projects through different modes of communication, such as in-person meetings, after class meetings, online meetings, discussion boards, phones, emails, etc.

(15) Even though students work on their SL projects individually based on the class structure or teaching approaches, it is helpful to create students' small groups at the beginning of class so that students can reach out to their small groups members in case they need any help over the course a semester. Students can also reach out to any teaching or graduate assistant if you have anyone who assists the instructor for this course.

(16) Instructors should also share the plagiarism and academic integrity policies with students so that they understand the principles, rules, and

circumstances related to it and appropriately follow the guidelines in completing their SL assignments and projects.

(17) It is essential for instructors to grade the SL assignments regularly, provide students with constructive and clear feedback, review the entire class feedback that they provided on an assignment, and share it with them. Instructors can either create a document and upload it to the learning management system (LMS) in the same module when the assignment was due or share it in their announcement.

(18) If instructors share any new information or documents during the week which was not uploaded or shared with students at the beginning of a week when the module was initially available to students, it is important to announce it after uploading that document to LMS and let students know how they can access it so that students can review and utilize it adequately. Sometimes, students complete their modules early in the week and don't go back to the same module that they have already completed.

(19) There is a possibility that students may feel quite frustrated, stressed, and overwhelmed due to the additional work that they need to complete for their SL projects. Hence, it is important for instructors to keep in touch with their students, keep motivating and encouraging them, foster student engagement to support each other, and share resources and events, which can be useful for students to deal with these challenges. For instance, if any students feel overwhelmed or stressed, they can go to the counseling center for additional support and assistance.

(20) It is important for instructors to acknowledge and consider distinctive and unique student learning styles and needs and be prepared to facilitate those students who have special learning needs. If any student struggles to accurately follow all steps of a SL project assignments compared to class but that student is successfully learning the process and going through important steps to complete the project, it is essential for instructors to be flexible in supporting that student to ensure the success of each student in their SL projects.

(21) The instructor does not need to go through the entire MCEM program process if it feels quite complex, lengthy, beyond the scope of a specific course. They can make a brief MCEM project based on the nature, scope, and time they have for that course. As discussed in the book, the MCEM programs are quite adaptable and flexible, instructors can adapt

and use the MCEM framework based on students' needs, their expertise, and the nature and SL requirements for a course.

(22) Instructors can also divide a MCEM project into multiple courses and determine the degree of stakeholders' engagement, complexity, and rigor as the MCEM programs range from simple to complex programs.

(23) It is imperative for schools and universities to motivate students to participate in such SL projects because they provide students with a highly impactful learning experience and prepare them personally, ethically, and professionally. For this purpose, universities can award students a certificate (The MCEM Program Certificate) after successfully completing their MCEM SL project/program in 3–4 courses. Remember, the MCEM framework and programs can be used and offered in various forms, degrees, and modes. Hence, the instructors can decide how they want to design their curriculum for offering a MCEM Program Certificate. The MCEM certificate substantially increases students' academic credentials and marketability in their profession.

This book is a paradigm shift in school, community, and workplace engagement and SL. Due to the flexibility, adaptability, and effective operationalization of the MCEM framework, the MCEM programs can be developed on any topic, implemented in any settings, and engage any target population. The MCEM programs offer a good balance between scientific rigor and participants' real-life experiences, which makes these programs more inclusive, successful, and sustainable. A continuous, collaborative, and engaged process among all relevant stakeholders including program participants recognize the voice of all groups and provide them with an opportunity to actively participate in the decision-making process, which also addresses the issues of equity, inclusion, and social justice.

The MCEM framework and the programs offer a new direction in the field of SL and community engagement and in various domains, such as school, community, and workplace. Due to the flexibility of the MCEM framework, it can be used in various disciplines, such as family science and human development, education, business, medicine, health service, counseling, agriculture, sports, STEM, etc. to systematically develop, implement, and evaluate programs. The adaptability and generalizability of the MCEM framework makes it applicable to societies around the world. Hence, learners from any country can utilize the MCEM framework to develop, implement, and evaluate the MCEM programs.

Further directions for the MCEM framework and its' use are discussed as follows: (1) future books will focus on how the MCEM framework can be used to review and assess existing programs in a collaborative, engaged, and inclusive manner for sustainability and successful outcomes; (2) future books will also guide the audience on how to work outside of academic settings with culturally diverse individuals, families, groups, and organizations in local communities around the world to develop, implement, and evaluate the MCEM programs; and (3) future books will also guide the audience on how to foster and grow engagement and collaboration among relevant stakeholders globally in a process of program development, implement, and evaluation; and (4) future books will also describe the SAMREEN evaluation design and SAMREEN goals and objectives more extensively and how it can be used to assess non-MCEM programs.

In sum, the author developed the MCEM framework and programs after an extensive work of more than a decade, which offer a paradigm shift in SL and community engagement in various domains, such as school, community, and workplace. Due to the flexibility, adaptability, and effective operationalization of the MCEM framework, the MCEM programs are developed on any topic, used in any discipline, and implemented with any group of the population in any suitable settings around the world.

CASE STUDY

When Karen started thinking about developing and offering her program on parent–child attachment among young parents who have children aged between 0 and 12, she had several questions in her mind. For instance, this problem was quite prevalent in her community. The rate of child abuse and neglect was quite high in her community. Young parents were getting divorced due to additional demands associated with their children. Children were showing social, emotional, and behavioral problems. Due to unhealthy parenting practices, children's academic performance and achievement were also below the average. Parents were also stressed and felt bad about their parenting skills. This problem was also quite important because she believes that childhood attachments with primary caregivers are extremely important for optimal development of children. She had good childhood experiences, but she observed many adverse childhood experiences and situations in her community. Moreover, the purpose of her program was not only to focus on the problem and specific group of families but to bring community groups together and provide them with a platform through this program to collaboratively work on this problem and other important and immediate community needs and issues. She knew that such a multilevel and complex program that ultimately invites different stakeholder groups and fosters stakeholders' engagement and collaboration can be challenging but she knew that it would pay off. Moreover, she is a big advocate of sustainability. Hence, another purpose of inviting and engaging different stakeholder groups in the program was to ensure the transformation of knowledge and skills to ensure program success and sustainability. She is so glad that her program brought many groups and organizations together who also have been working on similar issues, fostered their engagement, provided them with opportunities to learn about each other and make social connections, promoted a teamwork, raised community engagement, and made important contributions in existing sustainable efforts.

DISCUSSION QUESTIONS

(1) What is MCEM program sustainability?

(2) Why is it important for a MCEM program?

(3) How do MCEM programs foster broader community engagement and sustainability?

(4) What are the factors that learners need to consider in determining the degree of program rigor and complexity?

(5) How do MCEM programs bring people from different areas of society to work together?

(6) How do the MCEM programs address broader community needs and issues?

(7) How do the MCEM programs contribute to sustainable community efforts?

(8) How do the MCEM programs grow stakeholders' engagement among school, community, and workplace?

ASSIGNMENT QUESTIONS

(1) How do you see your program sustainability?

(2) Why is sustainability important for your program?

(3) How does your MCEM program foster sustainability?

(4) What degree of rigor, engagement, and complexity do you prefer in your program? Why?

(5) How does your program foster broader community engagement?

(6) How does your program contribute to sustainable community efforts?

(7) What did you learn from this assignment?

ABOUT THE AUTHOR

Muhammad Hassan Raza is an Associate Professor at Missouri State University, United States. He is a Theorist and a Methodologist. He is the author of Two Souls One Reflection. He has been teaching at the undergraduate level and the graduate level for almost a decade. He has experience of teaching in three large-scale public universities in the United States. He teaches courses on family development, couple relationships, diversity in early childhood education, research methods, statistics, service-learning, theories of family science and human development. He also writes poetry and songs in English and Urdu. In addition to writing poetry and songs, he writes drama and films. After work, he likes to spend time with his family, which includes his spouse and three young children. He also likes to travel and visit new places to explore and enjoy.

APPENDIX

THE MCEM SAMPLE PROJECTS

The following are some examples of the MCEM SL projects. Please note that due to limited space, brief information about these SL projects is shared.

Questions	Group 1	Group 2	Group 3	Group 4	Group 5	Group 6
What is the topic/title of your program?	Daily stressors	Family relationship issues and functioning.	Children with special needs and family development.	Transitions in family life and family development.	Children with special needs and family functioning.	Impacts of mass violence on family experiences and functioning.
Describe your program based on the definition provided. For instance, what comprises your program?	Resources, activities, and instructions. Sharing, discussions, and presentation. Participants will watch videos on daily stressors and their impacts on their lives. A list of coping strategies to deal with daily stressors will be provided to participants as a resource. Small and large group discussions will be held.	Resources and activities. Engagement, collaboration, various modalities of teaching. Participants will be provided with an informational resource which informs participants on different ways and processes to resolve relationship problems. Participants learn research on relationship problems and conflict.	Resources, activities, and services. Real-life experiences and application. Discussions, and performance. Participants will learn and receive information on those organizations which provide services and support to children with special needs. Activities and discussion will be held to foster participants' understanding of	Resources and activities. Class activities, discussions, sharing, and collaboration. Participants will learn and practice important coping strategies to adapt to new transitions and changes in the family due to the arrival of a new family member. Participants will have small and large group discussions on how to deal with new family	Resources, activities, and instructions. Poster presentation, chart writing and sharing, and class engagement activity. Participants will learn about the resources and support systems in school and community that support families and children with special needs. Participants will also learn and practice how to provide	Resources and services. Class survey, discussion, performance, collaboration, and real-life application. Participants will watch videos on situations when individuals, families, and communities face and experience mass violence during and after mass shooting. Participants will also learn about different interventions and strategies to prevent and cope

204 Appendix

Appendix

		Participants will also receive contact information of organizations and professional which provide counseling to couples and families on relationship problems and conflict.		members, form healthy relationships, and address their social emotional needs. Participants will receive tips and information on additional community support for these families.	social, emotional, financial, and instrumental support to these families.	with mass shooting. Participants will receive information on who to contact in case of any mass shooting and safety procedures.
What is the purpose of your program? Why is your program important in fostering family development?	Help families manage their daily stressors to foster their relationships and functioning.		Reflect on how couple relationship can become a stressor and affects their children.			
		children and families with special needs.	Provide important information and services to facilitate and help these families.	Help families through transitions that occur with the addition of a family member.	Supporting family functioning and address the family's needs.	Cope with a traumatic experience and learn to connect with other people.
Describe the demographic characteristics of your potential program participants, such as age, gender,	Low socioeconomic status families with children.		Parents with children ages 12 and under, counselors, and therapists.	Families from all backgrounds.	Any families of children with special needs, school, community organizations.	All families who are affected, community organization, counselors.
			Family of children with special needs, school, community groups.			

(Continued)

(Continued)

Questions	Group 1	Group 2	Group 3	Group 4	Group 5	Group 6
race, income, family structure, etc. Describe the Multilevel Community Engagement Model. How will you use it to systematically develop, implement, and evaluate your SL program?						
Identify all relevant stakeholders who belong to the proximal level. How are these stakeholders influencing your program participants at the proximal level (the first level) of the MCEM in relation to your program? For instance, your	Schools, community support groups, and employers. Program participants, friends, and extended family members.	Program participants, friends, and extended family members. Community partner and organizations.	Program participants, friends, and extended family members. Community partner and support groups.	Program participants, friends, and extended family members. Community partner.	Program participants, friends, and extended family members. Community partner.	Program participants, friends, and extended family members. Community partner and other relevant organizations.

participants may be influenced by their family members, friends, community support groups, schools, local organizations, etc.				
Identify all relevant stakeholders who belong to the influential level. How are these stakeholders influencing your program participants at the influential level (the second level) of the MCEM in relation to your program? For instance, your participants may be influenced by social media, the internet, television, phones, magazines, donor agencies, public institutions etc.).	Social media users, government personnel.	Electronic, social media, and phone users	Social media, internet, and TV users.	People who are running foster care programs. Media users. People from the medical field.	Social media, government, and donor agencies.	Social media, TV, and government.

(Continued)

(Continued)

Questions	Group 1	Group 2	Group 3	Group 4	Group 5	Group 6
Identify all relevant stakeholders who belong to the holistic level. How are these stakeholders influencing your program participants at the holistic level (the third level) of the MCEM in relation to your program? For instance, your participants may be influenced by any diversity areas such as, socioeconomic status, disability, gender, sexual orientation, ethnicity, etc., or culture.	Multigenerational families, families of different SES, rural and urban, minority families	Parents who have children older than 12 years.	Families who belong to different SES and have a member who have disability different from the program participants.	Families who experience normal developmental changes over time.	Families who are different from program participants based on SES and disability.	Families who are not US born.

Appendix

Discuss your participants' developmental, societal, and historical experiences in relation to your program. For instance, if your program focuses on parental stress, then discuss parenting and parental stress in the current society and how it was before the 1960s. Describe the changes over time. How are the influences of these stakeholders you identified at the three engagement levels on your program participants	The interactions between program participants and social media users are more prevalent and frequent in the current society compared to the past. Consequently, they can provide additional support and make positive influence on program participants.	Gender roles are changing, which influence the nature and extent of couple and family conflict.	Awareness and recognition about families and children with disability are growing in the current society compared to the past.	More support is prevalent for LGBTQ families for adoption compared to the past.	Stakeholders are engaging and creating additional support and resources for the program participants compared to the past.	Awareness is growing along with the problem in the current society compared to the past.

(Continued)

(Continued)

Questions	Group 1	Group 2	Group 3	Group 4	Group 5	Group 6
changed over time and are shaped by developmental, sociocultural, and historical contexts.						
Based on the stakeholders that you identified for your program participants at the proximal level (the first level) of the MCEM, what resources and vulnerabilities can those stakeholders create for your program participants at the proximal level in relation to your program? For instance, your participants (e.g., children or adolescents) may	School can provide more flexibility in education. Students can receive counseling services from school. Student support groups are also a resource for program participants. Employers' lack of flexibility, rural areas, and lack of transportation create vulnerabilities for program participants.	Children are involved in community and school. They are creating social connections for the program participants including themselves. These social connections create support for children and their families. Program participants are learning through these connections, which is minimizing their relationship conflicts in the family.	Family can offer support including childcare and finance. Organizations for children provide support and awareness for families with special need children.	Families and friends can share important resources with each other to function well and make successful transitions. Personality traits can affect the transitions and create challenges for family members. Managing the transition with foster care children who went through a traumatic experience can create	Families experience a grieving process differently. Due to technological advancement, work-family demands, and community support, the grieving process has changed. Consequently, most families with special needs can deal with their family needs.	Social emotional support from extended family members and friends. Community lack of cohesion and connections. Lack of school and workplace trainings on the topic.

210 Appendix

Appendix 211

experience a resource of positive parenting practices and a vulnerability of lack of peer support at the proximal level.	Lack of time in children's lives took time away from them to make connection. This hinders their ability to learn additional skills to manage their family relationship conflict and get emotional social support from other children and their families. Consequently, it creates vulnerabilities for program participants.	vulnerabilities for families.
	Extended families create support for program participants, particularly the grandparents are	

(Continued)

(Continued)

Questions	Group 1	Group 2	Group 3	Group 4	Group 5	Group 6
		teaching their adult children (who are the parents) and grandchildren about managing family relationship conflict. Negative examples which are prevalent in the extended families can create vulnerabilities for program participants because adult parents neither learned nor currently learning any appropriate skills from their parents to manage and cope with their family relationship conflict.				

Appendix

Based on the stakeholders that you identified for your program participants at the influential level (the second level) of the MCEM, what resources and vulnerabilities can those stakeholders create for your program participants at the influential level in relation to your program? For instance, your participants (e.g., children or adolescents) may experience a resource of social media platforms	Online tips on coping with daily stressors and webinars are resources. Lack of supportive state and federal policies and programs are vulnerabilities.	Social media users help program participants by creating online groups, events, and additional online support through which program participants are learning on how to cope with their family relationship conflict. Increased comparison on social media in terms of parent roles and expectations caused relationship conflicts among program participants. When	More platforms on the internet and through media can provide additional resources to participants. Misinformation about children and families with special health needs create vulnerabilities for program participants.	State foster care program offers support regarding behavioral interventions and support foster care families. Social media and the internet can be used to connect with other families to learn and share each other's experiences.	State level support, options, and programs provide support and resources with additional guidance to program participants. State and federal level support offer to those who are eligible based on certain criteria, which decreases these support systems to limited individuals and families.	School administrative offices and districts have limited resources to help and support local schools in the community to deal with school shooting. Hands-on trainings are offered to local school teachers and staff.

(Continued)

(Continued)

Questions	Group 1	Group 2	Group 3	Group 4	Group 5	Group 6
and a vulnerability due to high students' loan related policies/programs at the influential level.		program participants watch other parents who are doing poor in coping with their family relationship conflict, they feel guilty.				
Based on the stakeholders that you identified for your program participants at the holistic level (the third level) of the MCEM, what resources and vulnerabilities can those stakeholders create for your program participants at the holistic level in	High SES families can generate funds to support program participants. Other families can share additional strategies and resources with program participants. Discussions and sharing of high SES and urban families can be frustrating and stressful for	Parents with children older than 12 years old can support and guide the program participants and share important strategies with them. These families who are different from program participants and have children older	Diverse families will share their experiences and strategies with program participants. Expert families who successfully went through these situations can provide important suggestions to program participants.	Families with no experience or success with similar situations can create confusion. Different families can offer social support to the program participants.	Families of different SES backgrounds provide support and guide the program participants. Due to limited time, families may not get sufficient support.	Lack of awareness on the prevalence and facts on mass shooting among immigrant families can create confusion.

relation to your program? For instance, your participants (e.g., children or adolescents) may experience a resource of cultural belonging or support and a vulnerability due to their disability, sexual orientation and/or family structure (e.g., single parent family) at the holistic level.	program participants.	than 12 years have different views and cultures, which can create challenges for program participants. These different cultural families can share their parenting practices in their cultural context with program participants, which may help to expand the knowledge and skills or at least their learning on how to cope with relationship conflict in the family in different cultures. Program participants may find some coping strategies or practices useful to help themselves in handling their family relationship conflict.

(Continued)

(Continued)

Questions	Group 1	Group 2	Group 3	Group 4	Group 5	Group 6
How have these resources and vulnerabilities of your participants changed over time, and affected by developmental, sociocultural, and historical contexts in relation to your program? For instance, your participants (e.g., children or adolescents) currently use social media as a resource more actively compared to 1960s. Describe the changes over time.	Daily stressors are more frequent in today's society due to additional demands from work, school, and families, which affect the development and functioning of program participants.	In the past before 1960, the comparison was less on social media but in the current society social media users are quite active and program participants can access, watch, and interact with them more frequently that was not possible in the past, consequently, when they compare them with their current family situation and conflicts, the negative influences and the vulnerabilities of social media users on program participants is much greater than the past.	More awareness and sensitivity for families and children with special needs compared to the past. Technology and its use are also more prevalent in the current society compared to the past.	The government programs and policies are changing and improving to support these families. Due to this additional support, foster care families are growing and developing well.	Families with special needs became more inclusive and supportive language is used.	The perception of safety among children has been changed. Due to an increased understanding and its effects about school shooting helped children and their families to cope and survive compared to the past.

Appendix 217

Include a SAMREEN program objective(s).	Participants will learn research on daily stressors, their impacts on participants' lives, and practice effective coping strategies to deal with daily stressors.	Participants will learn the reasons and factors that lead to relationship problems and poor family functioning, and practice important steps for problem solving.	Participants will learn about important resources in school, community, and family which parents can use to support their children and family development.	Participants will learn and practice tips and coping strategies to effectively adapt to new situations, transitions, and relationships due to an addition of a new family member.	Participants will learn how to support themselves and local community families who have children with special needs.	Participants will learn the impacts of mass violence on individuals and family functioning, learn, and practice effective coping strategies to deal with this trauma.
The MCEM program curriculum (learners also complete the MCEM lesson plan template which is included at the end of Chapter 10).	Participants will watch videos on daily stressors and their impacts on their lives. A list of coping strategies to deal with daily stressors will be provided to participants as a resource. Small and large group discussions will be held.	Participants will be provided with an informational resource which informs participants on different ways and processes to resolve relationship problems. Participants learn research on relationship problems and conflict. Participants will also receive contact	Participants will receive information on those organizations which provide services and support to children with special needs.	Participants will learn and practice important coping strategies to adapt to new transitions and changes in the family due to a new family member. Participants will have small and large group discussions on how to manage and adapt to new family members. Participants will receive tips and information on	Participants will learn about the resources and support systems in school and community that support families and children with special needs. Participants will also learn and practice how to provide social, emotional, financial, and instrumental support to these families.	Participants will watch videos on situations and experience of individuals, families, and communities during and after mass shooting. Participants will also learn about different interventions and strategies to prevent and cope with mass shooting. Participants will receive information on who to contact in case of any mass

(Continued)

(Continued)

Questions	Group 1	Group 2	Group 3	Group 4	Group 5	Group 6
		information of organizations and professionals which provide counseling to couples and families on relationship problems and conflicts.		additional community support for these families. Games will be held to demonstrate the topic.		shooting and safety procedures. Role plays will be performed to demonstrate a real-life application of the topic.
The MCEM program implementation and delivery	Sharing, discussions, and presentation.	Engagement, collaboration, various modalities of teaching.	Real-life experiences and application. Discussions and performance.	Games, class activities, discussions, sharing, and collaboration.	Debates, class engagement, reflection activities, and discussions in class will be conducted.	Class survey, discussion, performance, collaboration, and real-life application.
Participants' learning styles and needs	Various audio/visual ads for learning. Learners' friendly instructions.	Foster social, individual, and collaborative learning.	Respect and welcome participants' views and opinions.	Provide participants additional time and safe environment when they needed to follow along the contents.	Poster presentation, chart writing and sharing, and class engagement activity. Learners' friendly instructions and various modes of learning.	Creativity, excitement, and relevance. Inclusion and active participation.

Appendix

Cultural and ethical challenges	Respect and promote all cultures. Ask participants to share their cultures and family life. Provide fair opportunities to all participants. Provide additional help and support to those participants who need it.	Share diverse cultures and provide participants with opportunities to share their cultures. Respect the views and opinions of all participants.	Provide additional accommodation to participants with special needs.	Learn about participants' culture, ensure inclusion, and respectful environment. Ask participants to share the cultures and family life.	Provide additional accommodation to participants with special needs. Respect the views and opinions of all participants.	Promote and encourage participants of all backgrounds. Remove barrier and stigma to participate, share, and speak. Use audio/visual aids which are appropriate, effective, and representative of all cultures. Ask participants to share their cultures and family life.
Overall reflections and lesson learned	Learned use and application of the MCEM framework in developing programs. Learned coping to manage daily stressors.	Learned how to manage and resolve personal relationship problems and conflicts.	Learn the challenges and support systems of children and families with special needs.	Learned how to use the knowledge and skills in real-world situations.	Increased knowledge and skills on working with children and families with special needs.	Learned how to help families in case of any mass violence by providing them with appropriate resources and support.

REFERENCES

Abbak Kacar, B. S., & Deretarla Gul, E. (2024). Peer-mediated education and autism spectrum disorder (ASD) in preschool inclusive programs: The power of games. *Early Years: An International Journal of Research and Development.* https://doi.org/10.1080/09575146.2024.2349756

Abell, L., Downey, D., & Pacheco, P. (2023). Institutionalizing community-based research: A case study of articulated program development. *Metropolitan Universities, 34*(5), 1047–8485.

Ajaps, S. (2023). Deconstructing the constraints of justice-based environmental sustainability in higher education. *Teaching in Higher Education, 28*(5), 1024–1038. https://doi.org/10.1080/13562517.2023.2198639

al'Absi, M., Ginty, A. T., & Lovallo, W. R. (2021). Neurobiological mechanisms of early life adversity, blunted stress reactivity and risk for addiction. *Neuropharmacology, 188.* https://doi.org/10.1016/j.neuropharm.2021.108519

Aldaheri, N., Guzman, G., & Stewart, H. (2023). Reciprocal knowledge sharing: Exploring professional–cultural knowledge sharing between expatriates and local nurses. *Journal of Knowledge Management, 27*(5), 1483–1505. https://doi.org/10.1108/JKM-10-2021-0735

Alzahrani, A. S., Tsai, Y.-S., Aljohani, N., Whitelock-wainwright, E., & Gasevic, D. (2023). Do teaching staff trust stakeholders and tools in learning analytics? A mixed methods study. *Educational Technology Research & Development, 71*(4), 1471–1501. https://doi.org/10.1007/s11423-023-10229-w

Amjad, F., Rao, Y., Rahman, A. U., Mohsin, M., & Sarfraz, M. (2024). Fostering sustainability through the green HRM and green inclusive leadership: The dual mediating role of creative self-efficacy and green skill competency. *Current Psychology: A Journal for Diverse Perspectives on Diverse Psychological Issues.* https://doi.org/10.1007/s12144-024-06027-z

An, J. (2021). Learning to teach students with disabilities through community service-learning: Physical education preservice teachers' experiences. *International Journal of Disability, Development and Education, 68*(3), 442–455. https://doi.org/10.1080/1034912X.2019.1693034

An, T., Wu, P., Wang, J., Zhang, H., & Chen, Z. (2024). The relationship between teaching experience and teaching outcomes in online teaching during the COVID-19 pandemic: The mediating role of teaching engagement. *Psychology in the Schools.* https://doi.org/10.1002/pits.23204

Anderson, J. B. (2000). *Service-learning and preservice teacher education.* Learning in Deed Issue Paper. Education Commission of the States, Denver, CO. Kellogg Foundation, Battle Creek, MI.

Anderson, K. L., Pierce, M. E., & McNamara, K. M. (2022). NUMB3Rs revisited: Long-term impacts of reimagining service learning. *Journal of Experiential Education, 45*(1), 51–67. https://doi.org/10.1177/1053825920973692

Angel, C. M. (2021). Assessing student achievement of learning outcomes through academic service-learning: A constructive alignment study. *Journal of Higher Education Theory & Practice, 21*(8), 166–194. https://doi.org/10.33423/jhetp.v21i8.4513

Anona, K., Olaomi, O., Udegbe, E., Uwumiro, F., Tuaka, E.-B., Okafor, N., Adeyinka, A., Obijuru, C., Okpujie, V., Bojerenu, M., & Opeyemi, M. (2024). Co-occurrence of bipolar disorder and personality disorders in the United States: Prevalence, suicidality, and the impact of substance abuse. *Journal of Affective Disorders, 345*, 1–7. https://doi.org/10.1016/j.jad.2023.10.087

Apanasionok, M. M., Neil, J., Watkins, R. C., Grindle, C. F., & Hastings, R. P. (2020). Teaching science to students with developmental disabilities using the early science curriculum. *Support for Learning, 35*(4), 493–505. https://doi.org/10.1111/1467-9604.12329

Aranbarri, A., Stahmer, A. C., Talbott, M. R., Miller, M. E., Drahota, A., Pellecchia, M., Barber, A. B., Griffith, E. M., Morgan, E. H., & Rogers, S. J. (2021). Examining US public early intervention for toddlers with autism: Characterizing services and readiness for evidence-based practice implementation. *Frontiers in Psychiatry, 12.* https://doi.org/10.3389/fpsyt.2021.786138

Arnell, S., Jerlinder, K., Geidne, S., & Lundqvist, L.-O. (2022). Experiences of stakeholder collaboration when promoting participation in physical activity among adolescents with autism spectrum disorder. *Disability & Rehabilitation: An*

International, Multidisciplinary Journal, 44(9), 1728–1736. https://doi.org/10.1080/09638288.2021.1887944

Arvola, O., Pankakoski, K., Reunamo, J., & Kyttälä, M. (2021). Culturally and linguistically diverse children's participation and social roles in the Finnish early childhood education – Is play the common key? *Early Child Development and Care, 191*(15), 2351–2363. https://doi.org/10.1080/03004430.2020.1716744

Aubry, A. (2023). *Promoting healthy identity development and mitigating minority stress among Black and African American transgender and gender-expansive young people using children's literature [ProQuest Information & Learning].* In Dissertation Abstracts International Section A: Humanities and Social Sciences (Vol. 84, Issue 11–A).

Auriemma, D. L., Ding, Y., Zhang, C., Rabinowitz, M., Shen, Y., & Lantier, G. K. (2022). Parenting stress in parents of children with learning disabilities: Effects of cognitions and coping styles. *Learning Disabilities Research & Practice, 37*(1), 51–63. https://doi.org/10.1111/ldrp.12265

Ayton, K., & Capraro, K. (2021). Students lead the charge! Using project-based learning with preservice teachers to redesign a curriculum resource center. *Education Libraries, 44*, 1–19. https://doi.org/10.26443/el.v44i1.367

Azor, R. O., Asogwa, U. D., Ogwu, E. N., & Apeh, A. A. (2020). YouTube audio-visual documentaries: Effect on Nigeria students' achievement and interest in history curriculum. *The Journal of Educational Research, 113*(5), 317–326. https://doi.org/10.1080/00220671.2020.1819182

Bacci, J. L., Zaraa, S., Stergachis, A., Simic, G., & Steve White, H. (2021). Stakeholder perceptions of community pharmacist population health management of people living with epilepsy. *Epilepsy and Behavior, 125.* https://doi.org/10.1016/j.yebeh.2021.108389

Bagnall, C. L., Fox, C. L., & Skipper, Y. (2021). What emotional-centred challenges do children attending special schools face over primary–secondary school transition? *Journal of Research in Special Educational Needs, 21*(2), 156–167. https://doi.org/10.1111/1471-3802.12507

Bajaj, G., Mohammed, C. A., Sahoo, S., Datta, A., Badyal, D., & Singh, T. (2024). Online role-plays: An asynchronous pedagogy for introducing tenets of interprofessional education and practice among Indian healthcare professionals. *Innovations in Education & Teaching International, 61*(1), 114–127. https://doi.org/10.1080/14703297.2022.2160368

Baker, R. S., & O'Connell, H. A. (2022). Structural racism, family structure, and black–white inequality: The differential impact of the legacy of slavery on poverty among single mother and married parent households. *Journal of Marriage and Family*. https://doi.org/10.1111/jomf.12837

Ballard, S. M. (2020). The practice of family life education: Toward an implementation framework. *Family Relations: An Interdisciplinary Journal of Applied Family Studies*, 69(3), 461–478. https://doi.org/10.1111/fare.12443

Bannon, S. M., Taggart, T. C., Kehoe, C. M., & O'Leary, K. D. (2020). Collaborative communication efficiency is linked to relationship satisfaction in dating couples. *Personal Relationships*, 27(2), 385–400. https://doi.org/10.1111/pere.12319

Barajas-Gonzalez, R. G., Torres, H. L., Urcuyo, A., Salamanca, E., & Kourousias, L. (2022). Racialization, discrimination, and depression: A mixed-method study of the impact of an anti-immigrant climate on Latina immigrant mothers and their children. *SSM Mental Health*, 2. https://doi.org/10.1016/j.ssmmh.2022.100084

Barth, M., Adomßent, M., Fischer, D., Richter, S., & Rieckmann, M. (2014). Learning to change universities from within: A service-learning perspective on promoting sustainable consumption in higher education. *Journal of Cleaner Production*, 62(1), 72–81. https://doi.org/10.1016/j.jclepro.2013.04.006

Basilici, M. C., Palladino, B. E., & Menesini, E. (2022). Ethnic diversity and bullying in school: A systematic review. *Aggression and Violent Behavior*, 65, 1–12. https://doi.org/10.1016/j.avb.2022.101762

Batastini, A. B., Jones, A. C. T., Lester, M. E., & Davis, R. M. (2020). Initiation of a multidisciplinary telemental health clinic for rural justice-involved populations: Rationale, recommendations, and lessons learned. *Journal of Community Psychology*, 48(7), 2156–2173. https://doi.org/10.1002/jcop.22424

Behmanesh, F., Bakouei, F., Nikpour, M., & Parvaneh, M. (2022). Comparing the effects of traditional teaching and flipped classroom methods on midwifery students' practical learning: The embedded mixed method. *Technology, Knowledge and Learning: Learning Mathematics, Science and the Arts in the Context of Digital Technologies*, 27(2), 599–608. https://doi.org/10.1007/s10758-020-09478-y

Bell, J., Lim, A., Williams, R., Girdler, S., Milbourn, B., & Black, M. (2021). 'Nothing about us without us': Co-production ingredients for working alongside stakeholders to develop mental health interventions. *Advances in Mental Health*. https://doi.org/10.1080/18387357.2021.2020143

Bennett Murphy, L., Thornton, J., & Thornton, E. (2022). Psychological adjustment of siblings of children with Prader-Willi syndrome. *Journal of Intellectual and Developmental Disability*. https://doi.org/10.3109/13668250.2022.2132630

Berezan, O., Krishen, A. S., & Garcera, S. (2023). Back to the basics: Handwritten journaling, student engagement, and Bloom's learning outcomes. *Journal of Marketing Education, 45*(1), 5–17. https://doi.org/10.1177/02734753221075557

Berger, E., Reupert, A., Stewart, S., Miko, A., Holford, T., & Stracey, L. (2024). School-based well-being programs for children living in regional and rural Australia: Stakeholder views. *Current Psychology: A Journal for Diverse Perspectives on Diverse Psychological Issues*. https://doi.org/10.1007/s12144-024-05853-5

Berman, S. (2015). *Service learning: A guide to planning, implementing, and assessing student projects* (2nd ed.). Skyhorse Publishing.

Bibbo, C., Bustamante, A., Wang, L., Friedman, F., Jr., & Chen, K. T. (2015). Toward a better understanding of gender-based performance in the obstetrics and gynecology clerkship: Women outscore men on the NBME subject examination at one medical school. *Academic Medicine, 90*(3), 379–383. https://doi.org/10.1097/ACM.0000000000000612

Birrell, L., Barrett, E., Oliver, E., Nguyen, A., Ewing, R., Anderson, M., & Teesson, M. (2024). The impact of arts-inclusive programs on young children's mental health and wellbeing: A rapid review. *Arts & Health: International Journal of Research in Pharmacology & Pharmacotherapeutics*. https://doi.org/10.1080/17533015.2024.2319032

Bjerke, M. B., & Renger, R. (2017). Being smart about writing SMART objectives. *Evaluation and Program Planning, 61*, 125–127.

Blocklin, M., Crouter, A. C., & McHale, S. M. (2012). Youth supervision while mothers work: A daily diary study of maternal worry. *Community, Work & Family, 15*, 233–249.

Bődi, C. B., Ortega, D. P., Hawkins, L. B., James, T. G., & Bright, M. A. (2023). Parents' and professionals' perspectives on school-based maltreatment prevention education for children with intellectual and developmental disabilities. *Child Abuse & Neglect, 145*, 1–9. https://doi.org/10.1016/j.chiabu.2023.106428

Bolger, L., & Murphy, M. (2024). Understanding the impact of international music therapy student placements on music therapy practice and professional identity. *Nordic Journal of Music Therapy, 33*(3), 189–207. https://doi.org/10.1080/08098131.2023.2268692

Bonesso, S., Cortellazzo, L., & Gerli, F. (2024). Developing leadership behaviours in higher education: A quasi-experimental study on the effect of experiential learning. *Innovations in Education & Teaching International, 61*(1), 70–84. https://doi.org/10.1080/14703297.2023.2214125

Bong, J. Y., Cho, K., Liu, Z., & He, D. (2024). A dual-process motivation mediation model to explain female high school students' cognitive engagement and disengagement in emergency remote teaching and online learning in South Korea. *British Journal of Educational Technology, 55*(3), 1020–1040. https://doi.org/10.1111/bjet.13415

Bowlby, J. (1958). The nature of the child's tie to his mother. *International Psychoanalysis, 39*, 350–373.

Bowlby, J. (1960). Grief and mourning in infancy and early childhood. *Psychoanalytic Study of the Child, 15*, 9–52.

Boye, K., & Evertsson, M. (2021). Who gives birth (first) in female same-sex couples in Sweden? *Journal of Marriage and Family, 83*(4), 925–941. https://doi.org/10.1111/jomf.12727

Boysen, G. A. (2024). Lessons (not) learned: The troubling similarities between learning styles and universal design for learning. *Scholarship of Teaching and Learning in Psychology, 10*(2), 207–221. https://doi.org/10.1037/stl0000280

Bredehoft, D. J., & Cassidy, D. (Eds.). (1995). *Family life education curriculum guidelines*. National Council on Family Relations.

Bredehoft, D. J., & Walcheski, M. J. (Eds.). (2011). *The family life education framework poster and PowerPoint*. National Council on Family Relations.

Brewster, M., Velez, B., Sawyer, J., Motulsky, W., Chan, A., & Kim, V. (2021). Family religiosity, support, and psychological well-being for sexual minority atheist individuals. *Psychology of Religion and Spirituality, 13*(3), 266–275. https://doi.org/10.1037/rel0000356

Broadbent, J., Sharman, S., Panadero, E., & Fuller-Tyszkiewicz, M. (2021). How does self-regulated learning influence formative assessment and summative grade? Comparing online and blended learners. *The Internet and Higher Education, 50*, 1–8. https://doi.org/10.1016/j.iheduc.2021.100805

References

Bronfenbrenner, U. (1978). The social role of the child in ecological perspective. *Zeitschrift fur Soziologie, 7*, 4–20.

Bronfenbrenner, U. (1979). *The ecology of human development: Experiments in nature and design.* Harvard University Press.

Brown, C. E., Boness, C. L., & Sheerin, K. M. (2022). Supporting students in health service psychology training: A theory-driven approach to meeting the diverse needs of trainees. *Training and Education in Professional Psychology, 16*(1), 78–86. https://doi.org/10.1037/tep0000354

Brown, S., Carbone, J. T., Hicks, L. M., Saini, E. K., Panisch, L. S., & Dayton, C. J. (2023). The moderating role of social support on the cortisol stress response of expectant fathers exposed to adverse childhood experiences. *Journal of Family Violence.* https://doi.org/10.1007/s10896-023-00555-1

Brown, C. P., Ku, D. H., & Englehardt, J. (2023). Mixed understandings: A case study of how a sample of preschool stakeholders made sense of the changed kindergarten. *Early Childhood Education Journal, 51*(3), 545–557. https://doi.org/10.1007/s10643-022-01315-4

Brown, J., McDonald, M., Besse, C., Manson, P., McDonald, R., Rohatinsky, N., & Singh, M. (2020). Anxiety, mental illness, learning disabilities, and learning accommodation use: A cross-sectional study. *Journal of Professional Nursing, 36*(6), 579–586. https://doi.org/10.1016/j.profnurs.2020.08.007

Bruck, S., Webster, A. A., & Clark, T. (2022). Transition support for students on the autism spectrum: A multiple stakeholder perspective. *Journal of Research in Special Educational Needs, 22*(1), 3–17. https://doi.org/10.1111/1471-3802.12509

Brummett, E. A., & Afifi, T. D. (2019). A grounded theory of interracial romantic partners' expectations for support and strain with family members. *Journal of Family Communication, 19*(3), 191–212. https://doi.org/10.1080/15267431.2019.1623220

Buldu, E. (2022). What is the state of play? Reintroducing 'role-playing' in higher education as an extension of dramatic play. *International Journal of Play, 11*(4), 357–362. https://doi.org/10.1080/21594937.2022.2136635

Bush, K. R. & Price, C. A. (Eds.). (2020). *Families & change: Coping with stressful events and transitions* (6th ed.). Sage Publications. ISBN: 9781544371245.

Cahill, P. T., Ng, S., Dix, L., Ferro, M. A., Turkstra, L., & Campbell, W. N. (2022). Outcomes management practices in tiered school-based speech–language therapy: A Canadian example. *International Journal of Language & Communication Disorders*. https://doi.org/10.1111/1460-6984.12822

Cahill, P. T., Reitzel, M., Anaby, D. R., Camden, C., Phoenix, M., Romoff, S., & Campbell, W. N. (2023). Supporting rehabilitation stakeholders in making service delivery decisions: A rapid review of multi-criteria decision analysis methods. *Disability and Rehabilitation: An International, Multidisciplinary Journal, 45*(12), 1933–1946. https://doi.org/10.1080/09638288.2022.2080285

Çakın, B., Glas, S., & Spierings, N. (2024). Polarization, religiosity, and support for gender equality: A comparative study across four Muslim-majority countries. *Women's Studies International Forum, 103*, 1–10. https://doi.org/10.1016/j.wsif.2024.102880

Calderon, P. S. P., Wong, J. D., & Hodgdon, B. T. (2022). A scoping review of the physical health and psychological well-being of individuals in interracial romantic relationships. *Family Relations: An Interdisciplinary Journal of Applied Family Studies, 71*(5), 2011–2029. https://doi.org/10.1111/fare.12765

Camus, R. M., Lam, C. H. Y., Ngai, G., & Chan, S. C. F. (2022). Service-learning exchange in developed cities: Dissonances and civic outcomes. *Journal of Experiential Education, 45*(4), 453–476. https://doi.org/10.1177/10538259211065971

Camus, R. M., Ngai, G., Kwan, K. P., Lau, K. H., & Chan, S. (2023). Teaching reflection in service-learning: Disciplinary differences in conception and practice. *Reflective Practice, 24*(6), 766–783. https://doi.org/10.1080/14623943.2023.2264204

Caravita, S. C. S., Stefanelli, S., Mazzone, A., Cadei, L., Thornberg, R., & Ambrosini, B. (2020). When the bullied peer is native-born vs immigrant: A mixed-method study with a sample of native-born and immigrant adolescents. *Scandinavian Journal of Psychology, 61*(1), 97–107. https://doi.org/10.1111/sjop.12565

Carlson, D. L. (2022). Reconceptualizing the gendered division of housework: Number of shared tasks and partners' relationship quality. *Sex Roles: Journal of Research*. https://doi.org/10.1007/s11199-022-01282-5

Carlson, R. G., Barden, S. M., Locklear, L., Taylor, D. D., & Carroll, N. (2022). Examining quality time as a mediator of dyadic change in a randomized controlled trial of relationship education for low-income couples. *Journal of Marital and Family Therapy, 48*(2), 484–501. https://doi.org/10.1111/jmft.12554

Carpenter, J. G., Scott, W. J., Kononowech, J., Foglia, M. B., Haverhals, L. M., Hogikyan, R., Kolanowski, A., Landis, L. Z., Levy, C., Miller, S. C., Periyakoil, V. J., Phibbs, C. S., Potter, L., Sales, A., & Ersek, M. (2022). Evaluating implementation strategies to support documentation of veterans' care preferences. *Health Services Research, 57*(4), 734–743. https://doi.org/10.1111/1475-6773.13958

Casquero, M. N., Núñez, A. M. A., & Iniesto, A. M. J. (2022). Effects of small-group learning on the assessment of professional skills through a PBL activity. *Transactions in GIS, 26*(4), 1735–1753. https://doi.org/10.1111/tgis.12897

Castellini, G., Tarchi, L., Cassioli, E., Rossi, E., Sanfilippo, G., Innocenti, M., Gironi, V., Scami, I., & Ricca, V. (2022). Attachment style and childhood traumatic experiences moderate the impact of initial and prolonged COVID-19 pandemic: Mental health longitudinal trajectories in a sample of Italian women. *International Journal of Mental Health and Addiction.* https://doi.org/10.1007/s11469-022-00798-x

Cecilia, K. Y. C. (2022). *Assessment for experiential learning.* Routledge.

Centers for Disease Control and Prevention. (2018). Evaluation briefs. https://www.cdc.gov/healthyyouth/evaluation/pdf/brief3b.pdf

Chambers, D., & Lavery, S. (2017). Introduction to service-learning and inclusive education. In S. Lavery, D. Chambers, & G. Cain (Eds.), *Service-learning: Enhancing inclusive education* (Vol. 12, pp. 3–19). Emerald Publishing Limited.

Chambers, D., & Lavery, S. (2022). International service learning: Benefits, challenges, and experiences of pre-service teachers. *Asia-Pacific Journal of Teacher Education, 50*(5), 498–514. https://doi.org/10.1080/1359866X.2022.2050355

Chan, C. K. Y. (2022). *Assessment for experiential learning.* Routledge Research in Education. https://www.routledge.com/Assessment-for-Experiential-Learning/Chan/p/book/9781032318196

Chan, S., Maneewan, S., & Koul, R. (2023). An examination of the relationship between the perceived instructional behaviours of teacher educators and pre-service teachers' learning motivation and teaching self-efficacy. *Educational Review, 75*(2), 264–286. https://doi.org/10.1080/00131911.2021.1916440

Charlesworth, T. E. S., & Banaji, M. R. (2022). Patterns of implicit and explicit stereotypes III: Long-term change in gender stereotypes. *Social Psychological and Personality Science*, *13*(1), 14–26. https://doi.org/10.1177/1948550620988425

Chen, Y.-L., Murthi, K., Martin, W., Vidiksis, R., Riccio, A., & Patten, K. (2022). Experiences of students, teachers, and parents participating in an inclusive, school-based informal engineering education program. *Journal of Autism and Developmental Disorders*, *52*(8), 3574–3585. https://doi.org/10.1007/s10803-021-05230-2

Chen, S., & van Ours, J. C. (2022). Mental health effects of same-sex marriage legalization. *Health Economics*, *31*(1), 42–56. https://doi.org/10.1002/hec.4441

Cho, Y., & Egan, T. (2023). The changing landscape of action learning research and practice. *Human Resource Development International*, *26*(4), 378–404. https://doi.org/10.1080/13678868.2022.2124584

Choi, S., Byoun, S.-J., & Kim, E. H. (2020). Unwed single mothers in South Korea: Increased vulnerabilities during the COVID-19 pandemic. *International Social Work*, *63*(5), 676–680. https://doi.org/10.1177/0020872820941040

Chow, E. H. Y., & Tiwari, A. (2020). Addressing the needs of abused Chinese women through a community-based participatory approach. *Journal of Nursing Scholarship*, *52*(3), 242–249. https://doi.org/10.1111/jnu.12546

Chung, S. (2020). *Teachers' conception of reflection in service-learning*. Routledge.

Clark, S. K., & Andreasen, L. (2021). Exploring elementary teacher self-efficacy and teacher beliefs: Are we preparing teachers to teach culturally diverse students? *Asia-Pacific Journal of Teacher Education*, *49*(1), 128–142. https://doi.org/10.1080/1359866X.2020.1777528

Clarke, L. (2022). The need to include intellectual/developmental disability in medical school curriculum: The perspective of a student advocate. *Journal of Intellectual and Developmental Disability*. https://doi.org/10.3109/13668250.2022.2111770

Coba-Rodriguez, S., & Lleras, C. L. (2022). Nonstandard work and preschool child development in single mother families: Exploring the role of maternal depression and parenting stress. *Marriage & Family Review*, *58*(8), 726–747. https://doi.org/10.1080/01494929.2022.2042883

References

Coenraad, M., Palmer, J., Eatinger, D., Weintrop, D., & Franklin, D. (2022). Using participatory design to integrate stakeholder voices in the creation of a culturally relevant computing curriculum. *International Journal of Child-Computer Interaction, 31*, 1–14. https://doi.org/10.1016/j.ijcci.2021.100353

Coleman, O. F., McDonnell, J., Jameson, J. M., Johnston, S. S., Farrell, M., Malbica, A., & Conradi, L. A. (2023). Curricular content of the individualized education programs of students with a significant cognitive disability. *Education and Training in Autism and Developmental Disabilities, 58*(4), 396–407.

Colistra, R., & Johnson, C. B. (2021). Framing the legalization of marriage for same-sex couples: An examination of news coverage surrounding the US Supreme Court's landmark decision. *Journal of Homosexuality, 68*(1), 88–111. https://doi.org/10.1080/00918369.2019.1627128

Compare, C., Pieri, C., & Albanesi, C. (2022). Community-university partnership in service-learning: Voicing the community side. *Journal of Higher Education Outreach and Engagement, 26*(2), 79–102.

Connors, S. K., Leal, I. M., Nitturi, V., Iwundu, C. N., Maza, V., Reyes, S., Acquati, C., & Reitzel, L. R. (2021). Empowered choices: African-American women's breast reconstruction decisions. *American Journal of Health Behavior, 45*(2), 352–370. https://doi.org/10.5993/AJHB.45.2.14

Cooper, J. R. (2014). Ten years in the trenches: Faculty perspectives on sustaining service-learning. *Journal of Experiential Education, 37*(4), 415–428. https://doi.org/10.1177/1053825913513721

Cooper, L. A., & Kotys-Schwartz, D. (2022). Designing the project-based learning experience using motivation theory. In Proceedings of the ASEE Annual Conference & Exposition (pp. 1–21).

Corneli, A., McKenna, K., Hanlen, R. E., Calvert, S. B., Mah, E., & Rosenfeld, S. J. (2023). Stakeholder reflections on implementing the National Institutes of Health's policy on single institutional review boards. *Ethics & Human Research, 45*(5), 15–26. https://doi.org/10.1002/eahr.500179

Costanzo, A., Santoro, G., & Schimmenti, A. (2023). Self-medication, traumatic reenactments, and dissociation: A psychoanalytic perspective on the relationship between childhood trauma and substance abuse. *Psychoanalytic Psychotherapy, 37*(4), 443–466. https://doi.org/10.1080/02668734.2023.2272761

Crabtree, R. D. (2013). The intended and unintended consequences of international service-learning. *Journal of Higher Education Outreach and Engagement, 17*(2), 43–66.

Cress, C. M., Stokamer, S. T., Van Cleave, T. J., & Kaufman, J. P. (2022). *Faculty service-learning guidebook: Enacting equity-centered teaching, partnerships, and scholarship*. Routledge.

Cress, C. M., Stokamer, S. T., Van Cleave, T. J., & Kaufman, J. P. (2023). *Faculty service-learning guidebook: Enacting equity-centered teaching, partnerships, and scholarship*. Routledge.

Creswell, J. W., & Creswell, J. D. (2018). *Research design: Qualitative, quantitative, and mixed methods approaches* (5th ed.). Sage Publications.

Cross, A. J., Etherton-Beer, C. D., Clifford, R. M., Potter, K., & Page, A. T. (2021). Exploring stakeholder roles in medication management for people living with dementia. *Research in Social and Administrative Pharmacy, 17*(4), 707–714. https://doi.org/10.1016/j.sapharm.2020.06.006

Cuesta-Hincapie, C., Cheng, Z., & Exter, M. (2024). Are we teaching novice instructional designers to be creative? A qualitative case study. *Instructional Science, 52*(3), 515–556. https://doi.org/10.1007/s11251-023-09656-2

Dai, X., Chu, X., Qi, G., Yuan, P., Zhou, Y., Xiang, H., & Shi, X. (2024). Worldwide perinatal intimate partner violence prevalence and risk factors for post-traumatic stress disorder in women: A systematic review and meta-analysis. *Trauma, Violence, & Abuse, 25*(3), 2363–2376. https://doi.org/10.1177/15248380231211950

Daif-Allah, A. S., & Al-Sultan, M. S. (2023). The effect of role-play on the development of dialogue skills among learners of Arabic as a second language. *Education Sciences, 13*(1), 1–12. https://doi.org/10.3390/educsci13010050

Darling, C. A., Cassidy, D., & Ballard, S. M. (2022). *Family life education: Working with families across the lifespan* (4th ed.). Waveland Press, Inc..

Darling, C. A., Cassidy, D., & Powell, L. (2014). *Family life education: Working with families across the lifespan* (3rd ed.). Waveland Press, Inc..

Darling, C. A., Cassidy, D., & Rehm, M. (2020). The foundations of family life education model: Understanding the field. *Family Relations: An Interdisciplinary Journal of Applied Family Studies, 69*(3), 427–441. https://doi.org/10.1111/fare.12372

Dashtestani, R., & Mohamadi, A. (2023). In-service teachers' conceptualization of implementing interactive learning in online and face-to-face teaching contexts: Challenges and opportunities. *Interactive Learning Environments.* https://doi.org/10.1080/10494820.2023.2255240

Davis, S. A., Howard, K., Ellis, A. R., Jonas, D. E., Carey, T. S., Morrissey, J. P., & Thomas, K. C. (2022). Feasibility of a best–worst scaling exercise to set priorities for autism research. *Health Expectations: An International Journal of Public Participation in Health Care & Health Policy.* https://doi.org/10.1111/hex.13508

Davis, C., Chan, B. Y.-L., Ong, A. S. Z., Koh, Y., Yap, A. F. H. W., Goh, S. H., & Vidyarthi, A. R. (2021). An evaluation of a medical student international service-learning experience in Southeast Asia. *Education for Health: Change in Learning & Practice, 34*(1), 3–10. https://doi.org/10.4103/efh.EfH_265_17

de Heer, B., Heffern, J. K., Cheney, J. S., Secakuku, A., & Baldwin, J. (2020). A community-based evaluation of a culturally grounded, American Indian after-school prevention program: The value of practitioner-researcher collaboration. *American Indian & Alaska Native Mental Health Research, 27*(1), 1–20. https://doi.org/10.5820/aian.2701.2020.1

Deng, L., Shen, Y. W., & Chan, J. W. W. (2021). Supporting cross-cultural pedagogy with online tools: Pedagogical design and student perceptions. *TechTrends: Linking Research & Practice to Improve Learning, 65*(5), 760–770. https://doi.org/10.1007/s11528-021-00633-5

Dholakia, K., & Hartman, J. (2023). Transforming society through critical service-learning: A position for a justice-based approach to experiential learning in physical therapy education. *Journal, Physical Therapy Education, 37*(4), 264–270. https://doi.org/10.1097/jte.0000000000000299

DiGregorio, N. (2021). Language appropriation practices of gay men after the legalization of same-sex marriage. *Journal of Homosexuality, 68*(9), 1525–1544. https://doi.org/10.1080/00918369.2019.1701335

Dirix, J., Peeters, W., Eyckmans, J., Jones, P. T., & Sterckx, S. (2013). Strengthening bottom-up and top-down climate governance. *Climate Policy, 13,* 363–383. https://doi.org/10.1080/14693062.2013.752664

DiSantostefano, R. L., Smith, I. P., Falahee, M., Jiménez-Moreno, A. C., Oliveri, S., Veldwijk, J., de Wit, G. A., Janssen, E. M., Berlin, C., & Groothuis-Oudshoorn, C. G. M. (2024). Research priorities to increase confidence in and acceptance of health preference research: What questions should be prioritized now? *The Patient: Patient-Centered Outcomes Research, 17*(2), 179–190. https://doi.org/10.1007/s40271-023-00650-x

Domagala-Zyśk, E. (2021). Remote teaching and learning – Challenges and opportunities for students with special educational needs. *Revista Portuguesa de Investigação Educacional, 21.* https://doi.org/10.34632/investigacaoeducacional.2021.10042

Domenech Rodríguez, M. M., Reveles, A. K., Litson, K., Patterson, C. A., & Vázquez, A. L. (2022). Development of the awareness, skills, knowledge: General (ASK-G) scale for measuring cultural competence in the general population. *PLoS One, 17*(9). https://doi.org/10.1371/journal.pone.0274505

Donadio, M., Valera, P., & Sinangil, N. (2021). Understanding attachment styles, adverse childhood events, alcohol use, and trauma in black and Latino men with criminal justice histories. *Journal of Community Psychology.* https://doi.org/10.1002/jcop.22773

Doran, G. T. (1981). There's a SMART way to write management's goals and objectives. *Journal of Management Review, 70,* 35–36.

Duffy, K. A., Sammel, M. D., Johnson, R. L., Morrison, K. E., Bale, T. L., & Epperson, C. N. (2024). Sex differences in stress-induced cortisol response among infants of mothers exposed to childhood adversity. *Biological Psychiatry.* https://doi.org/10.1016/j.biopsych.2024.05.015

Dugan, K. A., Fraley, R. C., Gillath, O., & Deboeck, P. R. (2024). Testing the canalization hypothesis of attachment theory: Examining within-subject variation in attachment security. *Journal of Personality and Social Psychology, 126*(3), 511–541. https://doi.org/10.1037/pspp0000488

Duncan, S. F., & Goddard, H. W. (2017). *Family life education: Principles and practices for effective outreach* (3rd ed.). Sage Publications, Inc.

Dymond, S. K., Bonati, M. L., Plotner, A. J., & Neeper, L. S. (2024). Trends in secondary curriculum for transition-age students with severe disabilities. *Education and Training in Autism and Developmental Disabilities, 59*(1), 85–96.

Eagly, A. H., Nater, C., Miller, D. I., Kaufmann, M., & Sczesny, S. (2020). Gender stereotypes have changed: A cross-temporal meta-analysis of US public opinion polls from 1946 to 2018. *American Psychologist, 75*(3), 301–315. https://doi.org/10.1037/amp0000494

Egan, C. A., Orendorff, K. L., & Merica, C. B. (2024). Community partnership strategies to facilitate service-learning opportunities in PETE K–12 schools. *Journal of Physical Education, Recreation & Dance, 95*(3), 20–27. https://doi.org/10.1080/07303084.2023.2299879

Erchick, D. J., Gupta, M., Blunt, M., Bansal, A., Sauer, M., Gerste, A., Holroyd, T. A., Wahl, B., Santosham, M., & Limaye, R. J. (2022). Understanding determinants of vaccine hesitancy and acceptance in India: A qualitative study of government officials and civil society stakeholders. *PLoS One, 17*(6). https://doi.org/10.1371/journal.pone.0269606

Ermer, A. E., & Proulx, C. M. (2020). Social support and well-being among older adult married couples: A dyadic perspective. *Journal of Social and Personal Relationships, 37*(4), 1073–1091. https://doi.org/10.1177/0265407519886350

Esparza-Del Villar, O. A., Montañez-Alvarado, P., Gutiérrez-Vega, M., Quiñones-Rodríguez, S., & Gutiérrez-Rosado, T. (2022). Past child abuse and neglect in adults from northern Mexico: Development of a scale and prevalence. *Journal of Interpersonal Violence, 37*(5–6), 2851–2876. https://doi.org/10.1177/0886260520943729

Esper, S. C., Barin-Cruz, L., & Gond, J.-P. (2024). Engaging stakeholders during intergovernmental conflict: How political attributions shape stakeholder engagement. *Journal of Business Ethics, 191*(1), 1–27. https://doi.org/10.1007/s10551-023-05448-3

Evans, W., Gable, R. A., & Habib, A. (2021). Lessons from the past and challenges for the future: Inclusive education for students with unique needs. *Education Sciences, 11*(6), 1–10. https://doi.org/10.3390/educsci11060281

Fahmy, C. (2021). First weeks out: Social support stability and health among formerly incarcerated men. *Social Science & Medicine, 282*. https://doi.org/10.1016/j.socscimed.2021.114141

Fang, Y.-C., Ren, Y.-H., Chen, J.-Y., Chin, T., Yuan, Q., & Lin, C.-L. (2021). Inclusive leadership and career sustainability: Mediating roles of supervisor developmental feedback and thriving at work. *Frontiers in Psychology, 12*. https://doi.org/10.3389/fpsyg.2021.671663

Fatemi, M. J., Afrashteh, S., Zahmatkesh, S., Hemmati, A., & Fararouei, M. (2022). Prevalence and determinants of caregivers' self-reported child abuse among children aged 3–6 years in the south of Iran. *Child Abuse Review, 31*(6). https://doi.org/10.1002/car.2763

Faulconer, E., & Kam, C. J. Y. (2023). Service-learning in undergraduate general chemistry: A review. *Journal of Experiential Education, 46*(1), 32–51. https://doi.org/10.1177/10538259221092141

Feubli, P., MacKevett, D., & Schwarz, J. (2024). Hybrid teaching and learning: A conjoint analysis of student preferences in online and onsite scenarios. *Journal of Computer Assisted Learning, 40*(2), 761–774. https://doi.org/10.1111/jcal.12913

Feuerherm, E., Hiramatsu, K., Miller, N. S., & Williams, K. (2022). Assessing outcomes of service learning: Student, instructor, and community reflections. *Journal of Community Engagement and Higher Education, 14*(2), 4–18.

Finley, L. L. (2021). Showcasing the wealth of service-learning initiatives in Asia. *International Journal of Research on Service-Learning & Community Engagement, 9*(1), 1–3. https://doi.org/10.37333/001c.31309

Flack, C. E., Garbacz, S. A., Stormshak, E. A., & McIntyre, L. L. (2023). A longitudinal study of home-based involvement and dyadic adjustment during the transition to early elementary school. *School Psychologist, 38*(5), 287–293. https://doi.org/10.1037/spq0000543

Flanagan, J. C., Jarnecke, A. M., Leone, R. M., & Oesterle, D. W. (2020). Effects of couple conflict on alcohol craving: Does intimate partner violence play a role? *Addictive Behaviors, 109.* https://doi.org/10.1016/j.addbeh.2020.106474

Fleet, A., Shalev, D., Spaeth, R. B., Patterson, T., Wardlow, L., Simoun, A., Tomy, M., & Pincus, H. A. (2023). Behavioral health integration in the Program of All-Inclusive Care for the Elderly (PACE): A scoping review. *Journal of the American Geriatrics Society, 71*(9), 2956–2965. https://doi.org/10.1111/jgs.18416

Flicker, S. M., Sancier, B. F., Afroz, F., Saif, S. N., & Mohsin, F. (2020). Attachment hierarchies in Bangladeshi women in couple-initiated and arranged marriages. *International Journal of Psychology, 55*(4), 638–646. https://doi.org/10.1002/ijop.12619

Fogarty, A., Seymour, M., Savopoulos, P., Talevski, T., Ruthven, C., & Giallo, R. (2022). The COVID-19 pandemic and Australian parents with young children at risk of interparental conflict. *Journal of Reproductive and Infant Psychology.* https://doi.org/10.1080/02646838.2022.2084055

Forsyth, V. (2023). Can a picture book teach history? An investigation into the authority and relevance of informational history picture books for Australian, upper primary, school students. *Education 3–13*, *51*(7), 1064–1076. https://doi.org/10.1080/03004279.2022.2042829

Frame, N. (2021). Intragroup differences of the non-religious: Attitudes towards same-sex marriage and same-sex adoption in the United States. *Journal of Homosexuality*, *68*(13), 2285–2300. https://doi.org/10.1080/00918369.2020.1736430

Friedman, E. J., & Rodríguez Gustá, A. L. (2023). Feminists, popular feminists, and transfeminists: Young argentine activists define their own identities. *Journal of Youth Studies*. https://doi.org/10.1080/13676261.2023.2298318

Gallop, C. J., Guthrie, B., & Asante, N. (2023). The impact of experiential learning on professional identity: Comparing community service-learning to traditional practica pedagogy. *Journal of Experiential Education*, *46*(4), 474–490. https://doi.org/10.1177/10538259231154888

Gamage, K. A. A., Gamage, A., & Dehideniya, S. C. P. (2022). Online and hybrid teaching and learning: Enhance effective student engagement and experience. *Education Sciences*, *12*(10), 1–13. https://doi.org/10.3390/educsci12100651

Gao, J., Yang, L., Zhao, J., Wang, L., Zou, J., Wang, C., & Fan, X. (2020). Comparison of problem-based learning and traditional teaching methods in medical psychology education in China: A systematic review and meta-analysis. *PLoS One*, *15*(12). https://doi.org/10.1371/journal.pone.0243897

García, R. S. (2023). A service-learning program assessment: Strengths, weaknesses and impacts on students. *Intangible Capital*, *19*(1), 4–24. https://doi.org/10.3926/ic.2093

Garner, P. W., & Parker, T. S. (2016). Service-learning linking family child care providers, community partners, and preservice professionals. *Early Child Development and Care*, *186*(9), 1466–1475. https://doi.org/10.1080/03004430.2015.1102136

Garvey, W., O'Connor, M., Quach, J., & Goldfeld, S. (2020). Better support for children with additional health and developmental needs in school settings: Perspectives of education experts. *Child: Care, Health and Development*, *46*(4), 522–529. https://doi.org/10.1111/cch.12766

Garvin, M. C., & Acosta Lewis, E. (2022). Reasons faculty teach, or do not teach, service-learning courses in a pandemic: The role of faculty investment and clues for the future of service-learning. *Higher Learning Research Communications, 12*, 46–58.

Garwood, J. D., Peltier, C., Ciullo, S., Wissinger, D., McKenna, J. W., Giangreco, M. F., & Kervick, C. (2023). The experiences of students with disabilities actually doing service learning: A systematic review. *Journal of Experiential Education, 46*(1), 5–31. https://doi.org/10.1177/10538259221109374

Gato, J., Henriques, M. R., & Leal, D. (2021). Adoption by lesbian women and gay men: Perceived challenges and training needs for professionals in Portugal. *Adoption Quarterly, 24*(2), 152–175. https://doi.org/10.1080/10926755.2020.1834044

Gillispie, M. (2021). Culturally responsive language and literacy instruction with Native American children. *Topics in Language Disorders, 41*(2), 185–198. https://doi.org/10.1097/TLD.0000000000000249

Godier, M. L. R., Gillin, N., & Fossey, M. J. (2022). *'Treat everyone like they're a man': Stakeholder perspectives on the provision of health and social care support for female veterans in the UK.* Health & Social Care in the Community. https://doi.org/10.1111/hsc.13790

Godwin, K. E., Leroux, A. J., Seltman, H., Scupelli, P., & Fisher, A. V. (2022). Effect of repeated exposure to the visual environment on young children's attention. *Cognitive Science, 46*(2), 1–36. https://doi.org/10.1111/cogs.13093

Goldberg, M. J., & Iruka, I. U. (2023). The role of teacher–child relationship quality in Black and Latino boys' positive development. *Early Childhood Education Journal, 51*(2), 301–315. https://doi.org/10.1007/s10643-021-01300-3

Goldenberg, I., Stanton, M., & Goldenberg, H. (2017). *Family therapy: An overview* (9th ed.). Cengage.

Gong, X., Huebner, E. S., & Tian, L. (2021). Bullying victimization and developmental trajectories of internalizing and externalizing problems: The moderating role of locus of control among children. *Research on Child and Adolescent Psychopathology, 49*(3), 351–366. https://doi.org/10.1007/s10802-020-00752-2

Gong, Q., Kramer, K. Z., & Tu, K. M. (2023). Fathers' marital conflict and children's socioemotional skills: A moderated-mediation model of conflict resolution and parenting. *Journal of Family Psychology, 37*(7), 1048–1059. https://doi.org/10.1037/fam0001102

Gonzalez-DeHass, A. R., Willems, P. P., & Vásquez-Colina, M. D. (2021). Case study instruction experiences in educational psychology and pre-service teachers' achievement goals for learning. *Teaching of Psychology, 48*(3), 228–235. https://doi.org/10.1177/0098628320977267

Goodman, H. P., Yow, R., Standberry-Wallace, M., Dekom, R., Harper, M., Gomez, A. N., & Watson, A. D. (2023). Perspectives from community partnerships in three diverse higher education contexts. *Gateways: International Journal of Community Research and Engagement, 61*(2), 1–13. https://doi.org/10.5130/ijcre.v16i2.8693

Gradellini, C., Gómez-Cantarino, S., Dominguez-Isabel, P., Molina-Gallego, B., Mecugni, D., & Ugarte-Gurrutxaga, M. I. (2021). Cultural competence and cultural sensitivity education in university nursing courses. A scoping review. *Frontiers in Psychology, 12*. https://doi.org/10.3389/fpsyg.2021.682920

Graham, F., Boland, P., Grainger, R., & Wallace, S. (2020). Telehealth delivery of remote assessment of wheelchair and seating needs for adults and children: A scoping review. *Disability & Rehabilitation: An International, Multidisciplinary Journal, 42*(24), 3538–3548. https://doi.org/10.1080/09638288.2019.1595180

Greenberg, J., Hilton, E. C., Li, J. J., Lu, Q., & Mailick, M. R. (2021). The impact of parenting a child with serious mental illness: Accounting for the parent's genetic vulnerability to mental illness. *Journal of Family Psychology, 35*(3), 417–422. https://doi.org/10.1037/fam0000783

Hallé, M.-C., Bussières, A., Asseraf-Pasin, L., Storr, C., Mak, S., Root, K., Owens, H., Amari, F., & Thomas, A. (2024). Stakeholders' priorities in the development of evidence-based practice competencies in rehabilitation students: A nominal group technique study. *Disability & Rehabilitation: An International, Multidisciplinary Journal, 46*(14), 3196–3205. https://doi.org/10.1080/09638288.2023.2239138

Halsell, T. Y., & Gallant, D. J. (2022). Black undergraduate women: Intersectionality and engagement with high impact practices. In R. D. Mayes, M. C. Shavers, & J. L. MooreIII (Eds.), *African American young girls and women in preK12 schools and beyond: Informing research, policy, and practice* (Vol. 8, pp. 161–184). Emerald Publishing Limited. https://doi.org/10.1108/S2051-231720220000008008

Hamilton, P., & Dynes, R. (2023). From 'tiaras and twirls' to 'action and adventure' Eliciting children's gendered perceptions of Disney characters through participatory visual methodology. *International Journal of Early Years Education, 31*(2), 482–501. https://doi.org/10.1080/09669760.2022.2164259

Hamon, R. R., & Smith, S. R. (2014). The discipline of family science and the continuing need for innovation. *Family Relations: An Interdisciplinary Journal of Applied Family Studies, 63*(3), 309–322. https://doi.org/10.1111/fare.12068

Hamon, R. R., & Smith, S. R. (2017). Family science as translational science: A history of the discipline. *Family Relations: An Interdisciplinary Journal of Applied Family Studies, 66*(4), 550–567. https://doi.org/10.1111/fare.12273

Harding, J. F., Keating, B., Walzer, J., Xing, F., Zief, S., & Gao, J. (2022). How accurately can we predict repeat teen pregnancy based on social ecological factors? *Developmental Psychology, 58*(9), 1793–1805. https://doi.org/10.1037/dev0001394

Harkness, S., Super, C. M., Bonichini, S., Bermudez, M. R., Mavridis, C., Schaik, S. D. M., Tomkunas, A., & Palacios, J. (2020). Parents, preschools, and the developmental niches of young children: A study in four Western cultures. *New Directions for Child and Adolescent Development, 2020*(170), 113–141. https://doi.org/10.1002/cad.20343

Harrison, A. G., & Armstrong, I. (2022). Accommodation decision-making for postsecondary students with ADHD: Treating the able as disabled. *Psychological Injury and Law, 15*(4), 367–384. https://doi.org/10.1007/s12207-022-09461-1

Hastings, O. P., & Schneider, D. (2020). Family structure and inequalities in parents' financial investments in children. *Journal of Marriage and Family.* https://doi.org/10.1111/jomf.12741

Hayward, E., Solaiman, K., Bee, P., Barr, A., Edwards, H., Lomas, J., Tindall, L., Scott, A. J., Biggs, K., & Wright, B. (2022). One-session treatment for specific phobias: Barriers, facilitators and acceptability as perceived by children & young people, parents, and clinicians. *PLoS One, 17*(9). https://doi.org/10.1371/journal.pone.0274424

He, S., Demmans Epp, C., Chen, F., & Cui, Y. (2024). Examining change in students' self-regulated learning patterns after a formative assessment using process mining techniques. *Computers in Human Behavior, 152*, 1–13. https://doi.org/10.1016/j.chb.2023.108061

Henry, L., Reinke, W. M., Herman, K. C., Thompson, A. M., & Lewis, C. G. (2021). Motivational interviewing with at-risk students (MARS) mentoring: Addressing the unique mental health needs of students in alternative school placements. *School Psychology Review*, *50*(1), 62–74. https://doi.org/10.1080/2372966X.2020.1827679

Hearne, A., Miles, A., Clark, E., Brasell, S., Divers, E., Tong, A., & Wielenga, S. (2024). Developing a stakeholder led stuttering resource for teachers in New Zealand. *Speech, Language and Hearing*. https://doi.org/10.1080/2050571X.2024.2330200

Heesch, K. C., Hepple, E., Dingle, K., & Freeman, N. (2020). Establishing and implementing a health promoting school in rural Cambodia. *Health Promotion International*, *35*(1), e11–e20. https://doi.org/10.1093/heapro/day114

Heidelburg, K., & Collins, T. A. (2023). Development of black to success: A culturally enriched social skills program for black adolescent males. *School Psychology Review*, *52*(3), 316–329. https://doi.org/10.1080/2372966X.2021.2001691

Henert, S., Jacobs, J., & Wahl-Alexander, Z. (2021). Let's play! Exploring the impact of summer day camp participation on the physical and psychosocial experiences of diverse urban youth. *Child and Adolescent Social Work Journal*, *38*(4), 381–391. https://doi.org/10.1007/s10560-021-00769-6

Heras-Colàs, R., Masgrau-Juanola, M., Guiu-Puget, E., Soler-Masó, P., & Albertín-Carbó, P. (2023). Service learning for sustainability in the practicum phase of initial teacher training. *Profesorado: Revista de Currículum y Formación Del Profesorado*, *27*(1), 425–445. https://doi.org/10.30827/profesorado.v27i1.21466

Heron, L. M., & Bruk-Lee, V. (2023). Informing inclusive management practices for employees with developmental disabilities: A supervisor training needs analysis. *Consulting Psychology Journal*, *75*(4), 322–353. https://doi.org/10.1037/cpb0000261

Herr, K. (1995). Action research as empowering practice. *Journal of Progressive Human Services*, (6), 45–58. https://doi.org/10.1300/J059v06n02_04

Herr, K. (1999). Unearthing the unspeakable: When teacher research and political agendas collide. *Language Arts*, *77*(1), 10–15. www.jstor.org/stable/41483020

Herr, K. (2017). Insiders doing PAR with youth in their schools: Negotiating professional boundaries and healing justice. *International Journal of Qualitative Studies in Education, 30*, 450–463. https://doi.org/10.1080/09518398.2017.1303213

Herr, K., & Anderson, G. L. (1993). Oral history for student empowerment: Capturing students' inner voices. *International Journal of Qualitative Studies in Education, 6*, 185–196. https://doi.org/10.1080/0951839930060301

Herr, K., & Anderson, G. L. (2015). *The action research dissertation: A guide for students and faculty* (2nd ed.). SAGE.

Hessel, V., Cortese, B., & De Croon, M. H. J. M. (2011). Novel process windows – Concept, proposition and evaluation methodology, and intensified superheated processing. *Chemical Engineering Science, 66*(7), 1426–1448. https://doi.org/10.1016/j.ces.2010.08.018

Hilliger, I., Miranda, C., Celis, S., & Pérez, S. M. (2024). Curriculum analytics adoption in higher education: A multiple case study engaging stakeholders in different phases of design. *British Journal of Educational Technology, 55*(3), 785–801. https://doi.org/10.1111/bjet.13374

Hoeh, E., Bonati, M. L., Chatlos, S., Squires, M., & Countermine, B. (2023). Stop, collaborate, and listen: A faculty learning community developed to address gaps in pre-service education about interdisciplinary collaboration. *International Journal for the Scholarship of Teaching & Learning, 17*(1).

Holcomb, J., Ferguson, G. M., Sun, J., Walton, G. H., & Highfield, L. (2022). Stakeholder engagement in adoption, implementation, and sustainment of an evidence-based intervention to increase mammography adherence among low-income women. *Journal of Cancer Education, 37*(5), 1486–1495. https://doi.org/10.1007/s13187-021-01988-2

Hollman, H., Updegraff, J. A., Lipkus, I. M., & Rhodes, R. E. (2022). Perceptions of physical activity and sedentary behaviour guidelines among end-users and stakeholders: A systematic review. *International Journal of Behavioral Nutrition and Physical Activity, 19*. https://doi.org/10.1186/s12966-022-01245-9

Holloway, S. M., Xu, S., & Ma, S. (2023). Chinese and Canadian preservice teachers in face-to-face dialogues: Situating teaching in cultural practices for west-east reciprocal learning. *Teaching and Teacher Education, 122*, 1–10. https://doi.org/10.1016/j.tate.2022.103930

References

Horton, A. G., Gibson, K. B., & Curington, A. M. (2021). Exploring reflective journaling as a learning tool: An interdisciplinary approach. *Archives of Psychiatric Nursing*, *35*(2), 195–199. https://doi.org/10.1016/j.apnu.2020.09.009

Hou, S.-I., & Wilder, S. (2015a). Changing pedagogy: Faculty adoption of service-learning: Motivations, barriers, and strategies among service-learning faculty at a public research institution. *Sage Open*, *5*(1). https://doi.org/10.1177/2158244015572283

Hou, S.-I., & Wilder, S. (2015b). How ready is higher education faculty for engaged student learning? Applying transtheoretical model to measure service-learning beliefs and adoption. *Sage Open*, *5*(1). https://doi.org/10.1177/2158244015572282

Huang, A., Hancock, D., Clemson, M., Yeo, G., Harney, D., Denny, P., & Denyer, G. (2021). Selecting student-authored questions for summative assessments. *Research in Learning Technology*, *29*. https://doi.org/10.25304/rlt.v29.2517

Huang, Y.-T., & Hang, Y.-C. (2024). Relational well-being among lesbian, gay, and bisexual young adults in Taiwan: Before and after the legalization of same-sex marriage. *Sexuality Research and Social Policy: A Journal of the NSRC*, *21*(1), 240–252. https://doi.org/10.1007/s13178-023-00895-z

Hughes, S., Lewis, S., Willis, K., Rogers, A., Wyke, S., & Smith, L. (2020). Goal setting in group programmes for long-term condition self-management support: Experiences of patients and healthcare professionals. *Psychology and Health*, *35*(1), 70–86. https://doi.org/10.1080/08870446.2019.1623891

Humphries, B., & Clark, D. (2021). An examination of student preference for traditional didactic or chunking teaching strategies in an online learning environment. *Research in Learning Technology*, *29*. https://doi.org/10.25304/rlt.v29.2405

Hwang, W., & Jung, E. (2020). Unpartnered mothers' work-family conflict and parenting stress: The moderating effects of nonstandard work schedules. *Journal of Family and Economic Issues*, *41*(1), 158–171. https://doi.org/10.1007/s10834-019-09647-x

Isaacson, A., Coleman, J., Fok, K., & Tolchin, D. W. (2024). Creating an anti-ableist learning environment: Development of a novel disability-related microaggressions session for medical and dental students and mixed methods analysis of impact on learning and empowerment. *Disability and Health Journal*. https://doi.org/10.1016/j.dhjo.2024.101584

Ivers, M., Alderton, E., & Swanson, R. (2022). Nontraditional post-baccalaureate students: How to better provide support for perceived mental health needs. *Journal of American College Health*. https://doi.org/10.1080/07448481.2022.2120357

Jelinčić, D. A., Baturina, D., & Franić, S. (2022). Impact of service learning on social entrepreneurship and youth employment in Croatia. *Interdisciplinary Description of Complex Systems*, 20(4), 319–335. https://doi.org/10.7906/indecs.20.4.2

Ji, X., & Fu, Y. (2021). The role of sleep disturbances in cognitive function and depressive symptoms among community-dwelling elderly with sleep complaints. *International Journal of Geriatric Psychiatry*, 36(1), 96–105. https://doi.org/10.1002/gps.5401

Jin, G., & Bierma, T. (2023). Sustainability education and civic engagement through integration of undergraduate research with service learning. *Science Education and Civic Engagement*, 15(1), 17–21.

Johnston, K. (2022). Creating space for equity in early childhood educator's participation in documentation, assessment and evaluation. *European Early Childhood Education Research Journal*, 30(3), 360–371. https://doi.org/10.1080/1350293X.2021.2019291

Jones, K. S. (2022). *The personal influences that contribute to the success of six African American female educational leaders [ProQuest Information & Learning]*. In Dissertation Abstracts International Section A: Humanities and Social Sciences (Vol. 83, Issue 11–A).

Joseph, J., Varghese, A., Vijay, V. R., Grover, S., Sharma, S., Dhandapani, M., Khakha, D. C., Arya, S., Mahendia, N., Varkey, B. P., & Kishore, K. (2024). The prevalence of alcohol use disorders using alcohol use disorders identification test (AUDIT) in the Indian setting: A systematic review and meta-analysis. *Journal of Ethnicity in Substance Abuse*, 23(1), 2–20. https://doi.org/10.1080/15332640.2022.2056105

Jung, J. J. (2021). An examination of work-based learning implementation: A study of teacher perception and employer engagement [ProQuest Information & Learning]. In *Dissertation Abstracts International Section A: Humanities and Social Sciences* (Vol. 82, Issue 6–A).

Juwono, S., Flores Anato, J. L., Kirschbaum, A. L., Metheny, N., Dvorakova, M., Skakoon-Sparling, S., Moore, D. M., Grace, D., Hart, T. A., Lambert, G., Lachowsky, N. J., Jollimore, J., Cox, J., & Maheu-Giroux, M. (2024). Prevalence, determinants, and trends in the experience and perpetration of intimate partner violence among a cohort of gay, bisexual, and other men who have sex with men in montréal, toronto, and vancouver, canada (2017–2022). *LGBT Health*. https://doi.org/10.1089/lgbt.2023.0265

Kabir, U., Marty, A. H., Akinrinmade, B., & Zuilkowski, S. S. (2022). An analysis of teaching and learning materials for literacy instruction in Kano State Nigeria: Curricular relevance, cultural responsiveness and gender equity. *Literacy*, 56(2), 130–149. https://doi.org/10.1111/lit.12268

Kanan, A., Alqudah, R., & Al-Mousa, A. (2023). A systematic multi-level assessment approach to enhance students' academic performance in sequential logic design. *International Journal of Engineering Education*, 39(5), 1256–1267.

Kandakatla, R., Dustker, S. M., Bandi, S., & Oakes, W. (2023). Achieving Indian National Board of Accreditation engineering graduate attributes through project-based service-learning: Conceptual analysis. *International Journal for Service Learning in Engineering*, 18(1), 52–69.

Kaplan Sayı, A., & Yurtseven, N. (2022). How do gifted students learn? Their learning styles and dispositions towards learning. *Education 3–13*, 50(8), 1031–1045. https://doi.org/10.1080/03004279.2021.1929380

Kara, B. H., & Khawaja, N. G. (2024). Wellbeing programs for culturally and linguistically diverse population in Australia: Barriers and improvements. *Australian Psychologist*, 59(3), 200–211. https://doi.org/10.1080/00050067.2023.2299667

Karasik, R. J. (2020). Community partners' perspectives and the faculty role in community-based learning. *Journal of Experiential Education*, 43(2), 113–135. https://doi.org/10.1177/1053825919892994

Karatasas, K., Noujaim, G., & Grace, R. (2024). A cultural newsletter: Sharing information and embedding cultural conversations in practice. *Australian Social Work*. https://doi.org/10.1080/0312407X.2024.2340459

Kaufman, G., Aiello, A., Ellis, C., & Compton, D. (2022). Attitudes toward same-sex marriage, polyamorous marriage, and conventional marriage ideals among college students in the southeastern United States. *Sexuality & Culture: An Interdisciplinary Quarterly*, 26(5), 1599–1620. https://doi.org/10.1007/s12119-022-09960-y

Kaynak, D., Irgıt, Y., & Çakmak, S. (2022). Self-esteem in female adolescents and relationships of its predictors with culture. *Psikiyatride Güncel Yaklaşımlar*, 14(3), 358–370. https://doi.org/10.18863/pgy.1009942

Kearney, C. A. (2021). Integrating systemic and analytic approaches to school attendance problems: Synergistic frameworks for research and policy directions. *Child and Youth Care Forum, 50*(4), 701–742. https://doi.org/10.1007/s10566-020-09591-0

Keesey-Phelan, S. H., Axe, J. B., & Williams, A. L. (2022). The effects of teaching a problem-solving strategy on recalling past events with a child with autism. *The Analysis of Verbal Behavior, 38*(2), 190–198. https://doi.org/10.1007/s40616-022-00176-7

Kennedy, H. R., & Dalla, R. L. (2020). "It may be legal, but it is not treated equally": Marriage equality and well-being implications for same-sex couples. *Journal of Gay & Lesbian Social Services: The Quarterly Journal of Community & Clinical Practice, 32*(1), 67–98. https://doi.org/10.1080/10538720.2019.1681340

Kern, M. L., Arguís-Rey, R., Chaves, C., White, M. A., & Zhao, M. Y. (2024). Developing guidelines for program design, practice, and research toward a positive and well-being education practice. *The Journal of Positive Psychology.* https://doi.org/10.1080/17439760.2024.2352743

Khabir, M., Jabbari, A. A., & Razmi, M. H. (2022). Flipped presentation of authentic audio-visual materials: Impacts on intercultural sensitivity and intercultural effectiveness in an EFL context. *Frontiers in Psychology, 13.* https://doi.org/10.3389/fpsyg.2022.832862

Kim, C. (2024). University–community collaborative school violence prevention program during out-of-school time. *Children and Schools, 46*(3), 199–202. https://doi.org/10.1093/cs/cdae013

Kim, B., Kim, J., Moon, S. S., Yoon, S., & Wolfer, T. (2021). Korean women's marital distress and coping strategies in the early stage of intercultural marriages. *Journal of Ethnic & Cultural Diversity in Social Work: Innovation in Theory, Research & Practice, 30*(6), 523–541. https://doi.org/10.1080/15313204.2020.1753616

Kim, H. S., Lee, C. E., & Kim, K. M. (2023). Challenges of single parents raising children with intellectual and developmental disabilities. *Journal of Applied Research in Intellectual Disabilities, 36*(4), 777–786. https://doi.org/10.1111/jar.13093

Kimiecik, C., Gonzalvo, J. D., Cash, S., Goodin, D., & Pastakia, S. (2023). Building a university–school–community partnership to improve adolescent well-being. *Children and Schools, 45*(1), 27–34. https://doi.org/10.1093/cs/cdac029

King, T. S., Bochenek, J., Jenssen, U., Bowles, W., & Morrison-Beedy, D. (2021). Virtual study-abroad through web conferencing: Sharing knowledge and building cultural appreciation in nursing education and practice. *Journal of Transcultural Nursing*, *32*(6), 790–798. https://doi.org/10.1177/10436596211009583

Kinsella, A. T., & Hollins, N. R. (2022). Using a service learning – Peer mentoring project to prepare OT students for their role in post-secondary transition services. *Journal of Occupational Therapy Education*, *6*(3). https://doi.org/10.26681/jote.2022.060317

Klodnick, V. V., Malina, C., Fagan, M. A., Johnson, R. P., Brenits, A., Zeidner, E., & Viruet, J. (2021). Meeting the developmental needs of young adults diagnosed with serious mental health challenges: The emerge model. *The Journal of Behavioral Health Services & Research*, *48*(1), 77–92. https://doi.org/10.1007/s11414-020-09699-0

Kobayashi, K. (2021). Learning by teaching face-to-face: The contributions of preparing-to-teach, initial-explanation, and interaction phases. *European Journal of Psychology of Education*. https://doi.org/10.1007/s10212-021-00547-z

Koly, K. N., Saba, J., Rao, M., Rasheed, S., Reidpath, D. D., Armstrong, S., & Gnani, S. (2024). Stakeholder perspectives of mental healthcare services in Bangladesh, its challenges and opportunities: A qualitative study. *Global Mental Health*, *11*. https://doi.org/10.1017/gmh.2024.30

Kong, D., Yuan, R., & Zou, M. (2024). Pre-service EFL teachers' intercultural competence development within service-learning: A Chinese perspective. *Asia-Pacific Education Researcher*, *33*(2), 263–272. https://doi.org/10.1007/s40299-023-00725-1

Koseoglu, S., Ozturk, T., Ucar, H., Karahan, E., & Bozkurt, A. (2020). 30 years of gender inequality and implications on curriculum design in open and distance learning. *Journal of Interactive Media in Education*, *2020*(1). https://doi.org/10.5334/jime.553

Kouamé, S., Hafsi, T., Oliver, D., & Langley, A. (2022). Creating and sustaining stakeholder emotional resonance with organizational identity in social mission-driven organizations. *Academy of Management Journal*, *65*(6), 1864–1893. https://doi.org/10.5465/amj.2018.1143

Koyanagi, A., Veronese, N., Vancampfort, D., Stickley, A., Jackson, S. E., Oh, H., Shin, J. I., Haro, J. M., Stubbs, B., & Smith, L. (2020). Association of bullying victimization with overweight and obesity among adolescents from

41 low- and middle-income countries. *Pediatric Obesity*, *15*(1). https://doi.org/10.1111/ijpo.12571

Kracht, C. L., Redman, L. M., Bellando, J., Krukowski, R. A., & Andres, A. (2023). Association between maternal and infant screen time with child growth and development: A longitudinal study. *Pediatric Obesity*, *18*(7). https://doi.org/10.1111/ijpo.13033

Kröger, C., van Baarle, E., Widdershoven, G., Bal, R., & Weenink, J.-W. (2022). Combining rules and dialogue: Exploring stakeholder perspectives on preventing sexual boundary violations in mental health and disability care organizations. *BMC Medical Ethics*, *23*. https://doi.org/10.1186/s12910-022-00786-9

Kumar, S. S., James, M., & Case, J. (2022). Engineering design for community impact: Investigating constructive alignment in an innovative service-learning course. In *2022 IEEE Frontiers in Education Conference (FIE)* (pp. 1–5). https://doi.org/10.1109/FIE56618.2022.9962674

Kumar, R. M., & Singh, R. M. (2024). Couple identity in Indian arranged marriages: Perceived partner responsiveness as the mediator of attachment styles and couple identity. *Couple and Family Psychology: Research and Practice*, *13*(2), 143–155. https://doi.org/10.1037/cfp0000220

Kusujiarti, S. (2011). Service-learning in Asia: Curricular models and practices. *Journal of Higher Education Outreach & Engagement*, *15*(3), 159–163.

Lalloo, F., Hawkins, N., Lindley, R., & Kumar, S. (2021). Medical students as service learners: Opportunities, risks, and recommendations. *Education for Primary Care*, *32*(3), 135–139. https://doi.org/10.1080/14739879.2020.1869589

Lam, C.-M. (2021). The impact of philosophy for Children on teachers' professional development. *Teachers and Teaching: Theory and Practice*, *27*(7), 642–655. https://doi.org/10.1080/13540602.2021.1986693

Lara, L. C. (2020). Benefits of journal-writing for students in the emotional/behavior disorders classroom. *Journal of Poetry Therapy*, *33*(3), 187–193. https://doi.org/10.1080/08893675.2020.1776971

Lau, K. H., Snell, R. S., Chan, M. Y.-L., & Yeung, C. L. S. (2023). Reflections by community partners of Hong Kong-based universities on key process variables in service-learning: An exploratory study. *Metropolitan Universities*, *34*(1), 28–53.

Lawlis, T., Mawer, T., Andrew, L., & Bevitt, T. (2024). Challenges to delivering university health-based work-integrated learning to students with a disability: A scoping review. *Higher Education Research and Development*, 43(1), 149–165. https://doi.org/10.1080/07294360.2023.2228209

Le Gouais, A., Bates, G., Callway, R., Kwon, H. R., Montel, L., Peake-Jones, S., White, J., Hasan, M. N., Koksal, C., Barnfield, A., Bondy, K., & Ayres, S. (2023). Understanding how to create healthier places: A qualitative study exploring the complex system of urban development decision-making. *Health & Place*, 81, 1–12. https://doi.org/10.1016/j.healthplace.2023.103023

Le Pichon, E., Wattar, D., Naji, M., Cha, H. R., Jia, Y., & Tariq, K. (2024). Towards linguistically and culturally responsive curricula: The potential of reciprocal knowledge in STEM education. *Language Culture and Curriculum*, 37(1), 10–26. https://doi.org/10.1080/07908318.2023.2221895

Lee, J., & Allen, J. (2021). The role of young adult children's income in the relationship between single mothers' poverty and their young adult children's depression. *Journal of Family Issues*, 42(11), 2509–2528. https://doi.org/10.1177/0192513X20984497

Lee, M. T., & Raschke, R. L. (2020). Innovative sustainability and stakeholders' shared understanding: The secret sauce to "performance with a purpose". *Journal of Business Research*, 108, 20–28. https://doi.org/10.1016/j.jbusres.2019.10.020

Lee, H., Ryan, L. H., Ofstedal, M. B., & Smith, J. (2021). Multigenerational households during childhood and trajectories of cognitive functioning among US older adults. *Journals of Gerontology Series B: Psychological Sciences and Social Sciences*, 76(6), 1161–1172. https://doi.org/10.1093/geronb/gbaa165

Lefebvre, C., Hiestand, B., Glass, C., Masneri, D., Hosmer, K., Hunt, M., & Hartman, N. (2020). Examining the effects of narrative commentary on evaluators' summative assessments of resident performance. *Evaluation & the Health Professions*, 43(3), 159–161. https://doi.org/10.1177/0163278718820415

Leftwich, B. M., Ashby-King, D. T., & Boyd, K. D. (2022). Student-instructor relationships and ethics education: Examining student perceptions of the integrative ethical education model. *Qualitative Research Reports in Communication*, 23(1), 46–55. https://doi.org/10.1080/17459435.2021.1937295

Leijen, Ä., Pedaste, M., Baucal, A., Poom-Valickis, K., & Lepp, L. (2024). What predicts instructional quality and commitments to teaching: Self-efficacy, pedagogical knowledge or integration of the two? *Frontiers in Psychology, 15*. https://doi.org/10.3389/fpsyg.2024.1287313

LeNoble, C. A., & Roberts, D. L. (2020). At the frontier of teaching and practice: Relevant issues for nontraditional undergraduate I-O psychology. *Industrial and Organizational Psychology: Perspectives on Science and Practice, 13*(4), 487–491. https://doi.org/10.1017/iop.2020.82

Lessard, L. M., Watson, R. J., & Puhl, R. M. (2020). "Bias-based bullying and school adjustment among sexual and gender minority adolescents: The role of gay-straight alliances": Correction. *Journal of Youth and Adolescence, 49*(5), 1110. https://doi.org/10.1007/s10964-020-01243-9

Levasseur, M., Routhier, S., Demers, K., Lacerte, J., Clapperton, I., Doré, C., & Gallagher, F. (2021). Importance of collaboration and contextual factors in the development and implementation of social participation initiatives for older adults living in rural areas. *Australian Occupational Therapy Journal, 68*(6), 504–519. https://doi.org/10.1111/1440-1630.12761

Lewis, C. A. (2021). *K-12 teachers' perceptions of barriers to implementing service learning [ProQuest Information & Learning]*. In Dissertation Abstracts International Section A: Humanities and Social Sciences, (Vol. 82, Issue 9–A).

Lewis-Thames, M. W., Leahy, N., Kruse-Diehr, A. J., Ackermann, N., Maki, J., Davis, K. L., & Drake, B. F. (2023). Adapting a research and community capacity-building program to address rural cancer burden and facilitate partnership development between rural community stakeholders and an urban comprehensive cancer center. *Journal of Cancer Education, 38*(4), 1245–1255. https://doi.org/10.1007/s13187-022-02256-7

Li, H., Forbes, A., & Yang, W. (2021). Developing culturally and developmentally appropriate early STEM learning experiences. *Early Education and Development, 32*(1), 1–6. https://doi.org/10.1080/10409289.2020.1833674

Lin, T.-J., Chen, J., Lu, M., Sun, J., Purtell, K., Ansari, A., & Justice, L. (2023). The influence of classroom language contexts on dual language learners' language development. *Journal of Educational Psychology, 115*(6), 877–890. https://doi.org/10.1037/edu0000804

Linder, K. E., & Hayes, C. M. (Eds.). (2018). *High-impact practices in online education: Research and best practices* (1st ed.). Stylus Publishing.

Liu, J. (2021). Building education groups as school collaboration for education improvement: A case study of stakeholder interactions in District A of Chengdu. *Asia Pacific Education Review, 22*(3), 427–439. https://doi.org/10.1007/s12564-021-09682-0

Liu, J., He, X., & Dong, Y. (2024). Household debt and children's psychological well-being in China: The mediating role of parent–child relations. *Children and Youth Services Review, 157*, 1–8. https://doi.org/10.1016/j.childyouth.2023.107387

Liu, M., Kitto, K., & Buckingham Shum, S. (2021). Combining factor analysis with writing analytics for the formative assessment of written reflection. *Computers in Human Behavior, 120*. https://doi.org/10.1016/j.chb.2021.106733

Looi, J. C. L., Maguire, P., Bonner, D., Reay, R. E., Finlay, A. J. F., Keightley, P., Tedeschi, M., Wardle, C., & Kramer, D. (2021). Conduct and evaluation of final-year medical student summative assessments in psychiatry and addiction medicine during COVID-19: An Australian University Medical School experience. *Australasian Psychiatry, 29*(6), 695–698. https://doi.org/10.1177/10398562211014229

Lowe, K., Tennent, C., Moodie, N., Guenther, J., & Burgess, C. (2021). School-based Indigenous cultural programs and their impact on Australian Indigenous students: A systematic review. *Asia-Pacific Journal of Teacher Education, 49*(1), 78–98. https://doi.org/10.1080/1359866X.2020.1843137

Lu, J., Cayabyab, Y. M., Malik, S., & Lwin, M. O. (2022). The associations between mobile media use and food consumption in parent-child dyads. *Journal of Child and Family Studies.* https://doi.org/10.1007/s10826-022-02241-0

Lyness, S. A., Peterson, K., & Yates, K. (2021). Low inter-rater reliability of a high stakes performance assessment of teacher candidates. *Education Sciences, 11*(10), 1–16. https://doi.org/10.3390/educsci11100648

Ma, R., Zhou, Y., & Xu, W. (2023). Guardianship from being present: The moderation of mindfulness in the longitudinal relationship of loneliness to quality of life and mental health problems among the oldest old. *Current Psychology: A Journal for Diverse Perspectives on Diverse Psychological Issues.* https://doi.org/10.1007/s12144-023-04418-2

Madden, J. M., Foxworth, P. M., Ross-Degnan, D., Allen, K. G., Busch, A. B., Callahan, M. X., Lu, C. Y., & Wharam, J. F. (2021). Integrating stakeholder engagement with claims-based research on health insurance design and bipolar disorder. *Psychiatric Services*, 72(2), 186–194. https://doi.org/10.1176/appi.ps.202000177

Malone, D., Abrey, K., Afolayan, O. R., Pendleton, Z., & Osgood, L. E. (2023). Examining an international service-learning project through the lens of the graduate attributes. *International Journal for Service Learning in Engineering*, 18(2), 14–29.

Marchlewska, M., Górska, P., Green, R., Szczepańska, D., Rogoza, M., Molenda, Z., & Michalski, P. (2024). From individual anxiety to collective narcissism? Adult attachment styles and different types of national commitment. *Personality and Social Psychology Bulletin*, 50(4), 495–515. https://doi.org/10.1177/01461672221139072

Marcussen, J., Thuen, F., O'Connor, M., Wilson, R. L., & Hounsgaard, L. (2020). Double bereavement, mental health consequences and support needs of children and young adults—When a divorced parent dies. *Journal of Clinical Nursing*, 29(7–8), 1238–1253. https://doi.org/10.1111/jocn.15181

Markaki, A., Prajankett, O., Shorten, A., Shirey, M. R., & Harper, D. C. (2021). Academic service-learning nursing partnerships in the Americas: A scoping review. *BMC Nursing*, 20(1), 1–15. https://doi.org/10.1186/s12912-021-00698-w

Marsh, R. J., Baltodano-Van Ness, H. M., & Mathur, S. R. (2023). Improving engagement in the virtual environment through culturally relevant expectations and parent collaboration for students with emotional and behavioral disorders. *Beyond Behavior*, 32(2), 128–136. https://doi.org/10.1177/10742956231161010

Marsh, L., Brown, M., & McCann, E. (2020). The views and experiences of fathers of children with intellectual disabilities: A systematic review of the international evidence. *Journal of Policy and Practice in Intellectual Disabilities*, 17(1), 79–90. https://doi.org/10.1111/jppi.12328

Marshall, C. J., Nguyen, A., Arteaga, S., Hubbard, E., Armstead, M., Peprah-Wilson, S., Britt, S., McLemore, M. R., & Gomez, A. M. (2024). Building capacity for research on community doula care: A stakeholder-engaged process in California. *Maternal and Child Health Journal*. https://doi.org/10.1007/s10995-023-03883-2

Martínez, J., Piersol, C. V., Holloway, S., Terhorst, L., & Leland, N. E. (2021). Evaluating stakeholder engagement: Stakeholder-centric instrumentation process (SCIP). *Western Journal of Nursing Research*, 43(10), 949–961. https://doi.org/10.1177/01939459211004274

Mathur, S. K., & Rodriguez, K. A. (2022). Cultural responsiveness curriculum for behavior analysts: A meaningful step toward social justice. *Behavior Analysis in Practice*, 15(4), 1023–1031. https://doi.org/10.1007/s40617-021-00579-3

Mays, I., Flynn, J., McGuire, B., & Egan, J. (2021). The role of attachment style, adverse childhood experiences and dissociation in migraine. *Journal of Trauma & Dissociation*. https://doi.org/10.1080/15299732.2021.1989114

McCarthy, F. E., Damrogmanee, Y., Pushpalatha, M., & Yamamoto, K. (2005). The practices and possibilities of service learning among colleges and universities in Asia. *Pacific-Asian Education*. https://citeseerx.ist.psu.edu/document?repid=rep1&type=pdf&doi=3922e484793ed589c137832b0a838592118d0f65

McCurtin, A., & O'Connor, A. (2020). Building a collaborative research community of practice and supporting research engagement in speech-language pathology: Identification of stakeholder priorities. *JBI Evidence Implementation*, 18(4), 368–375.

McLennan, H., Roberts, J., & Johnson, G. (2023). Stakeholder experience evaluating whole-school practice designed to improve educational outcomes for autistic students. *Australasian Journal of Special and Inclusive Education*, 47(1), 14–27. https://doi.org/10.1017/jsi.2023.3

McMullan, J., Robinson, J., & Varley, N. (2023). The neglect of adolescent neglect. *Comprehensive Child and Adolescent Nursing*, 46(2), 98–101. https://doi.org/10.1080/24694193.2023.2166160

McNally, P., Irvine, M., Taggart, L., Shevlin, M., & Keesler, J. (2022). Exploring the knowledge base of trauma and trauma informed care of staff working in community residential accommodation for adults with an intellectual disability. *Journal of Applied Research in Intellectual Disabilities*. https://doi.org/10.1111/jar.13002

Meinhardt, I., Cuthbert, S., Gibson, K., Fortune, S., & Hetrick, S. E. (2022). Young people and adult stakeholders' reflections on how school staff should support students who self-harm: A qualitative study. *Journal of Adolescence*, 94(7), 969–980. https://doi.org/10.1002/jad.12078

Mendenhall, A., Hicks, C., Holder, M., Holmes, C., Jung, E., Ramirez, L., Fairman, M., Bulls, S. T., & Levy, M. (2024). Growing stronger together: Sharing a story of culturally responsive evaluation with indigenous families and communities. *Child Abuse & Neglect*, 148, 1–9. https://doi.org/10.1016/j.chiabu.2023.106344

Mendenhall, T., Plowman, E., & Trump, L. (2019). *Intimate relationships: Where have we been? Where are we going?* (3rd ed.). Kendall Hunt Publishing.

Meral, B. F., Wehmeyer, M. L., Palmer, S. B., Ruh, A. B., & Yilmaz, E. (2023). Parenting styles and practices in enhancing self-determination of children with intellectual and developmental disabilities. *American Journal on Intellectual and Developmental Disabilities, 128*(4), 282–301.

Messina, R., & Brodzinsky, D. (2020). Children adopted by same-sex couples: Identity-related issues from preschool years to late adolescence. *Journal of Family Psychology, 34*(5), 509–522. https://doi.org/10.1037/fam0000616

Metcalf, C. D., Ostler, C., Thor, P., Kheng, S., Srors, S., Sann, R., Worsley, P., Gates, L., Donnovan-Hall, M., Harte, C., & Dickinson, A. (2024). Engaging multisector stakeholders to identify priorities for global health innovation, change and research: An engagement methodology and application to prosthetics service delivery in Cambodia. *Disability and Rehabilitation: An International, Multidisciplinary Journal, 46*(4), 685–696. https://doi.org/10.1080/09638288.2023.2173313

Miller, R. L. (2020). Service learning: A review of best practices. In A. M. Schwartz & R. L. Miller (Eds.), *High impact educational practices: A review of best practices with illustrative examples* (pp. 570–583). Society for the Teaching of Psychology.

Moen, K. C. (2021). The impact of multi-media presentation format: Student perceptions and learning outcomes. *Scholarship of Teaching and Learning in Psychology, 7*(4), 278–287. https://doi.org/10.1037/stl0000265

Molloy, R., Hansen, A., Robinson, E., D'Astoli, P., Wood, T., & Buus, N. (2024). Stakeholder perspectives on co-designing a post-registration mental health nursing curriculum: A case study. *Journal of Psychiatric and Mental Health Nursing, 31*(3), 303–312. https://doi.org/10.1111/jpm.12988

Moore, L. D. (2024). *Tools of engagement: The role of technology in promoting interaction between college students with disabilities and their educators [ProQuest Information & Learning].* In Dissertation Abstracts International Section A: Humanities and Social Sciences (Vol. 85, Issue 6–A).

Moore, E. A., Winterrowd, E., Petrouske, A., Priniski, S. J., & Achter, J. (2020). Nontraditional and struggling: Academic and financial distress among older student clients. *Journal of College Counseling, 23*(3), 221–233. https://doi.org/10.1002/jocc.12167

References

Mörk, S. B. (2022). University–preschool collaboration in pre-school teacher education in Iceland. *Learning Environments Research*, 25(1), 1–16. https://doi.org/10.1007/s10984-021-09350-5

Morris, J. L., Chalkley, A. E., Helme, Z. E., Timms, O., Young, E., McLoughlin, G. M., Bartholomew, J. B., & Daly-Smith, A. (2023). Initial insights into the impact and implementation of Creating Active Schools in Bradford, UK. *International Journal of Behavioral Nutrition and Physical Activity*, 20(1). https://doi.org/10.1186/s12966-023-01485-3

Murphy, B., Franklin, M., Tsang, Y. T., Sala-Hamrick, K., Atalla, M., & Barnett, D. (2021). Trust and communication with a caregiver reduces behavior problems and protects against stress among urban adolescents. *Youth & Society*, 53(2), 296–319. https://doi.org/10.1177/0044118X20947583

Naidoo, B., & Devnarain, B. (2009). Service learning: Connecting higher education and civil society – Are we meeting the challenge? *South African Journal of Higher Education*, 23(5), 935–952. https://doi.org/10.4314/sajhe.v23i5.48809

Naidoo, D., Govender, P., Naidoo, S. N., Ngubane, N., Nkosi, Z., & Mulla, A. (2020). Occupational risks in occupational therapy service learning: A single-site "fear factor" study in South Africa. *Occupational Therapy International*, 1–7. https://doi.org/10.1155/2020/4746813

Najjarnejad, N., & Bromfield, N. (2022). Professional stakeholders' perceptions of child marriage in Lebanon among Syrian refugees. *Children and Youth Services Review*, 140, 1–8. https://doi.org/10.1016/j.childyouth.2022.106592

Nannemann, A. C. (2021). The student self-accommodation strategy for students with visual impairments. *Journal of Visual Impairment & Blindness*, 115(6), 506–524. https://doi.org/10.1177/0145482X211059545

National Council on Family Relations. (2014). *Family life education content areas*. National Council on Family Relations. https://www.ncfr.org

National Council on Family Relations. (2024). *CFLE credentials*. https://www.ncfr.org

National Council on Family Relations Certified Family Life Education Advisory Board. (2018). Family life education content areas: Content and practice guidelines. In *Tools for ethical thinking and practice in family life education* (4th ed., pp. 35–41). National Council on Family Relations.

Neeper, L. S., & Dymond, S. K. (2020). Incorporating service-learning in special education coursework: Experiences of university faculty. *Teacher Education and Special Education, 43*(4), 343–357. https://doi.org/10.1177/0888406420912373

Newcomb, M. E. (2020). Romantic relationships and sexual minority health: A review and description of the Dyadic Health Model. *Clinical Psychology Review, 82*. https://doi.org/10.1016/j.cpr.2020.101924

Newton, J. R., Batz, R., O'Grady, C., Vinh, M., & Blanchard, S. B. (2024). Beyond omission: Analysing the erasure of disability and inclusion in the developmentally appropriate practices. *International Journal of Early Years Education.* https://doi.org/10.1080/09669760.2024.2343075

Nguyen, A. (2023). Correction to: "Children have the fairest things to say": Young children's engagement with anti-bias picture books. *Early Childhood Education Journal, 51*(8), 1553. https://doi.org/10.1007/s10643-022-01360-z

Nicol, D. J., & Macfarlane-Dick, D. (2006). Formative assessment and self-regulated learning: A model and seven principles of good feedback practice. *Studies in Higher Education, 31*(2), 2–19.

Nordin, N., Halford, W. K., Barlow, F. K., & Mastor, K. A. (2023). Relationship standards and Malay Muslim couples' marital satisfaction. *Journal of Marital and Family Therapy.* https://doi.org/10.1111/jmft.12659

Novak, A. M., Lewis, K. D., & Weber, C. L. (2020). Guiding principles in developing equity-driven professional learning for educators of gifted children. *Gifted Child Today, 43*(3), 169–183. https://doi.org/10.1177/1076217520915743

Nozhovnik, O., Harbuza, T., Starosta, H., Radchenko, Y., & Zatserkovnyi, O. (2022). Best practices of fostering undergraduates' cross-cultural competence involving training them in foreign languages: Systemic review. *International Journal of Educational Methodology, 8*(4), 655–668. https://doi.org/10.12973/ijem.8.4.655

Nunes, C., Martins, C., Ayala-Nunes, L., Matos, F., Costa, E., & Gonçalves, A. (2021). Parents' perceived social support and children's psychological adjustment. *Journal of Social Work, 21*(3), 497–512. https://doi.org/10.1177/1468017320911614

Ochsen, S., Bernholt, A., Grund, S., & Bernholt, S. (2023). Interestingness is in the eye of the beholder—The impact of formative assessment on students' situational interest in chemistry classrooms. *International Journal of Science Education, 45*(5), 383–404. https://doi.org/10.1080/09500693.2022.2163204

O'Connor, M., Chong, S., Quach, J., & Goldfeld, S. (2020). Learning outcomes of children with teacher-identified emerging health and developmental needs. *Child: Care, Health and Development, 46*(2), 223–231. https://doi.org/10.1111/cch.12737

Offei-Dua, V., Morris, J., Mohammad, A., Jones, K., & Ross, W. (2022). Development of a cultural competency curriculum. *Journal of the National Medical Association, 114*(4), 363–368. https://doi.org/10.1016/j.jnma.2022.02.012

Ojilere, A. (2024). Discrimination on grounds of sexual orientation and gender identity: The limits of human rights in Africa. *Journal of Homosexuality, 71*(3), 803–827. https://doi.org/10.1080/00918369.2022.2132577

Okoyo, C., Njambi, E., Were, V., Araka, S., Kanyi, H., Ongeri, L., Echoka, E., Mwandawiro, C., & Njomo, D. (2022). Prevalence, types, patterns and risk factors associated with drugs and substances of use and abuse: A cross-sectional study of selected counties in Kenya. *PLoS One, 17*(9). https://doi.org/10.1371/journal.pone.0273470

Ólafsdóttir, S. M., & Einarsdóttir, J. (2021). Peer culture in an Icelandic preschool and the engagement of children with diverse cultural backgrounds. *International Journal of Early Childhood, 53*(1), 49–64. https://doi.org/10.1007/s13158-021-00283-x

O'Loughlin, V. D., & Griffith, L. M. (2020). Developing student metacognition through reflective writing in an upper level undergraduate anatomy course. *Anatomical Sciences Education, 13*(6), 680–693. https://doi.org/10.1002/ase.1945

Olson, D. H., Defrain, J., & Skogrand, L. (2021). *Marriages and families: Intimacy, diversity, and strengths* (10th ed.). McGraw-Hill.

Olsson, E. M., Gelot, L., Schaffer, J. K., & Litsegård, A. (2024). Teaching academic literacies in international relations: Towards a pedagogy of practice. *Teaching in Higher Education, 29*(2), 471–488. https://doi.org/10.1080/13562517.2021.1992753

One, K. (2022). The role of international service learning and student outcomes. *College of Education Theses and Dissertations, 251*. https://via.library.depaul.edu/soe_etd/251

O'Reilly, S., & Milner, J. (2020). Impact of technology-based reflective practice tools on student skill development. *International Journal of Technology and Human Interaction*, 16(1), 77–93. https://doi.org/10.4018/IJTHI.2020010106

Ornstein, A. C., & Hunkins, F. P. (2013). *Curriculum foundations, principles, and issues*. Person Education, Inc..

Orozco, M. (2024). Disclosing own reasoning while appraising the students' reasoning: Implications for developments in formative assessment in science-engineering education. *Assessment & Evaluation in Higher Education*, 49(2), 165–177. https://doi.org/10.1080/02602938.2023.2196008

Orr, K., Wright, F. V., Grassmann, V., McPherson, A. C., Faulkner, G. E., & Arbour-Nicitopoulos, K. P. (2021). Children and youth with impairments in social skills and cognition in out-of-school time inclusive physical activity programs: A scoping review. *International Journal of Developmental Disabilities*, 67(2), 79–93. https://doi.org/10.1080/20473869.2019.1603731

Ortega, D. P., Walsh, K., Bődi, C. B., Hawkins, L. B., & Bright, M. A. (2023). School-based prevention education for children and youth with intellectual developmental disabilities. *Child Abuse & Neglect*, 145, 1–10. https://doi.org/10.1016/j.chiabu.2023.106397

Osmani, M., Hindi, N. M., & Weerakkody, V. (2021). Developing employability skills in information system graduates: Traditional vs innovative teaching methods. In *Research anthology on developing critical thinking skills in students* (pp. 1331–1344). Information Science Reference/IGI Global. https://doi.org/10.4018/978-1-7998-3022-1.ch069

Pakdaman, S., Unger, J. B., Forster, M., Rogers, C. J., Sussman, S. Y., & Benjamin, S. M. (2021). Childhood trauma and prescription drug misuse in a college population. *Substance Use & Misuse*, 56(1), 140–144. https://doi.org/10.1080/10826084.2020.1846056

Palladino, B. E., Nappa, M. R., Zambuto, V., & Menesini, E. (2020). Ethnic bullying victimization in Italy: The role of acculturation orientation for ethnic minority adolescents with differing citizenship statuses. *Frontiers in Psychology*, 11. https://doi.org/10.3389/fpsyg.2020.00499

Pan, C.-C., Bittner, M., & Chou, C.-C. (2023). Developing an inclusive culture through unified champion schools programs: A pilot study on school awareness and attitudes toward students with intellectual disabilities among general students in taiwan. *International Journal of Developmental Disabilities*. https://doi.org/10.1080/20473869.2023.2231215

Papadopoulos, I., Lazzarino, R., Sakellaraki, O., Dadāu, V., Apostolara, P., Kuckert-Wöstheinrich, A., Mauceri, M., & Kouta, C. (2022). Empowering refugee families in transit: The development of a culturally competent and compassionate training and support package. *Journal of Research in Nursing*, 27(3), 200–214. https://doi.org/10.1177/17449871211018736

Paquette, M., Sommerfeldt, E. J., & Kent, M. L. (2015). Do the ends justify the means? Dialogue, development communication, and deontological ethics. *Public Relations Review*, 41(1), 30–39. https://doi.org/10.1016/j.pubrev.2014.10.008

Pasternak, D. L., Harris, S. D., Lewis, C., Wolk, M. A., Wu, X., & Evans, L. M. (2023). Engaging culturally responsive practice: Implications for continued learning and teacher empowerment. *Teaching and Teacher Education*, 122, 1–12. https://doi.org/10.1016/j.tate.2022.103976

Patrick, C.-J., Valencia-Forrester, F., Backhaus, B., McGregor, R., Cain, G., & Lloyd, K. (2019). The state of service-learning in Australia. *Journal of Higher Education Outreach and Engagement*, 23(3), 185–198. https://openjournals.libs.uga.edu/jheoe/article/view/1528

Patterson, L. (2020). Engineering students' empathy development through service learning: Qualitative results in a technical communication course. In *2020 IEEE International Professional Communication Conference (ProComm), Professional Communication Conference (ProComm)* (pp. 68–75). IEEE International. https://doi.org/10.1109/ProComm48883.2020.00017

Peplak, J., Bobba, B., Hasegawa, M., Caravita, S. C. S., & Malti, T. (2023). The warm glow of kindness: Developmental insight into children's moral pride across cultures and its associations with prosocial behavior. *Developmental Psychology*. https://doi.org/10.1037/dev0001613

Pepping, C. A., Girme, Y. U., Cronin, T. J., & MacDonald, G. (2024). Diversity in singlehood experiences: Testing an attachment theory model of sub-groups of singles. *Journal of Personality*. https://doi.org/10.1111/jopy.12929

Peter, H. L., Giglberger, M., Streit, F., Frank, J., Kreuzpointner, L., Rietschel, M., Kudielka, B. M., & Wüst, S. (2023). Association of polygenic scores for depression and neuroticism with perceived stress in daily life during a long-lasting stress period. *Genes, Brain and Behavior*, 22(6). https://doi.org/10.1111/gbb.12872

Pieper, M., Roelle, J., vom Hofe, R., Salle, A., & Berthold, K. (2021). Feedback in reflective journals fosters reflection skills of student teachers. *Psychology Learning and Teaching, 20*(1), 107–127. https://doi.org/10.1177/1475725720966190

Pinkerton, B., & Martinek, T. (2023). Teaching personal and social responsibility practitioners' perceptions of the application of culturally relevant pedagogies. *Sport, Education and Society, 28*(5), 553–564. https://doi.org/10.1080/13573322.2022.2057463

Poon, P.-L., & Tang, S.-F. (2024). An effective teaching pedagogy involving an online learning platform under a multi-campus teaching model. *Technology, Knowledge and Learning: Learning Mathematics, Science and the Arts in the Context of Digital Technologies.* https://doi.org/10.1007/s10758-024-09761-2

Porter, S., & Couper, P. (2023). Autoethnographic stories for self and environment: A reflective pedagogy to advance 'environmental awareness' in student outdoor practitioners. *Journal of Adventure Education and Outdoor Learning, 23*(1), 25–37. https://doi.org/10.1080/14729679.2021.1935284

Postmes, L., Bouwmeester, R., de Kleijn, R., & van der Schaaf, M. (2023). Supervisors' untrained postgraduate rubric use for formative and summative purposes. *Assessment & Evaluation in Higher Education, 48*(1), 41–55. https://doi.org/10.1080/02602938.2021.2021390

Preuss, L., Fischer, I., & Arora, B. (2024). How do stakeholder groups make sense of sustainability: Analysing differences in the complexity of their cognitive frames. *Business Strategy and the Environment, 33*(3), 2367–2383. https://doi.org/10.1002/bse.3611

Pritchard, C., Abdul Azeez, E. P., & Mirza, S. (2023). Women's health inequalities in 15 Muslim-populated countries: Evidence from population and mortality statistics. *Health Care for Women International.* https://doi.org/10.1080/07399332.2023.2233093

Pugh, P., Hemingway, P., Christian, M., & Higginbottom, G. (2021). Children's, parents', and other stakeholders' perspectives on the factors influencing the initiation of early dietary change in the management of childhood chronic disease: A mixed studies systematic review using a narrative synthesis. *Patient Education and Counseling, 104*(4), 844–857. https://doi.org/10.1016/j.pec.2020.09.021

Radey, M., Langenderfer-Magruder, L., & Brown Speights, J. (2021). "I don't have much of a choice": Low-income single mothers' COVID-19 school and care decisions. *Family Relations: An Interdisciplinary Journal of Applied Family Studies, 70*(5), 1312–1326. https://doi.org/10.1111/fare.12593

Radey, M., Lowe, S., Langenderfer-Magruder, L., & Posada, K. (2022). Showing Everybody's True Colors': Informal networks of low-income single mothers and their young children during the COVID-19 pandemic. *Children and Youth Services Review, 137*, 1–9. https://doi.org/10.1016/j.childyouth.2022.106479

Ramaj, S. (2023). Neighbourhood effects and the labour market outcomes of immigrant men in same-sex couples. *Journal of Ethnic and Migration Studies, 49*(7), 1723–1745. https://doi.org/10.1080/1369183X.2021.2011174

Rasegh, A., Zandi, H., Firoozi, T., & Rasooli, A. (2022). Teachers' conceptions of classroom justice: An empirical study. *Social Psychology of Education: International Journal.* https://doi.org/10.1007/s11218-022-09735-1

Raviv, T., Smith, M., Hurwitz, L., Gill, T. L., Baker, S., Torres, S. A., Bowen, I. E., & Cicchetti, C. (2022). Supporting school-community collaboration for the implementation of a multi-tiered school mental health program: The Behavioral Health Team model. *Psychology in the Schools, 59*(6), 1239–1258. https://doi.org/10.1002/pits.22683

Raza, H. (2017). Using a mixed method approach to discuss the intersectionalities of class, education, and gender in natural disasters for rural vulnerable communities in Pakistan. *The Journal of Rural and Community Development, 12*(1), 128–148. https://journals.brandonu.ca/jrcd/article/view/1671

Raza, H. (2018). Participatory action research: Working beyond disaster towards prevention. *Natural Hazards, 90*(1), 1–15. https://link.springer.com/article/10.1007/s11069-017-3114-x

Raza, H. (2020a). The role of reflexivity in participatory action research to empower culturally diverse communities in Pakistan. *Journal of Rural and Community Development, 15*(1), 71–88. https://journals.brandonu.ca/jrcd/article/view/1671

Raza, H. (2020b, September 24). *3rd international online seminar [Webinar].* ASEAN Journal of Community Engagement. https://scholarhub.ui.ac.id/ajce/

Raza, H. (2021). Social justice and community development: A multilevel community engagement model to effectively working with families living in culturally diverse communities in Pakistan. *ASEAN Journal of Community Engagement, 5*(1), 25–48.

Raza, H. (2022). A global framework: Step-by-step guidelines to apply the multilevel community engagement model to effectively work with culturally diverse communities around the world. *Community Psychology in Global Perspective, 8*(1), 20–40. http://siba-ese.unisalento.it/index.php/cpgp/index

Raza, M. H. (2024a). The components of multilevel engagement theory. *Canadian Journal of Family and Youth, 16*(3), 38–56. http://ejournals,library,ualberta.ca/index/php/cjfy

Raza, M. H. (2024b). The functions of the multilevel engagement theory. *Scottish Journal of Residential Child Care: An International Journal of Group and Family Care Experience, 23*(1), 79–106. https://doi.org/10.17868/strath.00088900

Raza, M. H. (2024c). *The multilevel community engagement model: School, community, workplace engagement and service-learning.* Emerald Publishing.

Raza, H., Baron Cortes, L. M., van Eeden-Moorefield, B., & Khaw, L. (2023b). Using mixed models to examine the factors associated with intimate partner violence among married women in Pakistan. *Aggressive Behavior, 49*(3), 1–16. https://doi.org/10.1002/ab.22073

Raza, H., Grzywacz, J., Linver, M., van Eeden-Moorefield, B., & Lee, S. (2021). A longitudinal examination of work-family balance among working mothers in the United States: Testing bioecological theory. *Journal of Family and Economic Issues, 42*, 601–615. https://link.springer.com/article/10.1007/s10834-020-09747-z

Raza, H., Grzywacz, J., van Eeden-Moorefield, B., Linver, M., & Lee, S. (2023a). A content analysis of work-family conflict scholarship in the United States, 2010–2018. *Family Science Review, 27*(1), 1–23. https://www.familyscienceassociation.org/2023-volume-27-

Raza, H., & Richey, E. (2021). *Using multilevel community engagement model to develop, implement, and assess FLE programs that fosters community engagement and project sustainability.* [Conference session]. 2021 FLE Summit, National Council on Family Relations. ncfr.org

Reed, D. K., & Mercer, S. H. (2023). Potential scoring and predictive bias in interim and summative writing assessments. *School Psychologist, 38*(4), 215–224. https://doi.org/10.1037/spq0000527

Rego, M. A. S., Sáez-Gambín, D., González-Geraldo, J. L., & García-Romero, D. (2022). Transversal competences and employability of university students:

Converging towards service-learning. *Education Sciences*, *12*(4), 1–17. https://doi.org/10.3390/educsci12040265

Reid, N., Buchman, D., Brown, R., Pedersen, C., Kozloff, N., & Stergiopoulos, V. (2022). The acceptability of financial incentives to support service engagement of adults experiencing homelessness and mental illness: A qualitative study of key stakeholder perspectives authorship. *Administration and Policy in Mental Health and Mental Health Services Research*. https://doi.org/10.1007/s10488-022-01217-y

Remler, D. K., & Van Ryzin, G. G. (2022). *Research methods in practice: Strategies for description and causation* (3rd ed.). Sage Publications.

Riepe, V. A., McCluskey-Titus, P., & Illinois State University Department of Educational Administration and Foundations. (2011). *What students learn as a result of being a chairperson and/or officer of a programming board.* Dissertation.

Ripoll Gonzalez, L., & Gale, F. (2020). Combining participatory action research with sociological intervention to investigate participatory place branding. *Qualitative Market Research: An International Journal*, *23*(1), 199–216. https://doi.org/10.1108/QMR-02-2018-0028

Riser, Q. H., Meyer, D. R., Berger, L. M., & Kamble, V. (2023). Noncustodial parents, instrumental networks, and child support compliance. *Social Science Research*, *110*, 1–21. https://doi.org/10.1016/j.ssresearch.2023.102850

Robinson, G. (2021). Cultural competency, social responsibility and community service attitudes assessment of health professions students participating and not participating in service learning programs [ProQuest Information & Learning]. In *Dissertation Abstracts International: Section B: The Sciences and Engineering* (Vol. 82, Issue 11–B).

Rodgers, S. T., Bayne, G. U., & Archimandritis, J. (2023). The color of education: Discriminación y comportamientos. *Journal of Latinos and Education*, *22*(3), 1223–1235. https://doi.org/10.1080/15348431.2021.1935259

Rodriguez, A., Fei, Z., Barrera, W. A., Tsao, E. H., Waterman, J., Franke, T. M., Mogil, C. E., Bonilla, B., Cugley, G. M., Gillams, T., & Langley, A. (2022). Leveraging leadership in child welfare systems: Large-scale trauma- and resilience-informed training initiative. *The Journal of Behavioral Health Services & Research*. https://doi.org/10.1007/s11414-022-09815-2

Rönnlund, M., Bergström, P., & Tieva, Å. (2021). Teaching in a non-traditional classroom: Experiences from a teacher-initiated design project.

Teachers and Teaching: Theory and Practice, 27(7), 587–601. https://doi.org/10.1080/13540602.2021.1977274

Rosenthal, L., Deosaran, A., Young, D. L., & Starks, T. J. (2019). Relationship stigma and well-being among adults in interracial and same-sex relationships. *Journal of Social and Personal Relationships, 36*(11–12), 3408–3428. https://doi.org/10.1177/0265407518822785

Rusu, A. S. (2020). Connectedness behind social distancing in times of COVID-19: Qualitative analysis of civic engagement of students and teachers in Romania. *Journal of Educational Sciences & Psychology, 10*(1), 35–41.

Saarikallio, S., Alluri, V., Maksimainen, J., & Toiviainen, P. (2021). Emotions of music listening in Finland and in India: Comparison of an individualistic and a collectivistic culture. *Psychology of Music, 49*(4), 989–1005. https://doi.org/10.1177/0305735620917730

Samad, M. (2022). Tabletop: An experiential approach to teach sport. *Sport Management Education Journal (Human Kinetics), 16*(2), 171–174. https://doi.org/10.1123/smej.2021-0020

Samraj, J. R., Wright, D. J., & McMurtrie, H. (2023). Age and adult attachment style predict psychological distress in the Singapore general population during COVID-19. *Psychology Health & Medicine*. https://doi.org/10.1080/13548506.2023.2216466

Sartor-Harada, A., Azevedo-Gomes, J., & Torres-Simón, E. (2022). Developing teaching competences with service-learning projects. *Journal of Higher Education Outreach and Engagement, 26*(2), 65–78.

Schneider, A. R., Stephens, L. A. M., Ochoa Marín, S. C., & Semenic, S. (2018). Benefits and challenges of a nursing service-learning partnership with a community of internally-displaced persons in Colombia. *Nurse Education in Practice, 33*, 21–26. https://doi.org/10.1016/j.nepr.2018.08.002

Sellmaier, C., & Kim, J. (2021). Disability accommodation experiences of social work students in the United States. *Social Work Education, 40*(7), 872–887. https://doi.org/10.1080/02615479.2020.1738375

Sheen, M., Yekani, H. A. K., & Jordan, T. R. (2023). The good, the bad and the hijab: A study of implicit associations made by practicing Muslims in their native Muslim country. *Psychological Reports, 126*(6), 2886–2903. https://doi.org/10.1177/00332941221103532

Shrout, M. R., Renna, M. E., Madison, A. A., Malarkey, W. B., & Kiecolt-Glaser, J. K. (2023). Marital negativity's festering wounds: The emotional, immunological, and relational toll of couples' negative communication patterns. *Psychoneuroendocrinology, 149*, 1–11. https://doi.org/10.1016/j.psyneuen.2022.105989

Shurygin, V., Anisimova, T., Orazbekova, R., & Pronkin, N. (2023). Modern approaches to teaching future teachers of mathematics: The use of mobile applications and their impact on students' motivation and academic success in the context of stem education. *Interactive Learning Environments.* https://doi.org/10.1080/10494820.2022.2162548

Smith, S. R., & Hamon, R. R. (2022). *Exploring family theories* (5th ed.). Oxford University Press.

Smith, L. H., Hernandez, B. E., Joshua, K., Gill, D., & Bottiani, J. H. (2022). A scoping review of school-based prevention programs for indigenous students. *Educational Psychology Review, 34*(4), 2783–2824. https://doi.org/10.1007/s10648-022-09698-x

Smith, M. D., & Wesselbaum, D. (2023). Well-being and income across space and time: Evidence from one million households. *Journal of Happiness Studies: An Interdisciplinary Forum on Subjective Well-Being, 24*(5), 1813–1840. https://doi.org/10.1007/s10902-023-00660-4

Smith, T., Zou, A., Nelson, G., & Al-Ghaithi, A. (2020). *Overcoming institutional barriers to service learning.* Center for Engagement and Community Development. https://newprairiepress.org/cgi/viewcontent.cgi?article=1232&context=cecd

Snell-Rood, C., Willging, C., Showalter, D., Peters, H., & Pollini, R. A. (2021). System-level factors shaping the implementation of "hub and spoke" systems to expand MOUD in rural areas. *Substance Abuse, 42*(4), 716–725. https://doi.org/10.1080/08897077.2020.1846149

Snyder, J. S., & Henry, P. J. (2023). Regional measures of sexual-orientation bias predict where same-gender couples live. *Psychological Science, 34*(7), 794–808. https://doi.org/10.1177/09567976231173903

So, M., Almeida Rojo, A. L., Robinson, L. R., Hartwig, S. A., Heggs Lee, A. R., Beasley, L. O., Silovsky, J. F., Morris, A. S., Stiller Titchener, K., & Zapata, M. I. (2020). Parent engagement in an original and culturally adapted evidence-based parenting program, Legacy for Children™. *Infant Mental Health Journal, 41*(3), 356–377. https://doi.org/10.1002/imhj.21853

Song, B., & Ferguson, M. A. (2023). The importance of congruence between stakeholder prosocial motivation and CSR attributions: Effects on stakeholders' donations and sense-making of prosocial identities. *Journal of Marketing Communications*, 29(4), 339–357. https://doi.org/10.1080/13527266.2021.2021971

Soneson, E., Burn, A.-M., Anderson, J. K., Humphrey, A., Jones, P. B., Fazel, M., Ford, T., & Howarth, E. (2022). Determining stakeholder priorities and core components for school-based identification of mental health difficulties: A Delphi study. *Journal of School Psychology*, 91, 209–227. https://doi.org/10.1016/j.jsp.2022.01.00

Song, M. J. (2021). Teacher professional development in integrating digital fabrication technologies into teaching and learning. *Educational Media International*, 58(4), 317–334. https://doi.org/10.1080/09523987.2021.1989766

Strait, J. R. & Nordyke, K. (Eds.). (2015). *eService-learning: Creating experiential learning and civic engagement through online and hybrid course.* Stylus Publishing.

Stuhlsatz, G. L., Kavanaugh, S. A., Taylor, A. B., Neppl, T. K., & Lohman, B. J. (2021). Spirituality and religious engagement, community involvement, outness, and family support: Influence on LGBT+ Muslim well-being. *Journal of Homosexuality*, 68(7), 1083–1105. https://doi.org/10.1080/00918369.2021.1888585

Suarez, B. Y., Francisco, V. T., & Rubén Chávez, N. (2020). Applying community-based participatory approaches to addressing health disparities and promoting health equity. *American Journal of Community Psychology*, 66(3–4), 217–221. https://doi.org/10.1002/ajcp.12487

Suarez, M. L., & Torres, C. (2021). Understanding the factors associated with overprotective parenting behaviors in Latino parents. *Family Relations: An Interdisciplinary Journal of Applied Family Studies*, 70(5), 1556–1570. https://doi.org/10.1111/fare.12548

Suarez-Morales, L., & Harris, A. P. (2023). Relationship of parent cultural stress, overprotective parenting practices, and hispanic children's anxiety. *Journal of Child and Family Studies*. https://doi.org/10.1007/s10826-023-02560-w

Subban, P., Woodcock, S., Bradford, B., Romano, A., Sahli Lozano, C., Kullmann, H., Sharma, U., Loreman, T., & Avramidis, E. (2024). What does the village need to raise a child with additional needs? Thoughts on creating a framework to support collective inclusion. *Teachers and Teaching: Theory and Practice*. https://doi.org/10.1080/13540602.2024.2338398

Sundberg, A. D., & Koehler, E. N. (2023). Bridges to civic health: Enhancing shared service-learning collaboration in nursing and history. *Journal of Experiential Education, 46*(3), 261–280. https://doi.org/10.1177/10538259221146745

Sundqvist, A., Barr, R., Heimann, M., Birberg, T. U., & Koch, F. (2024). A longitudinal study of the relationship between children's exposure to screen media and vocabulary development. *Acta Paediatrica, 113*(3), 517–522. https://doi.org/10.1111/apa.17047

Sur, M. H., Kim, S.-Y., Zittel, L., & Gilson, T. A. (2021). Parental self-efficacy and practices in physical activity of young children with and without disabilities. *Journal of Child and Family Studies, 30*(6), 1567–1576. https://doi.org/10.1007/s10826-021-01967-7

Tan, K. L., & Adams, D. (2023). Leadership opportunities for students with disabilities in co-curriculum activities: Insights and implications. *International Journal of Disability, Development and Education, 70*(5), 788–802. https://doi.org/10.1080/1034912X.2021.1904504

Tao, Y., Bi, X.-Y., & Deng, M. (2020). The impact of parent–child attachment on self-injury behavior: Negative emotion and emotional coping style as serial mediators. *Frontiers in Psychology, 11.* https://doi.org/10.3389/fpsyg.2020.01477

Tapia, G., Teysseyre, J., Bréhonnet, R., Baud, A., Gauvreau, G., Gray, M., & Oprescu, F. (2024). Childhood trauma and alcohol misuse in college students: The moderating role of minimization. *Child Abuse & Neglect, 152,* 1–10. https://doi.org/10.1016/j.chiabu.2024.106749

Tatkin, B. T. (2016). *Improving high school service-learning to increase long-term impact on volunteerism [ProQuest Information & Learning].* In Dissertation Abstracts International Section A: Humanities and Social Sciences (Vol. 77, Issue 3–A(E)).

Terry, A. N., & Qi, Z. (2024). Unveiling the transformative power of service-learning: Student-led mental health roundtable discussions as catalysts for ongoing civic engagement. *Journal of Service-Learning in Higher Education, 18,* 101–112.

Temelturk, R. D., Yurumez, E., Cıkılı Uytun, M., & Oztop, D. B. (2021). Parent-child interaction, parental attachment styles and parental alexithymia levels of children with ASD. *Research in Developmental Disabilities, 112.* https://doi.org/10.1016/j.ridd.2021.103922

Terrizzi, B. F., Woodward, A. M., & Beier, J. S. (2020). Young children and adults associate social power with indifference to others' needs. *Journal of

Experimental Child Psychology, 198. https://doi.org/10.1016/j.jecp.2020. 104867

Theall, M., & Franklin, J. L. (2010). Assessing teaching practices and effectiveness for formative purposes. In K. J. Gillespie & D. L. Robertson (Eds.), *A guide to faculty development*. Jossey Bass.

Tinto, V. (1993). In *Leaving college: Rethinking the causes and cures of student attrition* (2nd ed.). University of Chicago Press.

Torres, Y., Walsh, N., & Tahvildary, N. (2022). Impact of mediator mentors service-learning on college student social-emotional expertise and cultural competence. *Journal of Practical Studies in Education, 3*(1), 3–13.

Troller-Renfree, S. V., Sperber, J. F., Hart, E. R., Costanzo, M. A., Gennetian, L. A., Meyer, J. S., Fox, N. A., & Noble, K. G. (2023). Associations between maternal stress and infant resting brain activity among families residing in poverty in the US. *Biological Psychology, 184*, 1–10. https://doi.org/10.1016/j.biopsycho.2023.108683

Trumbull, E., & Lash, A. (2013). *Understanding formative assessment: Insights from learning theory and measurement theory*. WestEd.

Türk, B., Yayak, A., & Hamzaoğlu, N. (2021). The effects of childhood trauma experiences and attachment styles on cyberbullying and victimization among university students. *Kibris Türk Psikiyatri ve Psikoloji Dergisi, 3*(4), 241–249.

Twohig, A., Lyne, J., & McNicholas, F. (2024). Attachment theory: Survival, trauma, and war through the eyes of bowlby. *Irish Journal of Psychological Medicine*. https://doi.org/10.1017/ipm.2024.12

Tyndall, D. E., Kosko, D. A., Forbis, K. M., & Sullivan, W. B. (2020). Mutual benefits of a service-learning community–academic partnership. *Journal of Nursing Education, 59*(2), 93–96. https://doi.org/10.3928/01484834-20200122-07

Umberson, D., & Thomeer, M. B. (2020). Family matters: Research on family ties and health, 2010 to 2020. *Journal of Marriage and Family, 82*, 404–419.

Vaarzon-Morel, P., Barwick, L., & Green, J. (2021). Sharing and storing digital cultural records in Central Australian Indigenous communities. *New Media & Society, 23*(4), 692–714. https://doi.org/10.1177/1461444820954201

Valdez, C. E., & Lovell, J. L. (2022). What psychology students want from service-learning. *Teaching of Psychology, 49*(3), 258–268. https://doi.org/10.1177/00986283211021075

Vamos, C. A., Kline, N., Vázquez-Otero, C., Lockhart, E. A., Lake, P. W., Wells, K. J., Proctor, S., Meade, C. D., & Daley, E. M. (2021). Stakeholders' perspectives on system-level barriers to and facilitators of hpv vaccination among Hispanic migrant farmworkers. *Ethnicity and Health*. https://doi.org/10.1080/13557858.2021.1887820

Vanderbilt, K. E., & Andreason, C. (2023). The influence of popular media characters on children's object choices. *British Journal of Developmental Psychology*, 41(1), 1–12. https://doi.org/10.1111/bjdp.12434

Vanner, C. (2024). What do you want your teachers to know? Using intergenerational reflections in education research. *International Journal of Qualitative Studies in Education*, 37(6), 1788–1803. https://doi.org/10.1080/09518398.2023.2233916

Vartiainen, H., Vuojärvi, H., Saramäki, K., Eriksson, M., Ratinen, I., Torssonen, P., Vanninen, P., & Pöllänen, S. (2022). Cross-boundary collaboration and knowledge creation in an online higher education course. *British Journal of Educational Technology*, 53(5), 1304–1320. https://doi.org/10.1111/bjet.13186

Vetri, L., Elia, M., Vitello, G. A., Greco, D., Gagliano, C., Costanzo, M. C., Romeo, G., & Musumeci, S. A. (2021). Impact of daytime routine modifications on people with severe intellectual disability amid COVID-19 pandemic. *Perspectives in Psychiatric Care*, 57(3), 1536–1537. https://doi.org/10.1111/ppc.12696

Vicente, F. S., Escuder, Á. V., Pérez Puig, M. Á., & López, F. S. (2021). Effect on procrastination and learning of mistakes in the design of the formative and summative assessments: A case study. *Education Sciences*, 11(8), 1–12.

Villar, A. A. (2022). To what extent a modern teaching style benefits students? Why do teachers act the way they do? *Journal of Computer Assisted Learning*. https://doi.org/10.1111/jcal.12765

Vo, L. K., Allen, M. J., Cunich, M., Thillainadesan, J., McPhail, S. M., Sharma, P., Wallis, S., McGowan, K., & Carter, H. E. (2024). Stakeholders' preferences for the design and delivery of virtual care services: A systematic review of discrete choice experiments. *Social Science & Medicine*, 340, 1–14. https://doi.org/10.1016/j.socscimed.2023.116459

Voith, L. A., Lee, H., & Russell, K. (2022). How trauma, depression, and gender roles lead to intimate partner violence perpetration among a sample of predominately low-income Black, Indigenous, Men of Color: A mixed methods study. *Journal of Interpersonal Violence, 37*(9–10), NP6487–NP6513. https://doi.org/10.1177/0886260520967139

von Bertalanffy, L. (1968). *General system theory: Foundation, development, and application.* Braziller.

Waisman-Nitzan, M., Ivzori, Y., & Anaby, D. (2023). Promoting participation-focused practices in inclusive educational settings: Stakeholders' perspectives following a knowledge translation initiative. *American Journal of Occupational Therapy, 77*(6), 1–8. https://doi.org/10.5014/ajot.2023.050262

Walker, A., Mercer, J., & Freeman, L. (2021). The doors of opportunity: How do community partners experience working as co-educators in a service-learning collaboration? *Journal of University Teaching and Learning Practice, 18*(7), 56–70.

Walsh, G., & Zadurian, N. (2022). Exploring the links between parental attachment style, child temperament and parent-child relationship quality during adolescence. *Journal of Child and Family Studies.* https://doi.org/10.1007/s10826-022-02447-2

Walther, A. K., & Pilarz, A. R. (2024). Associations between parental precarious work schedules and child behavior problems among low-income families. *Journal of Marriage and Family, 86*(3), 551–573. https://doi.org/10.1111/jomf.12933

Wang, Y. (2022). Music education: Which is more effective—Traditional learning or the introduction of modern technologies to increase student motivation? *Learning and Motivation, 77*, 1–11. https://doi.org/10.1016/j.lmot.2022.101783

Wang, Y. (2024). Examining the role of sense of belonging and formative assessment in reducing the negative impact of learning anxiety in mathematics. *European Journal of Psychology of Education, 39*(1), 431–453. https://doi.org/10.1007/s10212-023-00701-9

Wang, P., Ma, T., Liu, L.-B., Shang, C., An, P., & Xue, Y.-X. (2021). A comparison of the effectiveness of online instructional strategies optimized with smart interactive tools versus traditional teaching for postgraduate students. *Frontiers in Psychology, 12.* https://doi.org/10.3389/fpsyg.2021.747719

Wang, Y. C., & McLeroy, A. M. (2023). Poverty, parenting stress, and adolescent mental health: The protective role of school connectedness reexamined. *Children and Youth Services Review, 153*, 1–7. https://doi.org/10.1016/j.childyouth.2023.107127

Wang, Z., Zhao, L., Guan, J., & Zuo, G. (2023). The negative effects of positive gender stereotypes: Evidence from a collectivistic cultural context. *Sex Roles: Journal of Research*, *89*(11–12), 786–800. https://doi.org/10.1007/s11199-023-01413-6

Wassell, B. A., Coleman, N., Chen, X., & Browne, S. (2022). Families, resources, and community: Illuminating the structures of culturally relevant education in an urban early childhood center. *Education and Urban Society*, *54*(5), 538–559. https://doi.org/10.1177/00131245211004573

Weakley, S., Karlsson, P. S., Cullingworth, J., Lebec, L., & Fraser, K. (2021). Developing a university-voluntary sector collaboration for social impact. *Journal of University Teaching and Learning Practice*, *18*(7), 71–86. https://doi.org/10.53761/1.18.7.06

Webb, S. N., Kavanagh, P. S., & Chonody, J. M. (2020). Straight, LGB, married, living in sin, children out of wedlock: A comparison of attitudes towards 'different' family structures. *Journal of GLBT Family Studies*, *16*(1), 66–82. https://doi.org/10.1080/1550428X.2019.1577201

Westerman, J. W., Rao, M. B., Vanka, S., & Gupta, M. (2020). Sustainable human resource management and the triple bottom line: Multi-stakeholder strategies, concepts, and engagement. *Human Resource Management Review*, *30*(3). https://doi.org/10.1016/j.hrmr.2020.100742

Wetzl, A., & Lieske, P. (2020). The benefits and limitations of online peer feedback: Instructors' perception of a regional campus online writing lab. *Praxis*, *18*(1), 37–53.

White, J. M., Martin, T. F., & Adamsons, K. (2019). *Family theories: An introduction* (5th ed.). Sage Publishing.

Winberg, M., Tegmark, M., Vinterek, M., & Alatalo, T. (2022). Motivational aspects of students' amount of reading and affective reading experiences in a school context: A large-scale study of grades 6 and 9. *Reading Psychology*. https://doi.org/10.1080/02702711.2022.2118914

Wójcik, M., Eikeseth, S., Eldevik, S., & Budzińska, A. (2021). Teaching children with autism to request items using audio scripts, interrupted chain procedure and sufficient exemplar training. *Behavioral Interventions*, *36*(1), 40–57. https://doi.org/10.1002/bin.1761

Woods, J. B., Daniel, U. J., Kleven, L., Bucklin, R., Maldonado, A., Gilbert, P. A., Parker, E. A., & Baquero, B. (2021). Building leadership, capacity, and power to advance health equity and justice through community-engaged research in the Midwest. *American Journal of Community Psychology*, 67(1–2), 195–204. https://doi.org/10.1002/ajcp.12462

Wu, C.-F., Chang, Y.-L., Rhodes, E., Musaad, S., & Jung, W. (2020). Work-hour trajectories and associated socioeconomic characteristics among single-mother families. *Social Work Research*, 44(1), 47–57. https://doi.org/10.1093/swr/svz029

Wyche-Jonas, J. L. (2022). Good intentions are not enough: An examination of service-learning on a public charter high school campus. *LMU/LLS Theses and Dissertations*. https://digitalcommons.lmu.edu/cgi/viewcontent.cgi?article=2164&context=etd

Xing, J., & Ma, C. H. K. (Eds.). (2010). *Service-learning in Asia: Curricular models and practices*. Hong Kong University Press. http://www.jstor.org/stable/j.ctt1xwf3j

Yan, A., Hooyer, K., Asan, O., Flower, M., & Whittle, J. (2022). Engaging veteran stakeholders to identify patient-centred research priorities for optimizing implementation of lung cancer screening. *Health Expectations: An International Journal of Public Participation in Health Care & Health Policy*, 25(1), 408–418. https://doi.org/10.1111/hex.13401

Ye, M., Zhang, J., & Li, H. (2023). Twins, income, and happiness: Evidence from China. *PNAS Proceedings of the National Academy of Sciences of the United States of America*, 120(25), 1–8. https://doi.org/10.1073/pnas.2221884120

Yılmaz, A., Şahin, F., Buldu, M., Ülker Erdem, A., Ezmeci, F., Somer Ölmez, B., Aydos, E. H., Buldu, E., Ünal, H. B., Aras, S., Buldu, M., & Akgül, E. (2021). An examination of Turkish early childhood teachers' challenges in implementing pedagogical documentation. *Early Childhood Education Journal*, 49(6), 1047–1059. https://doi.org/10.1007/s10643-020-01113-w

Yoon, D., Kobulsky, J. M., Yoon, M., Park, J., Yoon, S., & Arias, L. N. (2024). Racial differences in early adolescent substance use: Child abuse types and family/peer substance use as predictors. *Journal of Ethnicity in Substance Abuse*, 23(1), 110–127. https://doi.org/10.1080/15332640.2022.2068720

Young, B. (2024). Benefits of volunteerism: From extracurricular to service learning and beyond. *International Journal of Art & Design Education*, 43(1), 37–50. https://doi.org/10.1111/jade.12475

Yusof, N., Tengku Ariffin, T. F., Awang-Hashim, R., Nordin, H., & Kaur, A. (2020). Challenges of service learning practices: Student and faculty perspectives from Malaysia. *Malaysian Journal of Learning and Instruction*, 17(2), 279–309.

Zhang Kudon, H., Herbst, J. H., Richardson, L. C., Smith, S. G., Demissie, Z., & Siordia, C. (2023). Prevalence estimates and factors associated with violence among older adults: National intimate partner and sexual violence (NISVS) survey, 2016/2017. *Journal of Elder Abuse & Neglect*. https://doi.org/10.1080/08946566.2023.2297227

Zhao, M., Fu, W., & Ai, J. (2021). The mediating role of social support in the relationship between parenting stress and resilience among Chinese parents of children with disability. *Journal of Autism and Developmental Disorders*, 51(10), 3412–3422. https://doi.org/10.1007/s10803-020-04806-8

Zhaoyang, R., & Martire, L. M. (2021). The influence of family and friend confidants on marital quality in older couples. *Journals of Gerontology Series B: Psychological Sciences and Social Sciences*, 76(2), 380–390. https://doi.org/10.1093/geronb/gbaa029

Zheng, Z., Layton, J., Stelmach, W., Crabbe, J., Ma, J., Briedis, J., Atme, J., Bourne, D., Hau, R., Cleary, S., & Xue, C. C. (2020). Using patient self-checklist to improve the documentation of risk of postoperative nausea and vomiting: An implementation project. *International Journal of Evidence-Based Healthcare*, 18(1), 65–74. https://doi.org/10.1097/XEB.0000000000000213

Zheng, Y., & Toribio, J. R. (2021). The role of transparency in multi-stakeholder educational recommendations. *User Modeling and User-Adapted Interaction*, 31(3), 513–540. https://doi.org/10.1007/s11257-021-09291-x

Zhou, S., Raat, H., You, Y., Santos, S., van Grieken, A., Wang, H., & Yang-Huang, J. (2024). Change in neighborhood socioeconomic status and childhood weight status and body composition from birth to adolescence. *International Journal of Obesity*, 48(5), 646–653. https://doi.org/10.1038/s41366-023-01454-7

Zhu, X., Cheong, C. M., Li, G. Y., & Wu, J. (2020). Primary school teachers' conceptions of reading comprehension processes and its formulation. *Frontiers in Psychology*, 11. https://doi.org/10.3389/fpsyg.2020.00615

Zorondo-Rodríguez, F., Gómez-Baggethun, E., Demps, K., Ariza-Montobbio, P., García, C., & Reyes-García, V. (2014). What defines quality of life? The gap between public polices and locally defined indicators among residents of Kodagu, Karnataka (India). *Social Indicators Research*, 115, 441–456. https://doi.org/10.1007/s11205-012-9993-z

INDEX

Collectivistic culture, 18–19
Community, 15–16
   engagement, 189–190, 196
Culturally valued education, 149, 152–153
Culture, 17–18

Developmental context, 20
Diversity, 19
Donor agency, 16–17

Ethically valued education, 149, 152
Evolved culture, 19

Family, 15

Historical context, 21–28

Individualistic culture, 18
Institutions, 17

Literature review, 99–106

Media, 16

Program, 61
   curriculum, 129, 131
   delivery, 129, 132
   review and share, 173
   sustainability, 190
   trustworthiness, 181
   vision, 109–110

Resources, 87

SAMREEN evaluation, 159–165
   attainable, 162–163
   engaged, 159–163
   evaluative, 162–163
   meaningful, 160–162
   neat, 161–163
   related, 161–163
   sustainable, 161–165
SAMREEN goal, 109, 115
   attainable, 125
   engaged, 127
   evaluative, 127
   meaningful, 125
   neat, 127
   related, 127
   sustainable, 125
SAMREEN objective, 109–123
   attainable, 125
   engaged, 125
   evaluative, 125
   meaningful, 125
   neat, 125
   related, 125
   sustainable, 125
Service-learning, 43–46
Sociocultural context, 20–21
Stakeholders, 77

Vulnerabilities, 87–88

Printed in the USA
CPSIA information can be obtained
at www.ICGtesting.com
JSHW011759031224
74704JS00004B/105